The Encyclopedia of Dog Sports and Activities

A Field Guide to 35 Fun Activities for You and Your Dog

D1531128

Diane Morgan

The Encyclopedia of Dog Sports and Activities

Project Team
Editor: Stephanie Fornino
Copy Editor: Joann Woy
Indexer: Dianne L. Schneider
Designer: Angela Stanford

T.F.H. Publications
President/CEO: Glen S. Axelrod
Executive Vice President: Mark E. Johnson
Publisher: Christopher T. Reggio
Production Manager: Kathy Bontz

T.F.H. Publications, Inc.
One TFH Plaza
Third and Union Avenues
Neptune City, NJ 07753

Printed and bound in China

09 10 11 12 13   1 3 5 7 9 8 6 4 2

Library of Congress Cataloging-in-Publication Data

Morgan, Diane, 1947-
   The encyclopedia of dog sports and activities : a field guide to 35 fun activities for you and your dog / Diane Morgan.
       p. cm.
   Includes index.
   ISBN 978-0-7938-1275-2 (alk. paper)
   1. Dog sports–Encyclopedias. I. Title.
SF424.M67 2009
   636.7–dc22
                                              2009010633

   This book has been published with the intent to provide accurate and authoritative information in regard to the subject matter within. While every reasonable precaution has been taken in preparation of this book, the author and publisher expressly disclaim responsibility for any errors, omissions, or adverse effects arising from the use or application of the information contained herein. The techniques and suggestions are used at the reader's discretion and are not to be considered a substitute for veterinary care. If you suspect a medical problem, consult your veterinarian.

   The sports included in this book are recognized by various organizations around the world and do not imply an endorsement by the publisher or author.

The Leader In Responsible Animal Care For Over 50 Years!®
www.tfh.com

Table of Contents

Introduction

So you want to get involved in a dog sport or activity! Good for you! Sharing activities with your canine companion will not only build a strong and trusting bond between you but can also make you both stronger, more agile, and more mentally alert.

No matter what sport you are considering, make sure that your dog is physically fit. Explain to your vet about the activity you are contemplating, and find out if your dog is a suitable candidate. (He should also be up to date on shots.) While some activities are more demanding than others, every dog performs better, both mentally and physically, when he is at the right weight and in peak condition. Age is important as well. Although older dogs *can* learn new tricks, it may take them longer. As for puppies, they are quick learners, but they are not fully developed and are easily distracted.

Some of the sports and activities described in this book require a high level of continuous involvement for you to be successful, while others are more casual. In the same way, some people wish to be an occasional "recreational" participant, while other people take their chosen activity very seriously and want to "go for the gold." Decide on a goal, and think about how much time you can realistically spend on working with your dog. The higher the goal, the more time and money it will take, especially for events that are not often held locally.

In any sport or activity, the greatest satisfaction comes from the knowledge that you have done the best that you could and given your dog every opportunity to make the most of his training and instincts. Overall, keep it fun! If you win, you can bask in the shared glory of it. If you lose—tomorrow is another day!

How to Use This Book

This book contains a selection of 35 sports and activities, separated out by chapter and alphabetized for easy reference. Each chapter contains the following topics:

DEFINITION
The definition gives a brief explanation of the sport or activity.

HISTORY
This section describes the history of the sport or activity and includes dates for when sponsoring organizations began to recognize it.

OVERVIEW
The overview outlines the general rules of the sport or activity, and when applicable, breaks down the information by sponsoring organization.

REQUIREMENTS
This section lists the dog and handler traits necessary for success in your chosen event.

EQUIPMENT AND SUPPLIES
The major equipment and supplies for each sport are outlined and described in detail. They include the main items required for training and practice, as well as the major tools present in an actual competition, which in some cases the sponsoring organization will supply. Not every single item that is conceivably needed is listed, but the basic ones are present. In all cases, you will need a basic rule book for your intended sport or activity.

SPONSORING ORGANIZATIONS
This section lists a selection of the sponsoring organizations for the sport or activity and were chosen based on whether they were a major US association or an international registry of which the United States is a part. The American Kennel Club (AKC) and United Kennel Club (UKC) were treated as the major organizations whenever applicable. (Other organizations that sponsor a sport but were not included in this section are listed, along with their websites, in the sidebar "Additional Organizations.")

Eligibility Requirements: Lists the breeds, age restrictions, spay/neuter restrictions, and registration rules for a particular organization.

Titles: Lists the titles for which a dog may be eligible.

Premier Events: Lists the major events held for the sport by the sponsoring organization.

How to Get Started

This section tells you what you need to do to get started in your sport or activity. Common topics include ensuring that your dog is ready, finding a mentor, and training and conditioning your dog for the event at hand.

The training techniques that you employ should be aimed not just at a particular sport but at your own particular dog. You know what stimulates him most—food, petting, or play—so you know what rewards will work best for him. This book offers some general training advice for each sport, but it is not a training book and is certainly not meant to take the place of working with an experienced group or mentor.

Strategies for Success

The strategies detailed in this segment will help you succeed in your chosen event by giving you helpful hints and tips. This section contains an array of topics specifically tailored to the chosen sport or activity.

Sidebars

The following four sidebars are present in every chapter:

Top Breeds: Reveals the breeds and types of dogs that are best suited to the sport or activity.

Fun Fact: Reveals an interesting tidbit about the sport or activity.

From the Expert: Gives a helpful tip from an expert in the sport or activity.

Additional Organizations: Lists the websites of those US and international sponsoring organizations that are applicable to the sport or activity but are not covered in detail within the chapter.

Chapter 1

Agility

Definition

Agility is a timed race over an obstacle course that includes tunnels, jumps, ramps, and weave poles. Both speed and accuracy are important.

Dogs who participate in agility must be smart, fast, and in top physical condition.

History of Agility

Canine agility arose from the equestrian sport of stadium jumping. Several unofficial agility trials were held during the 1970s in both England and the United States. In 1980, England's Kennel Club became the first organization to recognize agility as an official sport with a sanctioned set of rules; the first formal agility test to be held under the new regulations was the team event at the famous Crufts Dog Show that year. The United States Dog Agility Association (USDAA) was formed in 1986 in Texas. It soon began offering competitions, ribbons, and titles. The North American Dog Agility Council (NADAC) began offering agility trials in 1993, followed by the American Kennel Club (AKC) in 1994. Canine Performance Events (CPE) began offering agility trials in 1998.

Agility is currently the fastest-growing canine sport in North America, the United Kingdom, and continental Europe. Although it requires tremendous dedication and teamwork, it is also tremendously rewarding. Agility competitions are available for all breeds of dogs (and in some organizations, mixed breeds, too) at every level of expertise. Sanctioned tests are held throughout the year in the United States. Agility offers many benefits to both dogs and owners: quality training time, physical and mental stimulation, and confidence building.

Overview

In agility, the handler must direct her dog through an obstacle course within a set amount of time. Both accuracy and speed are important. The sport is designed to test a dog's intelligence, obedience, balance, flexibility, and versatility. It is also a race against the clock. Dogs compete against dogs of similar height, measured at the withers (shoulders)—it obviously would not be fair for a Bulldog to compete against a Saluki! The number of divisions varies from organization to organization.

Fun Fact
The American Kennel Club (AKC) held its first agility trial in 1994. That first year, only 23 AKC agility trials were held; today, the number is closer to 2,000.

The difficulty of agility is somewhat dependent upon the sponsoring organization. Organizations whose events conform to international rules, such as the USDAA, tend to be more rigorous than "domestic" events sponsored by the AKC, United Kennel Club (UKC), CPE, and NADAC.

There is no set rule about a course layout; each one is different. The judge determines a standard course time (SCT), which sets the parameters for completing the course. At entry-level competitions, the courses are simple. Higher-level courses are more complex, and at the highest level, the winning times are gauged in fractions of a second.

Before the event, handlers are permitted to walk the course without their dogs. During competition, the handler typically runs near the dog. Handlers are permitted to communicate with their dogs using any number of verbal or hand signals, as well as using body language (they can even cheer and clap their hands), but they are not allowed to touch their dogs or offer food or toys. Dogs who knock down a bar, refuse an obstacle, or fail to place their feet in a contact zone, or who navigate the obstacles out of sequence, are faulted. Dogs who fail to run the course within the SCT receive a time penalty. Dogs with the fastest time and fewest faults in their division are declared the winners.

Requirements

DOGS
- ability to jump, weave, climb, balance, and stay
- accuracy
- courage
- high level of intelligence
- obedience to voice/gesture commands
- reliability off lead
- speed
- top physical condition
- trust

HANDLERS
- ability to learn patterns
- good physical condition

Equipment and Supplies

No matter what the governing body, all agility trials offer the same basic course and equipment:
- A-frame
- dogwalk
- jumps (bar, spread, tire, broad)
- open and closed (chute) tunnels
- table
- teeter (seesaw)
- weave poles

A-Frame: The A-frame consists of two platforms, about 2 feet 6 inches to 4 feet (0.5 to 1 m) wide by 6 feet 8 inches to 8 or 9 feet (2 to 2.5 m or 3 m) long, hinged together and raised so that the apex is between 4 feet 1 inch and 5 feet 10 inches (1 and 2 m) above the ground, forming roughly an A shape. The bottom 42 inches (106.5 cm) of both sides

TOP BREEDS

Although individual dogs of almost any breed can perform well in agility, the top performers tend to be intelligent dogs of medium size and descended from herding and working dogs. Giant breeds, dogs with very long legs, and dogs with short legs and long backs are probably the least suited physically for this sport. In general, your dog should be able to jump his own height before entering an agility competition. Breeds that do especially well in agility include Shetland Sheepdogs, Belgian Tervurens, Border Collies, Australian Shepherds, Golden Retrievers, Labrador Retrievers, Cocker Spaniels, Welsh Corgis, and Papillons. However, any well-structured, sound, independent, and curious dog is a good candidate for this sport.

of the A-frame are painted a bright color, usually yellow, forming the contact zone. As is the case for every contact obstacle, dogs are required to have at least one paw touch the yellow painted areas on the way up and *especially* on the way down. Most sanctioning organizations require that A-frames have low-profile, narrow, horizontal slats all along their length to assist the dog's grip on the ascent and descent.

Dogwalk: This contact obstacle, usually made of wood, is like a large balance beam used in women's gymnastics. It consists of three 8-foot (2.5-m) or 11-foot 6-inch to 12-foot (3.5-m) planks, 11 to 12 inches (28 to 30.5 cm) wide, connected at the ends. The middle plank is raised above the ground so that the two end planks are essentially ramps leading to it. This obstacle also has contact zones, measuring from 36 to 48 inches (91.5 to 114.5 cm) from the bottom. Most sanctioning organizations also require slats on the dogwalk ramps.

Jumps: Jump heights are based on the competing dog's height. Types of jumps vary and include the bar jump, spread jump, and tire jump. Course designers have some latitude about which types of jumps to include, as well as their layout. The bar jumps can be "winged" or "wingless."

The **bar jump** challenges a dog's ability to jump high. It contains either a single bar or a solid panel over which the dog must jump.

The **spread jump**, which consists of two or three sets of uprights, each with horizontal poles, tests a dog's ability to jump high and wide. The double jump may have parallel or ascending horizontal bars; the triple jump always has ascending bars. The spread between the horizontal bars may be adjusted based on the dog's height.

The **tire jump** is usually suspended by a sturdy chain in a frame and set at the appropriate jump height. It is usually wrapped with brightly colored tape to make it visible. A chain is very easy to raise or lower by increments and so is almost infinitely adjustable. Dogs are faulted for going around the jump, under the tire, or between the tire and frame.

The **board jump**, **broad jump**, or **long jump** has two to five boards, depending on the jump height. The highest boards are placed in the middle, with marker poles at the corners. A dog jumping cleanly will not touch the boards or marker poles.

You might also see specialized jumps in some competitions, like the "picket fence," "wall," or even the picturesque "wishing well."

The open tunnel is constructed of flexible vinyl and wire.

Table: The purpose of this "obstacle," also known as the pause table, is to test a dog's control. It takes discipline to be able to stop in the middle of an exciting run to make a five-second *down-stay*, elbows touching the table. The dog can bark but is not allowed to get up until released by his handler's command. The height of the table is set at the dog's jump height category. The pause box is similar to the table except that it is on the ground. Usually a course will have one or the other style "rest stop," not both.

Teeter (Seesaw): This is an 8-, 10-, or 12-foot (2.5-, 3-, or 3.5-m) plank pivoting on a fulcrum. It is constructed slightly off balance so that the same end always returns to the ground. This obstacle also has contact zones. The balance point and the weight of the plank must be such that even a tiny dog can tip it.

Tunnels: The **open**, **rigid**, or **pipe tunnel** can range between 10 and 20 feet (3 and 6 m) long, with an opening of 18 to 24 inches (45.5 to 61 cm). A longer tunnel can have bends or curves in it, but it generally takes two people to manage. The tunnel is constructed of flexible vinyl and wire so that it can be configured in a straight line or curved.

The **closed tunnel (chute)** is a vinyl barrel with an opening of 24 inches (61 cm) in diameter. At the opposite end is a 12- to 15-foot (3.5- to 4.5-m) section of material (short tunnels are 6 to 8 feet [2 to 2.5 m]), which can be lightweight parachute material or heavy canvas. It is closed until the dog runs into the open end of the chute and pushes out through the chute part.

It sounds obvious, but for both the open and closed tunnels, the dog must exit the tunnel from the end opposite to that in which he entered. Otherwise there's a penalty. It's amazing how many dogs change their minds midway through. Of course, some breeds, such as terriers, are naturally attracted to tunnels and don't require any urging or special preparation. Other dogs are more skeptical.

Weave Poles: The weave poles are a series of poles about .75 to 1.5 inches (2 to 4 cm) in diameter and between 3 and 4 feet (1 m) high. They are spaced anywhere between 18 and 24 inches (46 and 61 cm) apart, according to the instructions of the judge. In competition, between 5 and 12 poles are used.

Dogs are required to enter to the right of the first pole and weave through each one until they exit the last pole, exiting to the left, rather like a slalom. This is the only obstacle that has a "correct" and "incorrect" side for entering and exiting. It is the most difficult obstacle for most dogs to learn to negotiate.

Sponsoring Organizations

AMERICAN KENNEL CLUB (AKC)

The AKC offers two types of agility classes. The first is the Standard Class, which includes obstacles such as the dogwalk, A-frame, and teeter. The second is Jumpers with Weaves, which has only jumps, tunnels, and weave poles. Both classes offer increasing levels of difficulty to earn titles. The classes are divided by jump heights to make the competition equal among the different sizes of dogs.

Eligibility Requirements: All AKC-registered dogs of at least 12 months of age can participate.

Titles: The AKC offers Novice, Open, Excellent, and Master titles in both its Standard and Jumpers with Weaves programs. After completing both an Excellent Standard title (AX) and Excellent Jumpers title (AXJ), a dog and handler team can compete for the Master Agility Champion (MACH) title.

FROM THE EXPERT

Agility expert Heather Smith of the United States Dog Agility Association (USDAA) says, "Forming a good working relationship is the cornerstone of any activity. By doing so, you learn what you can ask of and expect from the dog, and the dog learns to trust you and accept what you are asking him to do. When I started my first dog in agility in 1985 (the sport was brand new), I had a dog who I had trained through the Utility Level in obedience. We had also worked in tracking and field. When we started agility, I didn't "train" her—she just walked up the ramps and ran through the tunnels and learned it because I asked her to. Make it fun and positive for the dog and for yourself. Take your time and don't rush. Don't do anything with your dog that you don't feel comfortable with just because a trainer asks it of you."

The dogs run the same course but with adjustments in the expected time and jump height.

Premier Events: The AKC offers a National Agility Championship each year, as well as an Agility Invitational.

CANINE PERFORMANCE EVENTS (CPE)

The CPE offers Standard Classes and many Games Classes, including Snooker, Jackpot, Wildcard, and Colors. Junior and physically challenged handlers are welcomed.

Eligibility Requirements: All purebred and mixed-breed dogs are welcome, but dogs and their owners must be registered with the CPE. Dogs must be 15 months of age or older. Veterans six years or older may compete at lower jump heights.

Titles: The CPE currently offers five levels of titles from beginner to championship in various categories, including Regular, Veteran, Enthusiast, Specialist, and Champion, all at various levels. Important titles include CPE Agility Team Extraordinaire (C-ATE), CPE Agility Trial Champion (C-ATCH), Specialist Champion (SpCH), and Specialist Extraordinaire (SpEx).

Premier Events: The CPE holds a National Championship once a year.

NORTH AMERICAN DOG AGILITY COUNCIL (NADAC)

The NADAC was formed in 1993 specifically to foster and support agility competition. It holds separate classes for veterans and juniors, as well as a variety of games, ensuring fun for all levels of competition. Every class in a NADAC trial is split into two categories, Proficient and Skilled, with the former being more difficult. Courses are the same for both categories.

Eligibility Requirements: All dogs must be registered to compete in NADAC events. This is a one-time process, and the number assigned is permanent. Both purebred and mixed-breed dogs of at least 18 months are eligible to participate. Bitches in heat, as well as lame or blind dogs, are ineligible. Exhibitors are not required to be NADAC Associates to register their dogs or compete in NADAC-sanctioned events.

Titles: The NADAC offers Novice, Open, and Elite titles

All agility trials offer the same basic course and equipment.

in Regular Agility, Chances, Jumpers, Tunnelers, Touch 'n Go, Weavers, and their newest category, Hoopers. There are size divisions within each category. Major titles include NADAC Agility Trial Champion (NATCH), NADAC Versatility Champion (Vers-NATCH), and NADAC Agility Trial Medalist (MEDAL).

Premier Events: The NADAC offers an annual Championship competition.

UNITED KENNEL CLUB (UKC)

In UKC agility, the handler directs her dog through a course involving tunnels, a sway bridge (different from other clubs), jumps, and other obstacles in a race against the clock. Speed is important, but control and accuracy are as well. The dogs are scored on the manner in which they negotiate these obstacles and the time elapsed to complete the course. In general, UKC agility involves more control of the dog over complicated obstacles rather than speed and accuracy over simpler ones.

Eligibility Requirements: UKC-registered dogs of at least six months of age are eligible to participate.

Titles: The UKC offers United Agility I (UAGI) and United Agility II (UAGII) titles for earning three qualifying scores at three different UKC-licensed agility trials in the Agility I and II classes. From there, a dog can go on to earn his United Agility Champion (UACH), United Agility Champion Excellent (UACHX), and United Grand Agility Champion (UGRACH) titles.

Premier Events: The UKC offers an All-Stars series of awards. Although the UKC does not offer a National Championship in agility, it publicizes the names of the top winning dogs for the year on its website.

United States Dog Agility Association (USDAA)

The USDAA is the world's largest independent organization for the sport of dog agility, with more than 22,000 registered competitors and more than 30,000 dogs representing more than 200 different breeds, including mixed breeds. It represents more than 120 affiliated groups that conduct agility events in the United States, Puerto Rico, Canada, Mexico, Bermuda, Guatemala, Costa Rica, and Japan. It prides itself on conforming to international standards in the sport. In 2000, the USDAA became a charter member in the International Federation of Cynological Sports (IFCS), a nonprofit organization headquartered in Russia whose main purpose is to organize canine sports worldwide.

The USDAA offers two programs: Championship and Performance. The latter is more recreational, less competitive, and offers lower jumping heights for dogs, longer times for the course, and a lower A-frame for all height classes. The USDAA also has Jumpers Classes and other nonstandard classes (imported from the UK).

The USDAA has four basic height divisions within each of its competitive programs. It also offers other games like Gamblers and Snooker, which encourage handlers to design their own courses under rules established by the judge on the day of competition. Another option is Relay, which pairs two dogs and two handlers to take on a course together.

BEYOND STANDARD AGILITY: GAMES CLASSES

Games Classes offer something a little different.

Snooker: In the Snooker courses, dogs earn points by successfully negotiating a "red" obstacle, followed by the handler's choice of other obstacle. Because dogs are poor at distinguishing most colors, they rely on their handlers to pick out the right ones. After the opening sequence, the dog must complete the closing sequence before the clock runs out.

Pairs Agility: Another popular game course is Pairs Agility, which has two dogs in the ring at the same time. Each dog completes half the course separately; as in a relay race, the handlers carry a baton, which is passed to the next handler after completing each section.

Team Relay: Team Relay consists of a group of three or four dogs, each running the course separately.

Gamblers: In the Gamblers Class, the handler tries to pick up as many points as possible by choosing among various obstacles, each with a different point value.

Eligibility Requirements: Dogs must be registered with the USDAA to compete, and must be at least 18 months of age.

Titles: Participants may earn certification titles, such as Agility Dog®, Advanced Agility Dog®, and Master Agility Dog® in the Championship Program. Titles are also offered through the USDAA Junior Handler Program and Performance Program. Certification titles are offered for both standard and nonstandard classes: Standard Agility, Gambler's Choice, Snooker Agility, Jumpers, and Relay.

Premier Events: The USDAA top events include the Grand Prix of Dog Agility® World Championships, its flagship event; the Dog Agility Steeplechase® speed jumping tournament series; and the Dog Agility Masters® Three-Dog Team Championship. The Grand Prix has drawn competitors from 15 countries on 5 continents.

How to Get Started

Agility is tough work and involves movements that in some sense are unnatural to dogs. Wild dogs, for instance, have no need to negotiate weave poles or walk along seesaws. Problems are compounded when owners begin training their young dogs before their muscle and bone structures have matured. Twisting too much at the weave poles at an early age and jumping too early can spell trouble. Most trainers suggest that rigorous agility training begin with a young adult rather than a puppy. However, puppies are capable of learning some of the less strenuous groundwork, such as going through tunnels and learning obedience commands.

GET YOUR DOG A CHECKUP

Get your dog a health checkup before you begin training for agility. Explain to your vet what the dog will be doing to help her decide what tests are most important. (If you have a video of an agility competition, it might be very helpful.) Pre-existing conditions, such as hip or elbow dysplasia, must be ruled out.

WAIT UNTIL THE GROWTH PLATES CLOSE

You should wait until the growth plates in the long bones close completely before asking a small dog to jump more than 6 inches (15 cm) or a large dog to jump more than 12 inches (30.5 cm). The age of growth maturity varies. Ask your vet to X-ray your dog when he is about a year old to make sure that the plates have grown closed. In general, dogs whose adult weight is less than 50 pounds (22.5 kg) mature between 9 and 12 months of age. Larger dogs typically don't mature until they are between 10 and 14 months of age. This is not a sport in which "getting a head start" is an advantage.

At the other end of the scale, most healthy dogs are able to participate successfully in agility until they are eight to ten years old. Some trials even have "veteran" classes. Even if your dog is fully mature, he should have a complete health screening before attempting agility.

SPEND TIME IN CLASSES AND AT TRIALS

Spend as much time as possible in agility classes and at trials. You will learn an immeasurable amount merely by paying attention to the best people in the business. This doesn't mean that you should copy their every move; obviously, what works for one person might not work for another. Instead, learn from as many people as you can. Soon you'll have a

To learn the ropes, spend as much time as possible in agility classes and at trials.

storehouse of ideas and techniques from which to draw.

If you have access to an agility class, take advantage of it. Nothing replaces the hands-on, practical, personal tutelage of an experienced instructor. This sport is too complex and dangerous for do-it-yourselfers.

PHYSICALLY CONDITION YOUR DOG

If your dog has hair falling over his eyes, you will need to trim it or at least pin it back for agility work. The nails should be kept a proper length so that they don't catch in the equipment.

Weight is also an important consideration. As a trained athlete, your dog needs to be trim and fit. Most sports dogs weigh less than more sedentary dogs, even if the latter are not considered overweight. *Any* extra weight places strain on muscles, joints, and ligaments and can lead not only to slower times but to actual injuries. If your dog is at the proper weight, you can help him stay fit with regular walks interspersed with sprint activities. Games of fetch and endurance runs can also be helpful, as can swimming to improve cardiovascular strength.

OBEDIENCE TRAIN YOUR DOG

Good agility training begins with good obedience training. Your dog should know how to come, sit, down, and stay, all off lead. Ideally, he should also learn "right" and "left" (or "gee" and "haw," respectively). The most important thing your dog can learn is that you are his best friend, trusted leader, and happy playmate. Experts agree that dogs who have been trained in off-lead heelwork and who can fetch on command have an advantage.

Strategies for Success

Agility is a competitive event, but it's also a team sport and bonding activity between you and your dog. Your dog does not know that he is in a competition. He does know that he wants to please you and have fun at the same time. If you define success by having fun, staying active, and enjoying time with your dog, agility is bound to be winner for everybody.

ENCOURAGE YOUR DOG

This is a sport in which positive reinforcement yields its own rewards. Never punish your dog for making a mistake; instead, use encouragement to get him to do the right thing. The best agility dogs are highly motivated by playtime and enjoy games, such as tugging, which are not only pleasurable but interactive with the handler. The more play you can introduce, the better. It's easy to throw a treat at your dog when he makes the right moves, but that can ultimately be counterproductive, as he will soon be looking for the reward rather than having fun.

DON'T OVERPRACTICE

Don't burn your dog out by overpracticing—dogs have no ambition to become trophy winners. They want to have fun, and they enjoy being praised. Keep the sessions short. A 15-minute session is plenty of time to be actually working your dog. Slow, thorough preparation will pay off; don't let

> ## PAY ATTENTION!
>
> One of the simplest rules in agility is this: Pay attention to your dog! If you do, you'll be quicker to spot physical problems, training mistakes, and ways to make improvements. Best of all, paying attention to your dog will increase the likelihood of his paying attention to you.

Use encouragement to get your dog to do what you want on the agility course.

impatience get the better of you. It may take a year or more before your dog is ready to compete after you have started training.

Never push your dog to achieve a goal too quickly. On the other hand, don't repeat the same thing over and over. Although practice makes perfect, your dog is likely to conclude that he has done something wrong if you keep going over and over the same area.

START SLOWLY

Actual agility training begins with calmly introducing a dog to lower, simpler obstacles than those he will meet in trials.

Although some dogs require a leash at first, you may find that the leash is an impediment to learning because it can get tangled up in the equipment or your legs. On the other hand, judiciously used, a leash can show a dog how to negotiate obstacles.

After your dog can handle each individual obstacle, take him around the ring on a lead while he works them in a series. Once you are sure that your dog can handle the course, remove the leash.

DEVELOP A WORD CODE

You and your dog will need to develop a code that helps him understand which obstacle he needs to approach next. As you progress, he will be able to respond to your commands instantaneously and while running at full speed. Commands should be given in a sharp, clear voice and pronounced in advance of the obstacle that you wish your dog to take. However, don't start using your code words until your dog will go over the obstacle without fear. If you start by saying "Hoop!" to a dog who is afraid of the tire jump, the word itself can trigger a fear reaction.

WORK FROM ALL AREAS OF THE RING

Work from all areas of the ring—your dog should never have to rely on your being in one particular position in relation to him. He should also be prepared to negotiate any obstacle in any order. An agility dog needs to be alert in all directions.

ADDITIONAL ORGANIZATIONS

Agility Association of Canada (AAC)
www.aac.ca
British Agility Association (BAA)
www.baa.uk.net
Canadian Kennel Club (CKC)
www.ckc.ca
International Agility Link (IAL)
http://www.dogpatch.org/Agility/IAL/ial.html
The Kennel Club (KC)
www.thekennelclub.org.uk

Chapter 2

Bikejoring

Definition

Bikejoring is the sport of riding a bike (usually a mountain bike) overland while being pulled by one or two dogs. The rider can assist the dogs by pedaling if needed, especially on grassy, sandy, or mulch-chip paths. Occasionally, three smaller dogs may also be used, although this is rare. This sport is related to other dog mushing sports, such as canicross, scootering, skijoring, and sledding.

History of Bikejoring

There is no official history of this sport, although the idea of biking with dogs has been around for some time. The idea began with mushing, an activity carried on by Alaskan and Siberian people for thousands of years, and it has been a natural transition to other forms of nonmotored transport (carts, scooters, bikes, and skis, for example) with canine muscle. The first bikejorer's name is lost to history, and the sport is undoubtedly the result of an idea that many people came up with more or less simultaneously.

Overview

Bikejoring is the summertime version of skijoring. If you live in an area with no snow but hanker for the thrill of being pulled by a team of dogs, this is the sport for you. Bikejoring provides a great opportunity to allow your dog to run safely—and you get to keep up with him for once. It also

TOP BREEDS

All breeds are theoretically able to participate in bikejoring, but some are obviously better suited than others. While this makes it difficult to get mentored, it does mean that any dog who is big and strong enough to pull a bike can participate. The main considerations for a successful bikejoring dog are good conformation, good health, and a passionate desire to run. Usually, two dogs is a good number for bikejoring, with fewer dogs used on more difficult terrain. Most experts recommend using no more than two dogs.

The same breeds that make good mushing dogs, such as Samoyeds and Siberian Huskies, make excellent bikejorers, but so do some retrievers and other hunting dogs. Bulldogs and Basset Hounds make poorer candidates because of their short legs, and in the case of the Bulldog, inability to run for long periods. Dog with short muzzles usually cannot breathe well enough for this vigorous sport. Obviously, toy breeds (or anything under 30 pounds [13.5 kg]) are also unsuitable. Ideal bikejoring dogs are medium to large and strong, with the ability to run easily for a long distance.

allows you and your dog to work together as a team. This is one dog sport where you have to consider your own safety as well as that of the dogs; remember that wherever your dog goes, the bike goes and so do you.

Although some people (mostly in Europe) do bikejoring competitively, in the United States, it is largely done for fun and as summer training (dryland racing) for people who skijor.

Requirements

Dogs
- desire to pull
- endurance
- obedience to commands
- speed
- strength

Handlers
- competency in cycling
- good physical condition

Equipment and Supplies
- bike
- booties for dog
- eye protection
- gloves
- harness
- helmet
- line
- loop or bridle
- reflective vests

Bike: A good-quality mountain bike is pretty much a must, and it will need to be cleaned and lubricated frequently. Choose one with front suspension forks to add control to the bike; on the other hand, full-suspension bikes may require too-frequent maintenance.

The best brakes for bikejoring are the new V-brakes or disc brakes, which are more expensive and technologically complex. These brakes can be activated with a finger touch and give you great control. Some people opt for a single-

Purchase a good-quality mountain bike, and clean and lubricate it frequently.

speed bike with foot brakes as being satisfactory and in many ways safer than a bike with hand brakes. Biking while being pulled by dogs is tough on the brakes (especially in muddy conditions), so a frequent checkup is in order. It is also important to adjust the brake pads; they should be adjusted to align with the rim curvature. An improper adjustment could result in a blowout—not something you want when being pulled! Also, be sure that the bike has a mirror; you need to see what is coming up behind you.

One of the most critical elements of bikejoring maintenance is truing the tires. When you spin the wheels, there should be no wobble in any direction—either side to side or up and down. Careful bikejorers may take the time to true the wheels to 1/100th of an inch. This can be done with a wheel truing stand and spoke wrench.

A bike with a quick-release seat binder allows for quick seat adjustment on the trail without the need for tools. Many find this useful while they are getting used to the changes resulting from adding a dog to the bike.

Booties: Booties protect your dog's feet. The best dog booties allow maximum flexibility of your dog's foot and should fit properly.

Eye Protection: Dogs tend to kick up a lot of debris. Protect your eyes by wearing impact-resistant glasses.

Gloves: Gloves are needed to protect your hands from rope burn (or road rash if you fall). The best bikejoring gloves are made from leather or its equivalent. They should fit snugly and comfortably.

Harness: Use the same well-padded X-back harness used for sled-dog racing and skijoring. These can be purchased from any sled-dog equipment dealer. Make sure that the fit is a good one, and ask for expert help if you are not sure. Don't use a typical walking harness, in which the loop is attached near the shoulder area. The loop needs to be attached closer to the tail so that the dog has use of the front of his body; he needs to be able to move freely. The proper harnesses cannot be purchased in most pet-supply stores but are available from mushing specialty stores.

Helmet: It's pretty much a guarantee that you will fall off your bike sooner or later, so a good helmet is a necessity. Some bikers wrap reflective tape on theirs to make themselves more visible.

Line: Use a skijoring line, a 9- or 10-foot (2.5- or 3-m) length of hollow polyrope with a 3-foot (1-m) bungee cord integrated into the core of the rope. One end snaps to the dog's harness, and the other end has a loop that connects to the bridle snap. If you are running two dogs, you should also use a neckline between the dogs, attached to their collars. This will ensure that the dogs run side by side, close together—not veering off from each other and creating a trail hazard for others. If you are riding on very narrow trails, it is wise to use an inline lead that will position the dogs one in front of the other. This is also a great way to train a lead dog. You can buy such a lead from sled-dog suppliers.

Loop or "Bridle": The bridle loop attaches the line to the bike. Although several devices are on the market to attach dogs to bikes, look specifically for the kind that allows your dog to run in front, not tag along behind or beside you. A dog who is pulling to the side can unseat you; a dog who is trailing behind you can get into trouble before you even notice. Get a simple, snapped-loop (6 to 8 inches [15 to 20.5 cm] long when folded) nylon cord. Tie it under the stem of the bike with a nonslip knot; the snapped end of the loop should lie over the bars. This kind of connection allows you the most control of the bike because the dogs will be pulling in the direction of bike travel. Do not attach the line from the grips of the handlebar or indeed to any part of the bike that is not front and center. Because bikejoring alters the rider's center of gravity to some degree, you may need to compensate by positioning your body over the bicycle a little farther back, especially when going downhill. You can correct this by attaching the loop to the head tube of the bike, but that will drag the line over the wheel, causing premature wear to the line. A few dogs simply will not run in front of a bicycle. For these dogs, you can buy an attachment called a "springer" that attaches to the bicycle seat tube via a short

Many dogs are natural runners, so bikejoring is a good sport for them.

Fun Fact

An obedient dog trusts you to do what is right, respects your leadership, and responds to you instantly. You don't have time in bikejoring to repeat shouted commands. Good training is based on positive reinforcement, although firm but kind correction also has its place. Your dog should have plenty of fun, but there should be no room in his brain to doubt your authority. Dogs are very responsive to tone of voice, so use a bright, cheerful voice for praise, a firm tone for commands, and a darker tone for corrections.

leash and spring mechanism. This is ideal for dogs who are not "front runners." The shorter lead is also good for urban bikejorers, who need a shorter lead for more control. A disadvantage is the wider profile you'll create—not good for narrow tracks.

Reflective Vests: When bikejoring, you want your dog to be as visible as possible. Most such vests are orange and made of a mesh fabric with yellow and gray reflective strips (yellow is reflective during the day and gray at night). The width of the vest should equal the circumference of the rib cage, and the length should be slightly less than your dog's length from tail to collar to ensure a comfortable fit.

Sponsoring Organizations

Bikejoring is largely a recreational rather than a competitive sport, but things are beginning to change. Sponsors include the International Sled Dog Racing Association (ISDRA) and the International Federation of Sleddog Sports, Inc. (IFSS). Races are governed by the local entity or mushing club sponsoring the race. Bikejoring competitions may be divided into one- and two-dog classes, as well as among Pro, Novice, and Junior Classes. Men's and women's events may be held separately. Events may last for two or three days, but distances run in any one heat or race usually vary between 3 and 5 miles (5 and 8 km) over fairly level terrain.

Eligibility Requirements: Most clubs prohibit dogs under one year of age from competing, but unless it's a

You should be a competent cyclist before you attempt to bikejor, and your dog should be able to run in front of a bike.

breed-specialty club, all breeds and mixes are welcome. The IFSS requires dogs to be 18 months old.

Titles: At present, no titles can be earned in bikejoring.

Premier Events: Races are held all around the United States and Europe under various sponsorships, and several countries, like Switzerland, have championship races. The United States does not at present.

How to Get Started

Many dogs are natural runners, so bikejoring is a good sport for them. It is also a great opportunity for your dog to get some needed and wanted exercise.

FIND A MENTOR

If possible, find a mentor, group, or club to help you with the basics. Bikejoring is a complex sport in which both humans and dogs can sustain injuries because of poor training or unsafe practices. Even putting on the harness correctly can be a challenge, not to mention knowing how to buy and maintain the right bike. Getting together with an experienced bikejorer can enhance your experience and reduce the possibility of injury or accident.

PUT SAFETY FIRST

To keep both you and your dog safe, make your first attempts at bikejoring in a low-traffic, gravel-free area. Also, begin with just one dog; only time will tell if you become skillful enough to add a second one. Many bikers find that biking with just one dog is best. After all, you're not running the Iditarod in a heavy sled! Even if you have more than one dog, taking one out at a time gives you that all-important one-on-one quality time and teaches all of your dogs to be confident leaders. One dog at least should be trained to lead.

CONDITION YOUR DOG—AND YOURSELF

Both you and your dog must be in good condition for this often rigorous sport. First, you must be a competent cyclist before you attempt to bikejor. Second, your dog must be strong and able to run in front of a bike for several miles (km). He should have a health check, especially of his heart and lungs, before you begin. Your dog must also be obedient and not distractible. If paired with another dog, he must be able to get along with him.

DEVELOP VERBAL CUES

Because you will have very little, if any, physical control of your dog, you will need to depend on verbal cues. In bikejoring, as in skijoring, an unresponsive dog can be deadly. Bikejoring requires big-time obedience. A disobedient dog will not just "lose points"—he could kill you.

Begin by teaching your dog to heel and obey your commands while doing so. (Some bikejoring enthusiasts, however, maintain that dogs should be taught to always be in front.) Then move on to having your dog walk in front of you (leashed) while you work the same commands. When perfect, it's time to hook your dog up to the bike. Again, for safety's sake, always begin with just one dog.

Many bikejorers have discovered that it helps dogs settle if you remark upon what is happening without too much excitement. Words like "car," "cat," "people," "dog," "squirrel," and so forth, when pronounced calmly, let your dog know that you have observed these things as well, and they're nothing to get excited about. Even more complex information such as "front" or "behind" can be added to

FROM THE EXPERT

Bikejoring expert Bruce Crawford passed along some fabulous tips to help people get started. Bruce says, "I have more of an adventure bikejoring before work than most people have all week!"

- Find a mentor or group.
- Suit the sport to your dog, and check with your vet to make sure that you won't hurt him by running him.
- If you bikejor in traffic or busy places, be visible. Wear bright colors, tie flagging to the gang line, and have your dog wear a reflective vest.
- Watch out for and detour around broken glass.
- Be safe and be patient. Get your dog used to being around bikes before you hook him up to one. (A scared dog hooked to a bike or scooter that he fears is a disaster.)
- Always wear a bike helmet and other safety gear because you will likely take a spill when you least expect it. You are always one squirrel away from a spill!
- Learn in a quiet, straight, and flat location on a wide trail or road. Always make it fun, or take a break.
- Getting the gang line stuck between the front wheel and frame and being thrown from the bike or scooter is another common mistake. People I've talked with either use a length of hose or plastic pipe or a bay-o-net to help keep the gang line from getting caught in the front wheel. But you should still keep your hand on the rear brake to prevent a slack line.
- Always use the rear brake first and the front brake gently and only as a last resort. If you jam the front brake on, you will be thrown from the bike.

your dog's comprehension vocabulary over time. If you are running more than one dog and wish to make a correction to one dog only, it may make sense to preface the command with the dog's name, such as "Thunder, leave it!" That will reduce the likelihood of the other dogs being confused by an irrelevant (to them) comment.

Bikejoring commands are similar to those used in sledding. Teach them to your dog while you are on foot at first and when you presumably have some reinforcement power. Of course, you can use any words you like, but make them consistent and sufficiently different in sound from each other so as not to confuse him. Because your dog is moving fast, it's usually good idea to give him a few seconds (if possible) to obey, so an early command is best. Useful commands include:

- Gee: Turn right!
- Haw: Turn left!
- Hike: Get started!
- Leave it: Drop that dead possum!
- On by: Ignore whatever that it is and just keep moving.
- Out there!: Move to the very end of the line and pull.
- Slow: Take down the pace.
- Stop: Come to a complete halt.
- Straight: Continue in a straight line (to be used at crossroads).
- Turn: Turn completely around. If preceded by "Gee" or "Haw," your dog will know which way to begin the turn.
- Yield: Get off the trail.

If your dog ignores a command, it's time to get off the bike and do some retraining. Flying along at top speed is no time to have your commands disobeyed.

Strategies for Success

Success in bikejoring is defined as being able to enjoy the great outdoors, partner with your dog, and not fall off your bike—at least not too often. To that end, know and understand your bike and dog before you pair them together.

Success in bikejoring is being able to enjoy the outdoors with your dog—while not falling off your bike!

WALK FIRST, THEN RUN

It's best to train your dog to lead you at a walk first. Dogs who veer off the trail when they are just walking in front of you will also do it at a run when pulling a bike. A dog will not behave better when moving fast.

TAKE CARE OF YOUR DOG

It's important to take care of your dog as he works. Here are some tips when bikejoring to assure your dog's safety:

- Carry a first-aid kit.
- Ride when it's cool. Dogs can't handle heat as well as people can.
- Take along plenty of water for your dog, or ride where it is readily available. Running dogs should have water every 2 miles (3 km).
- Check his feet frequently, and constantly watch for

limping. Bring along booties to deal with cut pads. If your dog will learn to run with booties, so much the better; the best dog booties allow maximum flexibility of your dog's foot.

- Soft dirt or even a sandy surface is easier on your dog's paws than hard-packed dirt. Do not ride on concrete.

- Pay careful attention to your dog's behavior. You have little real control, and if he scents a deer or squirrel and charges into the woods after it, you will be dragged along for what will surely be an uncomfortable or even lethal (but undoubtedly short) ride.

- Don't go too fast. It's exhilarating, but the last thing you want is to lose control of your dog.

- Pay attention to your dog's body language, and stop right away if something seems wrong. Some dogs will literally run until they are dead.

- When braking, try to brake to the side of your dog, not directly behind. Although you should have no problems if the brakes are good and the conditions perfect, you might slide into your dog and hurt him. Even if you don't, it could make him lose confidence.

PRACTICE WITH A FRIEND

One way to practice, especially for hills, is to ask a good (and good-natured) friend to play the part of your dog and pull you up and down and around turns. This will give you some experience, at least as to what to expect under various conditions. It will also give the neighbors something to talk about.

ADDITIONAL ORGANIZATIONS

European Canicross and Bikejöring Federation (ECF)
www.ecf.cc
International Federation of Sleddog Sports, Inc. (IFSS)
www.sleddogsport.com
International Sled Dog Racing Association (ISDRA)
www.isdra.org

Chapter 3

Canicross

Definition

Canicross (also referred to as CaniX) is the sport of running cross-country with a dog or dogs attached to you and pulling you forward. The technical difference between canicross and just jogging along with your dog is that canicross is a hands-free activity. This is probably the only canine activity in which you actually encourage your dog to pull! The sport is unlike hiking or jogging in that the dog is a motivator and actually helps pull the runner up hills. It's been estimated that runners can go up to 30 seconds per mile (1.5 km) faster with a dog "pulling" them.

People who ski may use poles while canicrossing to keep their "poling muscles" in top shape, but it's not necessary, and nonskiers don't use them. People who do a lot of skijoring or other dog and snow sports call canicross a "dryland" sport, and many people participate in it only while the ground is bare of snow; for them, canicross is just a training exercise. For others, however, canicross is a sport to enjoy on its own merits, and many participants never skijor or bikejor.

History of Canicross

The term "canicross" is of European origin: "cani" is representative of your canine friend, and "cross" refers to traveling cross-country on foot. The sport is most popular in Europe, where it originated, and is gaining popularity in other parts of the world, including Asia. (One recent race in South Korea was plagued with dust storms blowing in from the Gobi Desert in China.) A relatively new sport, the first World Championships in canicross were held in Ravenna, Italy, in 2002.

Overview

Canicross is really a human speed sport. (Skijoring and sledding are dog speed sports.) Canicross is closely related to the winter sport of skijoring, in which the dog uses his strength to pull his human counterpart on skis. Many skijorers do canicross when there is no snow available or to travel from one snowy patch to another. Canicross is also a power sport for dogs when done uphill.

Two kinds of people take readily to this sport: competitive runners who want to improve their speed and endurance and mushers who are looking for a snowless way to keep their dogs in condition. (It is also an excellent way to begin training a leader dog for other sports, as corrections can be more easily made on foot than from a bike or sled.) Many skijorers and mushers enjoy canicross when the snow is melted and it is too muddy to bike, while others enjoy the sport just for itself. And like all dog sports, canicross will build trust between you and your dog.

Competitive runners and mushers take readily to the sport of canicross.

Requirements

Dogs
- ability to pull
- obedience to commands
- top physical condition

Handlers
- good endurance
- top physical condition

Equipment and Supplies

The equipment required for canicross is quite similar to that used for skijoring (without the skis, of course).
- booties
- eye protection
- flexible line or lead
- head halter
- running harness
- waist belt

> ## FUN FACT
>
> Expert human distance runners run at about 12 miles (19.5 km) per hour (that's 1 mile [1.5 km] in 5 minutes), while experienced sled dogs have no trouble with 20 miles per hour (32 kph) for more than 20 miles (32 km)! Still, the fastest team is only as fast as the slowest dog. In canicross, that's you. It's important, though, not to try to "catch up" with your dog. He's faster than you are and always will be. Trying to keep pace with him will result in an unnatural lengthening of your stride, possibly resulting in injury.

Booties: Booties are essential for canicross; they can be used both to prevent and treat foot problems. (Always inspect your dog's feet before, during, and after a run.) Many booties come with Velcro fasteners to keep them in place. Different types of surfaces call for different types of booties: Cordura for snow, fleece or Toughtek for gravel or other hard surfaces. After the run is done, remove the booties immediately, partly so that your dog's paws don't "fall asleep" but mainly so that he doesn't eat his shoes.

Eye Protection: Many people choose to wear impact-resistant goggles or other eye protection, especially when running on a surface where dirt, grit, or gravel may be a problem. If you're running in the shade, choose light rather than dark lenses, of course.

Flexible (Elasticized or Bungee) Line or Lead: The purpose of the flexible line is to reduce jerks and shocks to both participants. Many people use the same line that is used for skijoring and scootering. It should be made of high-quality polyethylene. These lines come in various colors and can be purchased in both one- and two-dog versions. Lines with an internal bungee work best and are even mandated in some competitions. The line length is usually 7 to 12 feet (2 to 3.5 m). This is shorter than those used for skijoring, but abrupt stopping is not a consideration in canicross; however, in competition, specific rules may be laid out for line length and clipping requirements. In general, personal preference counts most.

If you are running two dogs, it's a good idea to attach the dogs to each other as well.

Head Halter: Many canicrossers add a head halter to their dog's running gear. The head halter is important for easy halts if you (the runner) should get into trouble.

Running Harness: Most participants select a padded X-back harness, which allows the dog to pull from his chest but which then disperses the stress over his entire body. Some Europeans prefer to use a "guard" harness similar to an ordinary walking harness. They believe it reduces stress on the mid or rear portions of the dog. The harness attaches to the mid-back area and may be a better choice if you are very tall or are using a short dog. Some people who use pointers, tall hounds, or similarly structured dogs prefer the split chest or hound harness, which features an open front. (Many hound-types dogs have a protruding sternum that makes other harness types uncomfortable.)

Waist Belt: Waist belts are designed to fit around the runner's waist. Some kinds come with leg loops, which are often preferred by women to keep the belt from riding up above the hips. A few manufacturers make belts specifically for canicross; these simple belts have less hardware and are lighter than belts needed for skijoring and scootering.

Sponsoring Organizations

For serious competitors, the International Sled Dog Racing Association (ISDRA) and the International Federation of

TOP BREEDS

All breeds and all mixes may participate, although some dogs are better suited to the sport than others. Obviously, toy breeds make poor candidates for this sport, as do flat-faced dogs who may develop breathing issues. Siberian Huskies, tall hounds, pointers, Border Collies, Weimaraners, Dalmatians, and strong mixes can excel. However, smaller, mellower dogs of any breed make excellent canicross companions, as long as you don't expect them to pull you.

In Europe, canicross races are much longer and are geared to long-distance runners. In the United States, they are shorter and are held mainly to condition the dogs.

Sleddog Sports (IFSS) are two governing bodies associated with canicross competitions worldwide. However, a variety of canicross hiking clubs have also been established that sponsor both leisurely hikes and yearly competitions. Many people enjoy canicross on their own time—for fun, not in competition. Rules for each sponsoring organization may differ slightly, but general guidelines are the same. Warm or excessively humid weather may cause the event to be cancelled or restricted in distance. The faster a dog runs, the faster he overheats.

Competitions may be divided into Pro, Novice, and Junior classes. In the United States, events are held over weekends in 1- to 3-mile (1.5- to 5-km) heats over fairly level ground, with the winners being those who have the fastest accumulated times. Competitors must use the same dog for all heats of the event. The line between the racer and the dog is usually regulated to between 7 and 12 feet (2 and 3.5 m).

Eligibility Requirements: Events are restricted to dogs who are 12 months of age or older, although for certain distance events, the limit may be raised to 18 months. Any breed is eligible.

Titles: Because canicross is not recognized as an event by major kennel clubs like the American Kennel Club (AKC) or United Kennel Club (UKC), no widely recognized titles are offered.

Premier Events: Although most national dog clubs do not offer canicross events yet, check with your local kennel club for fun events in your area.

How To Get Started
Almost anyone can enjoy canicross with the right training. In fact, it is a wonderful conditioning method for both dogs and humans. Canicross is not only an excellent sport in

itself but a good conditioning activity for other sports. If you hate running, then you can walk. If your dog is already used to sledding, skijoring, or bikejoring, the most difficult task will be to get him to slow down to human speed.

Canicross is a wonderful conditioning method for both dogs and humans.

CONDITION YOUR DOG

Conditioning your dog for canicross can be easy and fun for both of you. As in all sports, it is important to start slowly and make sure that you and your canine companion are both healthy before beginning canicross training. Your pet should also get a veterinary checkup before you start training.

Overheating is a concern in this sport, particularly because it is often run in warm weather. People who do canicross as summer conditioning for their Nordic-breed skijoring dogs must be particularly on the lookout for signs of overheating. Keep your dog hydrated at all times.

KNOW BASIC OBEDIENCE COMMANDS

The ideal canicross dog is well mannered and responsive, so work on basic obedience first. Your dog should already know basic heeling commands and be accustomed to wearing a head halter. The head halter is important for easy halts if you (the runner) should get into trouble. After all, the last thing you want is for Fido to drag you downhill.

In canicross, your dog will learn to keep tension on the line while traveling at human speeds. He must also learn to move with the line taut, or "line out," if you are looking to train a leader.

DEVELOP VERBAL CUES

Your dog should know the following common commands, which are similar to those used in sledding and bikejoring. They include:

- Hike!: Start or go a little faster
- Whoa!: Stop.
- Easy: Slow down, darn it!
- Gee: Go right.
- Haw: Go left.
- Straight ahead: Go straight.
- On by: Keep going, ignore that squirrel!
- Line out: Tighten the tow-line.
- Come around: Turn 180 degrees.

Start by giving your dog the *hike* command to move forward. Praise him when he responds appropriately by moving along. If he fails to respond properly, move forward yourself. Praise him as long as he is going forward. If you begin in a familiar place, you may get off to a better start.

To teach *whoa*, incorporate the command into

> ## FROM THE EXPERT
>
> Mike Callahan, in *Mushing Magazine*, recommends using a pair of old ski poles to build up muscle in your arms so that you can "bound up" mountainsides pulled by your dog. It's a great way, he says, to cover more ground (and give your dog a tremendous workout as well).

everyday work, when your dog is on a leash. Ask him to sit at the same time, and don't allow forward movement until you have given the release. Once he is familiar with these commands, they are easily transferrable to canicross.

STAY ON LEVEL GROUND IN THE BEGINNING

Running canicross puts the runner somewhat off balance at the moment both feet are in the air. A tugging dog can definitely be a handicap, and it's especially dangerous if you are going downhill. Beginners must stay on level ground. Most dogs will be trotting while you run, although a lope is a more efficient stride for them. (The lope generally covers between 7 and 9 miles per hour [11.5 and 14.5 kph].) If you want more solid control, you will need to walk, where you have one foot on the ground at all times.

Strategies for Success

As with every other dog sport, the main key to success is to have fun. Canicross is still mostly noncompetitive, so you can define for yourself what success means.

TAKE CARE OF YOUR DOG

Because canicross is often undertaken in warmer weather, you must keep your dog cool and well hydrated. (Dogs have very inefficient cooling systems and can easily overheat.) It is imperative that you monitor your dog's performance at all times and keep him hydrated. If

Keep an eye on your dog to ensure that he doesn't overexert himself

possible, train in areas where a supply of fresh, drinkable water is available, such as near a creek or stream. Encouraging your dog to swim is a great way to help him cool off, as is splashing his coat with water.

If the area where you train has no fresh supply of water, carry a bottle of water for him. Training at daybreak or in the evening is also an excellent way to avoid the heat, which is one of the main risks to dogs in this sport. In many competitive events, runners are required to carry a minimum of 1 liter of water plus a dog bowl.

Another and related danger is accidental overexertion. A finely tuned jogger may in fact have more endurance than her four-legged companion, so it is important to keep an eye on him. Dogs work hard to keep pace with their owners and will run past the point of exhaustion.

REWARD AT TRAINING CONCLUSION

Most experts recommend rewarding the dog at the conclusion of the training rather than during it; otherwise, the dog may continually be looking back and expecting to be fed. Some approve the use of food treats, while others do not because it encourages the dog to perform on the basis of expectations rather than on trust. In addition, if you use food, your dog is bound to be very disappointed when you run out. However, if food treats have worked for you in the past, you may continue to use them.

DON'T GET DISCOURAGED

Canicross should be a fun and positive experience for both dog and owner. If at first your dog refuses to pull, don't get discouraged. Remember, from puppyhood you have probably trained him *not* to pull on his leash, and now suddenly it is okay. This newfound freedom can be a bit confusing to him. But don't despair—with time, training, patience, and a great deal of encouragement, he will eventually get the idea. He'll learn that in this instance, pulling is more than acceptable—it's fun! It is also said that people who participate in canicross really know what it means to be attached to their dogs.

ADDITIONAL ORGANIZATIONS

CaniX UK
www.cani-cross.co.uk
European Canicross and Bikejöring Federation (ECF)
www.ecf.cc

Chapter 4

Canine Freestyle

Definition

Canine freestyle (also known as musical canine freestyle, canine dance, and dancing with dogs) generally refers to the rhythmical, choreographed movements of dogs and owners to music. Although some freestyle events include fancy costuming, others focus solely on the dog. It can be a competitive sport, but not all sponsoring organizations offer titles.

Some handlers choose to dress their dance partners in a costume.

History of Canine Freestyle

The concept of doggy dancing began in Canada and Europe in the late 1980s and moved to the United Sates in the early 1990s. It has no particular founder, although several people claim the honor. The inspiration seems to have come from a similar sport with horses: equine freestyle, a kind of dressage. One of the first recorded routines was performed at a seminar by Dawn Jecs and her Border Collie, Checkers, from Puyallup, Washington. The first formal musical freestyle group, founded in 1991 in Canada, was Musical Canine Sports International. Other groups around the world soon followed, with the Canine Freestyle Federation (CFF) forming in 1995, the World Canine Freestyle Organization (WCFO) in 2000, and the Musical Dog Sports Association (MDSA) in 2005.

Overview

Most people call it dancing with dogs, but *you* don't have to dance—in fact, it's probably better if you don't. You are not on *Dancing With the Stars*, and intricate, flashy movements will just take away from the dog. As Attila Szkukalek, a true shining light in the world of canine freestyle, says, "The team presents itself as partners, but the dog is always the STAR."

This sport combines obedience work with joyful movement, all performed to music— fun for spectators and dogs alike! Both subtle verbal and body cues are used

> ### DID YOU KNOW?
>
> American canine freestyle groups tend to feature more tricks and fancy costumes, while English groups focus more on heelwork.

to achieve results, but you must first have a well-trained, extremely responsive dog (with a sense of rhythm). Except for some beginner classes, routines are performed off lead. Altogether, there are about 40 accepted steps.

Different organizations have different rules for competition, but in general, the competition winner is the team that has acquired the most points in the event. The points are awarded based on a variety of technical and artistic criteria. Competition is often individual, with one dog–handler team pitted against another. However, sometimes full teams (three dogs and three handlers) are assembled. Almost always, though, there is one dog per person. Each team creates its own three- to six-minute

TOP BREEDS

Any dog can dance, but responsive, obedient, athletic dogs like Border Collies and Golden Retrievers can be especially successful. Size is no deterrent: Chihuahuas and Yorkshire Terriers can dance, too! And many times, of course, a good mixed breed is the best of all.

program based on instrumental or vocal music.

Performances that are judged are evaluated on two grounds: technical (difficulty of movements, precision, and the attitude and enthusiasm of the dog) and artistic (choreography, interpretation of the music by the handler, and synchronization of movement to music). This last criterion is quite important, as routines that do not match the music are penalized severely. Obviously, all of these technical and artistic elements blend into each other to create a harmonic whole.

A dog can participate in video events in some organizations, like the MDSA—this is a method of competing in which handlers send in videos of their work to be judged and scored. Titles can be won in this way.

Requirements

Dogs
- ability to follow commands
- close bond with handlers
- high intelligence
- highly athletic, with ability to leap, turn, prance, bow, and so on

Handlers
- creativity
- musical sensitivity
- topnotch training skills

Equipment and Supplies
- costumes
- music

- music player
- video camera

Costumes: Fancy clothes are optional. The costuming is mostly for the handler, though. Dogs are allowed a decorative collar and ankle bands.

Music: Any type of music or medley of selections can be used, but music with a strong beat is the easiest to interpret. It should be music that carries well over a sound system—some music is too soft or "blurry" to be clearly heard. It's best to pick something that can be easily interpreted, with enough variety to showcase different elements of your dog's work. It may seem counterintuitive, but faster pieces (as least as fast you can handle) generally work better for beginners than slower pieces. Music can have both vocals and instruments, depending on the handler's wish. Entrants are expected to supply their own music CD.

Music Player: A music player will be provided at the venue, but you still need something for your own use with which to practice.

Video Camera: A video camera is also an optional piece of equipment, but it's a terrific asset because it enables you to record and critique your own performance. .

Sponsoring Organizations

Canine Freestyle Federation (CFF)

For the CFF, canine freestyle showcases both the technical training and close bond between dog and handler. When done well, freestyle illustrates the free movement, drive, and graceful athleticism of the canine partner. CFF offers four levels of competition as well as two "non-regular" classes. Each of the four levels is offered in Individual and Multiple Dog Divisions. The Multiple Dog Division further includes Team, (two or more handlers each with a single dog) and Brace (one handler with two dogs). The very lowest level allows the handler to use a lead with her dog.

Eligibility Requirements: CFF freestyle is open to all dogs over one year of age, purebred or mixed heritage. Human exhibitors may enter at any level for which they feel qualified, except in Level IV. To compete in Level IV, a

When done well, canine freestyle illustrates the free movement, drive, and grace of the canine partner.

handler and dog must have previously competed in a CFF competition at Level I, IIA, IIB, or III.

Titles: There are a variety of titles available for regular classes Levels I, II, III, and IV only. Single handler and dog(s) and multiple handler and dog teams are eligible.

Premier Events: Exhibitions are held year-round all over the United States.

MUSICAL DOG SPORTS ASSOCIATION (MDSA)

MDSA freestyle features a choreographed "dance routine" that showcases the dog's athletic movement, grace, and beauty. MDSA events are not competitions. The participants simply attempt to meet performance guidelines set up by the organization. Their goal is to receive a title in each progressive class.

In the MDSA, a handler and dog team may compete in three different classes at three different levels: Novice, Standard, and Premier. Classes include Individual (one handler, one dog), Brace (two handlers, two dogs), and Team (three or more handlers, each with a dog). Participants may begin competing with a dog in any class, in either the On-Leash or Off-Leash Divisions, but must qualify from the Off-Leash Division to enter Masters.

Eligibility Requirements: Freestyle events are open to all dogs, purebred or mixed breeds. Dogs must be one year of age.

Titles: The titles of Novice Freestyle Dog (NFD), Standard Freestyle Dog (SFD), Premier Freestyle Dog (PFD) can be earned by a dog and handler earning two qualifying legs at each successive level. Performances for each qualifying leg must be earned with a new routine, with new choreography and new music. Legs may be earned at video or live events.

Premier Events: Freestyle events are held all around the United States.

World Canine Freestyle Organization (WCFO)

The WCFO seeks to promote canine freestyle as both sport and entertainment. It divides canine freestyle into two major divisions: Heelwork-to-Music and Musical Freestyle. Heelwork-to-Music focuses on a dog's ability to stay in variations of the *heel* position while the handler moves to music. The handler and dog remain in close contact (sort of like ice dancing in the figure skating world). It is not permitted to "send the dog away," and jumping, weaving, rolling, and other such "tricks" are not allowed either. The impression given is that of the dog and handler being invisibly tethered together. Typical performances include pivoting and forward, backward, and diagonal moves

The second division, "Musical Freestyle," is a choreographed musical program performed by handlers and their dogs. In Musical Freestyle, heelwork is also important, but it is combined with leg weaving, spins, pivots, jumps, send aways, bows, and rolls. It demands that the dog perform tricks and showcase other obedience skills. It puts more emphasis on the handler's own dance abilities and creativity.

Eligibility Requirements: Any athletic dog with a sense of rhythm and the ability to cue into his owner, whether purebred or a mixed breed, can participate. Dogs must be six months of age and older; female dogs in season are not

---

FROM THE EXPERT

Patie Ventre, the founder of the World Canine Freestyle Organization (WCFO), advises beginners to visit and join e-mail freestyle group lists and meet local people who are interested in this sport. When asked about what taught her the most about freestyling, she unabashedly says, "My dogs." She adds that when you learn to read your dog's movements, there is nothing you cannot accomplish together.

---

permitted to participate in live events, although they can perform in video events. You don't have be a member to take the Proficiency Tests. However, a person must be a member to enter titling competitions, both live and video.

Titles: The WCFO offers a Global Certified Progressive Proficiency Level Testing Program, which includes the following levels and titles: Bronze Bar Freestyle Dog (W-BBFD); Bronze Medal Freestyle Dog (W-BMFD); Silver Bar Freestyle Dog (W-SBFD); Silver Medal Freestyle Dog (W-SMFD); Gold Bar Freestyle Dog (W-GBFD); and Gold Medal Freestyle Dog (W-GMFD).

Premier Events: The WCFO sponsors an International Conference each year and a North American National. It also holds an annual Disco Doggie Dance Meet.

How to Get Started

Love of music, dance, and of course, dogs, is essential to success in canine freestyle. You don't have to be a good dancer yourself, however—you can leave that up to your dog. Your dog must have a high level of obedience, enthusiasm, and a sense of fun. An apparent feeling for music doesn't hurt, either. It seems likely that dogs can learn to recognize and respond to tempo, rhythm, and changes and accents in music. Animals apparently have an innate ability to harmonize their bodies with music, just as people tap their feet to a rhythm. This is something you can use to enhance the sharpness of your routine. (However, you will cue your dog yourself with visual cues—your dog does not have to "memorize" the routine. Memorization, in fact, is not desirable; the idea is to keep the dog focused on the handler.)

GET YOUR DOG A CHECKUP

Naturally, your dog should be in top physical and mental shape to participate in canine freestyle. Before you begin, get him checked out by a vet to ensure that he doesn't have any conditions, especially bone or joint abnormalities, that could be aggravated by dance moves. For example, animals disposed to hip dysplasia put a lot of pressure on the hip joint during a pivot—just what you don't want.

TAKE A BASIC OBEDIENCE CLASS

It's also a good idea to enter your dog in a basic obedience class; you'll not only have a better-behaved dog, but you'll have a closely bonded friend who will be more responsive to further training.

Sponsoring organizations have different levels of training and competition, so novices won't be verwhelmed. Beginners should complete a standard beginning obedience class with an experienced trainer and then buy a training video, available from most freestyle organizations. If your dog has attained the level of Companion Dog in standard obedience training (whether he actually has a title or not), he should be ready to begin canine freestyle work.

LEARN THE REQUIRED MOVES

Most organizations have certain required moves. Dogs need to learn to heel on both sides, not just the left. Additional skills for your dog to learn are walking backward in a straight line, pivoting in place (both in front and at the sides), and side stepping. Other important work includes front work or greeting, lateral work, and change of pace. Higher levels may require distance work in which the owner and the dog are separated by at least 6 feet (2 m). At these levels a dog may also walk backward through a handler's legs, weave backward, walk

FUN FACT

Famous canine freestyle performances have included everything from a gladiator simulation to a Charlie Chaplin routine!

Select music that is well suited to both you and your dog's style.

on his hind legs, and jump over the handler's head. Really, anything is possible.

Again, each sponsoring organization has somewhat different requirements, and these should be consulted before you develop a routine. However, even associations with required moves may offer creative interpretation or exhibition classes just for fun, which have no required moves. These classes may also allow props, cues, and costumes that would not be permitted in regular classes.

Strategies for Success

Success in canine freestyle is feeling the music, loving the steps, and enjoying a deep partnership with your dog. It's also giving pleasure to your audience, for above all, this is a performance sport.

WARM UP YOUR DOG

Warm-ups are critical in this sport. They serve the function of getting the dog ready to perform by increasing the physiological and metabolic rates in the body, which helps warm up the muscles. Nerve impulses travel faster in warm muscles, and a warm muscle is less prone to strain and tears than a cold one.

SELECT THE RIGHT MUSIC

Learn to select music that is suited to your dog's style—and your own. A beginning piece should be short, probably less than two minutes. Many trainers suggest that you evaluate your dog's personal style. Is he more of a Fred Astaire or Michael Jackson? Is he a jazz, boogie, or West Coast Swing type?

DEVELOP SOLID CHOREOGRAPHY

Good choreography uses both repetition and novelty, always with the idea of producing a balanced routine. For example, stationary moves might alternate with steps that cover the entire area. Repeating the same move on two different sides of the area (to give your audience or judges different views) is a good idea too, as is trying the same move at different speeds to really "wow" them. Many performers even freeze for a moment during the routine for effect!

LINK THE MOVES TOGETHER

Most trainers start with two or three moves and then work on linking them together fluidly. The key is not to get overwhelmed—each "trick" can be taught separately to your dog. It's your job to join them together in a pleasing way.

ADDITIONAL ORGANIZATIONS

Canine Freestyle GB
www.caninefreestylegb.com
The Kennel Club
www.thekennelclub.org.uk
Pawfect K9 Freestyle Club
www.pawfect.jp

Chapter 5

Canine Good Citizen® Program

Definition

The Canine Good Citizen (CGC) Program is an entry-level, ten-step, noncompetitive basic obedience and socialization test sponsored by the American Kennel Club (AKC). The CGC test is used as a basic training prerequisite for therapy dogs and is a key component in therapy dog assessment as well as a good measure of any dog's ability to serve as a good "citizen" in the community. The CGC test is often the first step that dog owners take in training because it prepares their dogs for other activities, such as agility, obedience, tracking, and performance events. It also creates a trusting bond between dog and owner and provides the means to a higher quality of life for both.

History of the Canine Good Citizen® Program

The CGC Program began in 1989 as a means of rewarding dogs (and their owners) for good manners and responsible behavior at home and in the community. Over the years, police, animal control agencies, and therapy dog groups have used the CGC test as a tool to train and evaluate dogs for service as well as for solving dog problems within the community. State legislatures have also used the program to promote responsible dog ownership within the community. In fact, 22 states now have CGC resolutions.

Overview

The CGC test is a wonderful way for an owner to bond with her dog and is also a useful way to assess a dog's temperament and ability to function as a welcomed member of the community. The skills assessed during the CGC test range from the dog's ability to respond to basic commands to his overall "politeness" when confronted with strangers. The CGC is a logical first step toward getting higher titles for your dog in obedience, rally, tracking, herding, and agility.

Test 1: Accepting a friendly stranger. Demonstrates that the dog will allow a friendly stranger to approach and speak to the dog owner while the stranger ignores the dog. As the owner and stranger shake hands and engage in conversation, the dog must show no signs of aggression, shyness, or resentment toward the stranger and must not break his position by the owner's side.

Test 2: Sitting politely for petting. Demonstrates the

TOP BREEDS

The Canine Good Citizen (CGC) Program is especially designed so that any dog of any breed or mix can pass! Don't hesitate to try just because your pet is not a Golden Retriever or another of the classic "obedient" breeds. Independent dogs like hounds and Bulldogs may take a little longer to be ready, but by using positive methods and patience, absolutely any dog can achieve this level of distinction.

dog's willingness to be touched by a stranger while with his owner. The evaluator will assess the dog by stroking his head and body and talking to him. As in the first test, the dog must not show any signs of aggression, shyness, or resentment toward the evaluator.

Test 3: Appearance and grooming. Demonstrates the dog's willingness to be groomed and examined. This test also evaluates the dog owner's sense of responsibility as a pet owner and caregiver. The evaluator will inspect the dog for cleanliness and grooming, as well as evaluate his appearance of health. Proper weight, cleanliness, and alertness are taken into account. The evaluator will then brush the dog gently with a brush provided by the owner, as well as check the dog's ears and paws. The owner may praise and encourage her dog throughout the test.

Test 4: Walking on a loose lead. Demonstrates the owner's control over the dog, taking into account his attention and response to his owner. The evaluator in some instances may use a pre-plotted course or specific instructions or commands. The evaluation should consist of a right and left turn and an about-turn with at least one stop in the middle and one at the end. The owner may praise and encourage her dog throughout the test, give commands, and have the dog sit at each stop if she wishes to do so.

Test 5: Walking through a crowd. Demonstrates the politeness and control of the dog in a heavily populated public venue. The dog owner will lead him through a crowd of at least three people. While doing so, he may show interest in the strangers but must continue to walk alongside his owner. The dog must not show any signs of aggression, shyness, or resentment, nor should he jump or pull on the leash. The owner may praise and encourage him throughout the test.

Test 6: Sit on command and stay. Demonstrates the dog's training and his ability to respond to *sit* and *stay* commands by his owner. At the beginning of this test, the dog will be put on a 20-foot (6-m) lead. He must respond to *sit* and *down* and must stay in the position that his owner has chosen without being forced to do so. The owner may use gentle guidance by touching her dog, but she cannot

During the Canine Good Citizen test, your dog will have to allow someone to groom and examine him.

force him into position. Once the dog is in place, the owner commands the dog to stay, walks the length of the line, and returns to the dog. Although the dog may change position, he must remain in place until the owner has been instructed by the evaluator to release him. The dog may be released from the front or side.

Test 7: Come when called. Demonstrates the dog's ability to respond to a command to come by his owner. The owner must walk 10 feet (3 m) from the dog, turn, and call him. The owner may use encouragement and may use the *stay* or *wait* command to have her dog remain in place until called.

Test 8: Reaction to another dog. Demonstrates the dog's ability to behave politely around other dogs. As in Test 1, two dog owners will approach from a distance of 20 feet (6 m), shake hands, and engage in conversation with one another. They will then continue to walk away from one another for a distance of 10 feet (3 m). The two dogs should show no more than a casual interest in one another and should remain with their owners.

Test 9: Reaction to distraction. Demonstrates confidence amid distractions. The evaluator will select two distractions (e.g., dropping a chair, having a jogger run in front of the dog, rolling a crate trolley past the dog). The dog may express interest or appear slightly startled but may not panic, run away, show aggression, or bark. The owner may encourage or praise him throughout the test.

Test 10: Supervised separation. Demonstrates the dog's ability to maintain good manners and training when left with a trusted person. The evaluator will approach the owner and ask if the owner would like her to watch the dog. The owner will hand the leash to the evaluator and leave the area for three minutes. The dog should not whine, bark, pace, or show signs of anything more than mild agitation or nervousness. The evaluator may talk to the dog but may not pet or try to manage him.

If a dog passes all but one exercise, the evaluator may at her discretion retest him on the particular task that he

FUN FACT

Once your dog has passed the Canine Good Citizen (CGC) test, the AKC will send you a certificate suitable for framing announcing the fact. Sometimes this certificate is more than just a piece of paper—people have used them to persuade landlords, for instance, that their dogs will really be excellent tenants after all. Unfortunately, a CGC certificate doesn't prove that your dog isn't a barker or that he doesn't eat drywall. But it's a start!

failed to complete. Owners are not permitted to use food as a reward during the test. Any dog who eliminates during the test (not including Test 10 when outdoors), growls, bites, snaps, attacks, or attempts to attack is immediately failed.

Requirements

Dogs

- ability to follow basic commands such as *come*, *down*, *heel*, *sit*, *stay*, and *wait*
- calmness in the presence of distractions
- sociability

Handlers

- willingness to teach basic obedience
- willingness to groom dog

Test 9 is "reaction to distraction"; in this case, the red umbrella serves to distract the dog.

Equipment and Supplies

Little is required in the way of equipment to participate in the CGC test. The supplies include:

- 20-foot (6-m) lead (supplied by the evaluator)
- buckle or slip collar
- dog brush or comb
- leash

20-Foot (6-M) Lead: This lead is supplied by the sponsoring organizers; it is used during the *sit* and *stay* exercise just to make sure that the dog doesn't run off.

Buckle or Slip Collar: Collars may be buckle, martingale, or slip and may be made of fabric, leather, or chain. Be sure that they fit correctly—you should be able to slide two fingers between the collar and the neck. So-called training collars (choke or prong), head halters, and harnesses are not permitted.

Dog Brush or Comb: Use a brush or comb that your dog is familiar with; his job is to show that he is relaxed about being groomed. (This also shows the evaluators that you are in the habit of grooming your dog!)

Leash: The leash is used throughout the test, except when it is exchanged for the long lead. There is no mandated length for the leash nor any regulations about its material. It's probably best to use a 4- or 6-foot (1- or 2-m) lead that your dog is comfortable with.

Sponsoring Organizations

AMERICAN KENNEL CLUB (AKC)

The AKC has developed the CGC test and offers the official certificate. However, local clubs, 4-H leaders, therapy dog evaluators, veterinarians, vet techs, groomers, private trainers, kennel operators, animal control personnel, and police K-9 officers can administer the test as long as they are certified evaluators. It is usually offered by dog clubs to the community as a whole. There is a small charge for the test, which may go to help the club offering the event.

Eligibility Requirements: The beauty of the CGC test is that it is open to all dogs, including unregistered purebreds and mixed breeds. Dogs with disabilities such as a loss of limb, deafness, or blindness in one eye are also welcome to take part in the CGC test. The only exceptions that may be applied to the test are in the case of an AKC-sponsored show (usually specialty or one-breed shows). In this case, age limits and breed restrictions may be limited to those stated in the regulations of the show.

Although there is no age limit for participation—even puppies may be tested—dogs must be old enough to have had all of their necessary vaccinations. (However, because a dog's behavior may change over time, it is wise that he be retested as an adult.) Dogs must also be in good health,

FROM THE EXPERT

Mary R. Burch, Ph.D., the American Kennel Club's (AKC) Canine Good Citizen Director and a Certified Applied Animal Behaviorist, says, "Getting your dog ready for the AKC CGC test can begin as soon as you bring your new puppy or adult dog home. One of the most important things you can do is to make sure that he is well socialized. This means that you should be taking your dog out in the world daily to meet new people, go new places, and see new things. While a responsible dog owner will work hard to ensure that the dog is well socialized, we also recommend that every dog attend at least a CGC course or basic training class. It is there that an owner can learn the best way to teach new skills and the dog can be exposed to a number of other dogs and distractions. Many CGC skills depend on the dog reacting appropriately to other people, dogs, and distractions. The ability to do this comes from having a lot of experience in the world beyond the dog's own home and yard.

"Other skills, such as *sit, down,* and *come,* are learned behaviors. You'll get better results with training, and you'll develop a wonderful relationship with your dog if you use a positive rather than a harsh physical approach to training. Short training sessions (about 15 minutes) every day are far better than trying to have one very long training session per week. (This does not mean an hour-long group class where the dog has downtime while other dogs take their turns; this means that you should not try to work with your dog one-on-one for an hour). You should be consistent, reinforcing, and make training fun!"

and owners must sign a Responsible Dog Owner's Pledge confirming that their dogs receive routine veterinary care, adequate nutrition, and daily exercise, as well as a great deal of love and attention.

An eligible dog can be trained by a certified CGC training facility, a club training program, or by his owner.

Titles: The CGC test may be included as a component of dog show events; however, it is not a title. Therefore, the AKC does not add the CGC to official registration papers.

Premier Events: Canine Good Citizen tests are held around the country at various venues, often as a fundraiser for the officiating group.

How to Get Started

The key to getting started is to have a well-groomed, happy, fairly obedient, well-socialized pet. Each aspect is well within the abilities of the average pet owner—it only take some commitment.

SOCIALIZE YOUR DOG

Your dog must be socialized to be a canine good citizen. The best way to accomplish this is to take him out for long walks in different environments every day, especially when he is likely to meet other dogs and people of all walks of life—of different ages and races, wearing different clothing, and using different appurtenances, including canes, wheelchairs, walkers, bikes, and baby carriages. You should also keep your dog updated on all vaccinations, especially because he'll be out and about in the world.

TEACH BASIC COMMANDS

Because CGC training is basic obedience, your goal is to make sure that your dog knows the standard commands. Using nonpunitive training methods will ensure the best results because they will be based on trust rather than on fear. Choose a quiet time to train your dog, and practice for short periods every day.

COME

When you first begin teaching the *come* command, wait until your dog is already heading in your direction and then

Your dog will need to know basic obedience, including how to heel, before he can pass the Canine Good Citizen test.

call him. It's important to wait until he is already headed in your direction; don't initiate the command yourself. If he suddenly stops, call him again and use a small treat to lure him. When he gets to you, give him lots of praise, attention, or even a treat, like a Nylabone. The key is to look sharp and be prepared to call "Come!" in a cheery tone every time you see your dog doing it anyway. If he changes direction, don't chase him. Turn your back and walk in the opposite direction. He'll probably come to you. When he does, give him a treat and start walking again. The key is to make him think that coming to you and being by your side is the most rewarding activity there is. This is a tricky command that takes repeated, long-term application to make sink in.

DOWN

Down can be a bit difficult to learn because it places the dog in a vulnerable situation. The most successful trainers have established a relationship of absolute trust between themselves and their dogs. Begin training in a familiar place where your dog is already comfortable lying down. It's usually best to start with the dog in a sitting position, so be sure that he knows this command well first. When he is sitting, give the verbal command "Down" (or a visual equivalent if you prefer). Lure him down with a favorite treat or toy by placing it between his front paws. Stay near him. Say "Okay!" when it is all right for him to get up.

HEEL

A correctly heeling dog is a pleasure to walk. If you have a puppy, take heart; a puppy is much easier to teach to heel than is an older dog. He will naturally want to come with you and probably won't have bad habits to unlearn.

Use a 6-foot (2-m) nylon or leather lead for *heel* training exercises. It's always best if you have accustomed your dog to walk happily at your side before attaching a leash to him, and you can easily do this with the use of tiny treats. Be sure that he is sitting straight before you start—if he is veering inward, you might trip over him. Simply hold the treat at your side in about the same position you'll want your dog's head to be when he is heeling. You may offer the treat at intervals, which can decrease as he becomes accustomed to walking. Also, keep the leash loose—you don't want to be tugging and jerking at him. If you are both successful with this method, the leash will become an afterthought.

Some trainers prefer to train this command without food rewards, and some dogs respond better to things like squeaky toys. The key is to know your dog and do what works best for him. Don't let theory get in the way of practice.

SIT

To teach this command, simply say "Sit" and hold a treat slightly above your dog's eye level. This will encourage him to sit down. Praise him lavishly when he succeeds. Be careful

Praise your dog lavishly when he performs a command successfully, such as the *sit*.

to praise and treat him as he soon as he sits, not when he starts to get up. When you do want your dog to rise, give him a release command, such as "Break." Some trainers use a separate command for *stay* so that the dog does not expect to rise immediately. Others use only *sit* and expect the dog to sit until released.

WAIT

Some handlers use a special *wait* or *stay* command, while others prefer the simpler *sit*, knowing that the dog must sit until released. If you wish to teach a separate *wait* command, attach a short leash to your dog's collar. Tell him to sit and walk slowly away with your palm out facing him. Use his name and say "Wait." If he doesn't move, praise him generously and give him a treat. If he breaks position, simply start again. Gradually increase the distance and the time until he will stay reliably for several minutes.

Strategies for Success

Canine Good Citizen success doesn't mean a blue ribbon or a trophy, but it does give evidence that you have a happy and well-socialized dog. Here are two strategies you can use to make sure that you and your dog pass the test:

GROOM YOUR DOG

Groom your dog—and ask other people to do it, too. One of the main parts of the test involves grooming and handling. It's a cinch if you make sure that he's bathed and groomed before the show and that he's used to being handled. You don't need to involve a professional groomer for this. Just ask a friend—she doesn't have to do it "right."

PRACTICE SUPERVISED "LEAVES"

Ask a stranger (not a stranger to you of course, but someone your dog doesn't know) to hold your dog while you practice brief separations. Self-confident, happy dogs are most successful at this, but if you have a rescue dog, he may be more fearful. Frequent practice sessions are the key.

ADDITIONAL ORGANIZATIONS

Many countries have developed canine good citizen programs based on the AKC's program.

Australia
Canine Good Companion Programme
www.diydoggrooming.com/caninecompanionsoverview.php
Canada
Canine Good Neighbour Program
www.ckc.ca/en/Default.aspx?tabid=91
England
Good Citizen Dog Scheme
www.thekennelclub.org.uk/dogtraining
Denmark, Finland, Hungary, Japan, and Sweden also have similar programs.

Chapter 6

Carting

Definition

Carting is any event in which a dog pulls a wheeled vehicle. Although the word "pull" seems to say it all, a distinction is made between two- and four-wheeled vehicles. There is also a distinction between driven carts with a person aboard and those used only for freight. When a person is riding in the cart and controlling the movements of the animal(s), it is properly referred to as "driving" rather than "carting," although it is also sometimes called (half humorously) "dryland mushing."

Carting is more than a fun game for you and your dog—many certified assistance dogs help disabled owners fetch home the week's groceries. Others work in search and rescue and help rescuers bring supplies into remote areas.

Carting is largely a recreational sport, although competition programs are available.

History of Carting

Dogs have been assisting people with their transport needs for many centuries. Sled dogs are most familiar to us, but dogs have also contributed to human needs by hauling to market vegetables, milk, fish, and other products in carts. In times of war, the Bouvier des Flandres, for example, served the Belgian military as sentries, and they also hauled carts full of machine guns and wounded soldiers. During World War I, some armies had a canine corps that carried munitions and even a dog ambulance to pick up fallen canine soldiers. In some parts of the world, like Switzerland, working cart dogs are still a regular sight.

Overview

Carting is largely a recreational sport, although competitive programs and titles are available. Perhaps the most fun way to enjoy the carting experience is to enter your dog in a parade. A carting dog is still such an unusual sight in the United States that the dogs attract more attention than horses. However, carting dogs can also take the trash to the recycling center, carry away lawn debris, haul off the Christmas tree, or bring in firewood.

FUN FACT

Any event in which a dog pulls something is called drafting. Sledding, bikejoring, weight pulling, and carting are thus all subdivisions of drafting.

For a recreational jaunt, a typical carting distance is 2 to 5 miles (3 to 8 km).

Draft tests are often divided into four parts, as in this example from the Newfoundland Test:

Part 1: In the first part, which exhibits basic control, the unattached dog must exhibit competence in heeling and *recalls* and must perform a *down-stay* for three minutes with the handler out of sight.

Part 2: The second part involves harnessing and hitching. The dog must stand and wait while the handler gets the harnessing tack from a point 20 feet (6 m) away and cooperate while it is being put on. The dog must then back up on command from the judge a distance of 4 feet (1 m), preferably backing right in front of the cart. Once hitched to the empty cart, he must move forward at a reasonable working speed, change speed on direction from the handler, back up on command, and remain in position one minute with the handler out of sight.

Part 3: The third part demonstrates how well the dog can maneuver a course. The course is at least 150 yards (137 m) long and incorporates as many natural features as possible. It includes circular patterns, wide curves, at least two 90-degree turns, narrow spaces, a dead-end area to back out of, and a removable obstacle. The handler may walk in front of, beside, or behind the dog, or any combination of these positions. The dog must demonstrate knowledge of commands to go left, right, back up, speed up, and slow down.

Part 4: The fourth part of the test is the freight haul, a cross-country test of at least 1 mile (1.5 km) with a loaded cart, wagon, toboggan, sled, or travois. Dogs often set off in groups of four, with a maximum of five handlers. The course contains no obstacles other than natural objects such as bends in the trail, potholes, or bridges. The dog and handler may stop along the course as necessary to remove obstructions or obtain water if it is hot.

The tied-down load should be appropriate to the dog and apparatus and can vary from 5 to 100 pounds (2.5 to 45.5 kg). (A heavier load often creates a more stable cart.) The handler must accompany the dog, directing him by voice command. Handlers may not touch the apparatus except to adjust the load if necessary.

In most tests, teams will be disqualified if the dog refuses to accompany the handler, urinates, upsets the cart, or if the handler has to physically guide the dog or move in front of him to stop him. The owner may speak to the dog during distractions.

Requirements

Dogs
- ability to pull carts
- desire to pull
- obedience to commands
- patience
- strength

Handlers
- ability to maintain a harness and cart
- patience

Equipment and Supplies
- harness
- vehicle

Harness: Choose the vehicle before the harness! This is important because the cart is your main (and most expensive) concern, and different harnesses work differently with different carts. Several varieties of harness are available. Which one is right for you depends on your purpose, and equally important, your dog's preference. Some dogs just fare better in one type of harness than another. Whatever kind you and your dog choose, a proper fit is an absolute must.

TOP BREEDS

Some breeds were specifically developed to pull carts, like Newfoundlands, Bernese Mountain Dogs, and Greater Swiss Mountain Dogs, and these naturally make excellent candidates. Other successful breeds include Great Pyrenees, Rottweilers, Giant Schnauzers, and other large, strong breeds; the best carting dogs are lean and well muscled, with good joints (and no arthritis). In general, dogs who weigh 33 pounds (15 kg) or more are best suited to practical carting. However, even smaller dogs can pull carts with toys as passengers. The thumbnail rule is that the total load (cart and driver) should not exceed two and a half or three times the weight of the pulling dog on level ground. (Almost all carting is done on flat ground anyway.)

Measuring is critical; be sure to measure the dog, not his fur. Different kinds of harness require different measurements, so check with the manufacturer before ordering. If a weight measurement is needed, do actually weigh your dog—don't just guess.

A **parade harness** consists of padded leather or nylon straps. One strap goes across the withers and encircles the dog's chest; a second padded strap wraps around the front of the dog across the forechest. The straps are often buckled together. The disadvantage of this sort of harness is that it may limit the dog's range of motion.

A **siwash harness** resembles a sledding harness, with a series of straps crossing the dog's back between two other straps that extend past the rear of the dog, parallel to the ground. The dog's head comes out through a padded chest strap that follows down the breastbone and back through the front legs. A belly band provides the connection point for the cart shafts. This harness allows a great deal of freedom of movement and is often used when a lot of pulling power is required.

A **draft harness** features a large padded leather collar to provide the main pull. This permits good shoulder and leg motion while allowing the dog to lean into the collar to increase pulling force. A belly strap provides the shaft

Whatever harness you choose, a proper fit is a must.

connection point, while the traces (side straps) run back from the collar to the cart.

Vehicle: A two-wheeled vehicle is technically called a cart or sulky; a four-wheeled vehicle is called a wagon. A wagon can carry more weight than a cart and has the additional advantage of not pressing down on the dog; all the weight is supported directly by the vehicle itself. Carts, on the other hand, must be carefully balanced. In general, a cart has a driver, while a wagon is used for freight pulling only. A vehicle that simply drags along the ground is called a travois. These are quite useful for going over rough terrain and can be made from wood or aluminum. The most important question you must answer is whether you will be using one or more dogs for this activity. That decision will to some extent determine your choice of vehicle.

Sponsoring Organizations

The New England Drafting and Driving Club (NEDDC) offers some competitions, as do certain clubs. Many other organizations sponsor parades and recreational and competitive carting events. Some are breed specific, but many more are open to any breed that wishes to participate. Some groups, like the American Working Collie Association (AWCA), offer versatility titles that may include carting as an eligible activity. Check with your local kennel club or other local organization for more information.

NEW ENGLAND DRAFTING AND DRIVING CLUB (NEDDC)

The NEDDC offers a four-level program of classes, beginning with Novice (for on lead), Open (for off lead), Driving Excellent (for driving behind the axle), and Driving Sulky (for handlers seated in the cart or sulky). They also offer Brace (a pair of dogs) events in each division.

Eligibility Requirements: Any dog big enough to pull a cart or wagon is eligible in open clubs like the NEDDC.

Titles: Titles vary, and to win them, a dog must pass requisite tests. Examples include Draft Dog Excellent (DDx), Draft Dog Sulky (DDs), Brace Draft Dog (BDD), and Brace Draft Dog Excellent (BDDx).

Premier Events: Tests are held all over New England.

How to Get Started

Almost any dog can learn to pull a cart if the cart is small enough and the load is light enough. Many dogs take to the sport readily if introduced to the idea of cart and harness slowly—they will even start wagging their tails happily at the sight of them!

CHECK YOUR DOG'S CONFORMATION

Conformation is important in this sport, and participating

SPECIALTIES

At specialties, clubs may add Specialty Cart and Wagon classes, which involve running a maneuvering course on or off lead. They may also add a Decorative Carting class, which is a parade of creatively decorated carts. Competition and prizes may be offered in these classes, but no titles can be earned.

Many dogs readily take to the sport of carting.

dogs should have a good straight topline, which allows for more support while pulling. Legs should be straight in the right places; if the legs have an unnatural bow, added pressure is placed on the rest of the body. Stick to level ground and paved surfaces at first if possible.

GET YOUR DOG A CHECKUP

Have your dog checked by your vet before you start any training program. He should be fully mature, of proper weight for his age and build, and structurally sound. No dog under 18 months should pull anything heavier than the cart itself. Pups under 12 months can be trained to accept the harness but should not pull anything. Proper weight distribution is really critical for successful carting. Dogs should also be free of serious health problems, including hip dysplasia.

CONDITION YOUR DOG

Conditioning is also critical. Walking, jogging, and especially swimming help tone up those muscles for pulling a heavy load.

OBEDIENCE TRAIN YOUR DOG

Basic obedience training is a must. A dog who will not listen to you when he is unattached to the cart will not suddenly turn into Rin Tin Tin when he is hooked up. Teaching him to walk quietly on lead is of supreme importance. Carting dogs should be nondistractible, especially if they are entered in parades or competitions.

TRAIN ONE STEP AT A TIME

The most important concept with carting is to take things one step at time.

1. First, get your dog used to the harness by having him wear it during everyday activities. Have him drag the traces without anything attached.
2. When he's comfortable with this, attach something light, such as an empty plastic milk jug, to the traces to create some "disturbance."
3. Ask a friend to walk behind your dog and gently bump him while you praise him for not reacting. (Always keep your dog moving forward—don't let him stop to think about anything.) Harnessing up to the cart involves (usually unintentionally) lots of little bumps and minor jolts—the idea is to get your dog used to being harnessed and the movement it involves.
4. Attach the cart.

FROM THE EXPERT

Sharyl Mayhew, an experienced carter, recommends that when training a dog, you should attach empty milk jugs to the long traces and let the dog pull them around. Start with a straight line, and your dog probably won't even notice at first that he is pulling anything! Then start with the turns. For more tips on carting, check out Sharyl's site: http://users.erols.com/gr8rswis/IntroCarting.htm

The well-trained carting dog must respond to your cues.

Do not progress to the next step until your dog (and you) are comfortable and happy with the step that went before.

DEVELOP VERBAL CUES

The well-trained carting dog must learn to respond to verbal cues. Teach the commands first while he is unattached so that he can learn one thing at a time. Typical carting commands include:

- Back (hup): Turn backward.
- Forward (let's go, with me, follow me): Move forward.
- Gee: Turn right.
- Haw: Turn left.
- Let's go (faster): Move faster.

- Slow (easy): Go at a slow pace.
- Stand: Stand.
- Stay: Stay or wait.
- Stop (halt): Stop.

Strategies for Success

With carting, don't assume that you can just hook up your dog and take off. It will take months to train him even to the beginning level.

MAKE TRAINING FUN

Successful carting dogs love to pull, and this is something you can't force. If you try to force a dog to pull, he will probably end up lying down and shaking with fear. The most important thing is to make sure that he has fun!

FIT THE HARNESS AND CART PROPERLY

A correct fit on the harness is absolutely critical. You will probably need a mentor to see that you adjust it properly, but in general, make sure that the shaft is level at the point of your dog's shoulder and protrudes no farther than the point of the shoulder. The cart should be balanced, producing no more than 1 pound (0.5 kg) of pressure on the shafts. The cart should also be level—you can check this best by kneeling down and looking at the cart levelly, rather than down at it.

BE PATIENT

It is also important to know that success will not happen overnight. Be prepared to take the time to train your dog in the proper manner, and be patient. Be prepared to walk alongside your dog, or run if necessary, for miles (km) at a time while he learns to pull the cart without you in it. This training will last a minimum of three to six weeks and should be done over a variety of different terrains, with a variety of challenges, including hills, difficult turns, and distractions.

ADDITIONAL ORGANIZATIONS

Canadian Kennel Club (CKC)
www.ckc.ca

Chapter 7

Conformation

Definition

The sport of conformation is more informally and widely known as a dog show, a competition in which the contestants are each compared against the ideal as depicted in the written standard for the breed. When we think of dog shows, the image that immediately comes to mind is the beautiful lineup in February at the famed Westminster Dog Show in New York City. And it's a good image because a dog show is indeed a combination of Miss America and the television show *Survivor*—a giant beauty pageant that is an elimination contest as well.

History of Conformation

The historical purpose of the conformation show was to identify the best examples of a particular breed. These dogs would then be bred to pass on their good qualities to the next generation. The first dog show on record occurred on June 28, 1859, in Newcastle-upon-Tyne in the United Kingdom. This first show was limited to pointers and setters but proved so popular that the next show added spaniels. Hounds were added a year later, and so on. In 1870, the UK's National Dog Club met to establish a body with the purpose of controlling England's entire dog show activities. Three years later, the Kennel Club was founded. In 1874, it published a studbook with a Code of Rules to guide the management of future dog shows.

The American Kennel Club (AKC), which sponsors most dog shows today in the United States, was not organized until 1884, and modern dogs shows were first held in 1924. Originally emphasizing working trials and hunting and working dogs, the United Kennel Club (UKC) began its all-breed conformation shows in 1996. Unlike the AKC, it does not permit professional handlers in its conformation or obedience events. The Mixed Breed Dog Club of America (MBDCA) was founded in 1978 and began holding dogs shows that year. Because the MBDCA emphasizes obedience and companionship, it requires a conformation dog to obtain an obedience degree before obtaining a Championship.

The most famous dog show in the United States is undoubtedly the Westminster Dog Show. The first show was held in 1877, with an entry list of more than 1,000 dogs.

TOP BREEDS

As long as your breed is officially registered with the sponsoring organization, it can participate and win. And because the competitions are divided into breeds, every breed can attempt to get its championship.

Overview

During a conformation event, each dog is judged (a single judge for each breed) according to how well he conforms to the breed standard, a word picture of the ideal dog in each breed.

In a conformation show, a dog must stack, which shows his body off to advantage.

Each national parent breed club develops its own standard and is responsible for any changes or revisions to it. These breed standards delineate the ideal size, color, and temperament of each breed, as well as correct proportion, structure, and gait. Some standards are quite brief, while others go into great detail. In addition, some standards emphasize certain traits over others. In some breeds, for example, color is not important, while in others it is. Exhibitors should carefully study the standards for their breed.

Technically, dogs are not judged against each other but are evaluated on how well each matches up to the ideal dog outlined in its breed standard. AKC judges are not people pulled off the street to provide an opinion. To become a judge, a person must have 12 years' documented experience in the breed, having bred and raised at least five litters in the initial breeds being applied for. She must also have bred at least four champions in that breed and must pass a test on the breed standard, canine anatomy, and AKC rules. She must have spent time as a ring steward and pass an interview. Even then, approval is on a provisional basis, as she must judge the breed at least five times with an AKC field representative watching her at least three of those times. A written report is filled out on her performance.

The UKC requires its judging applicants to submit a resume, pass an exam, and apprentice with a senior judge. The MBDCA qualifies its own judges, who must have had experience in judging, training, and showing dogs.

AKC AND UKC SHOWS

Three kinds of conformation shows are held:

All-Breed Shows: In the AKC, these shows offer classes for more than 150 recognized breeds and varieties. This is the most common kind of show and the one you are most likely to see on television. The UKC holds shows for one breed, groups, and all-breeds, depending on the experience of the local club managing the show.

Specialty Shows: In the AKC, these shows are restricted to dogs of a specific breed or to varieties of one breed. For example, the Basset Hound Club of America Specialty is held once a year for Bassets only. However, the Poodle Club of America's specialty show includes all three varieties of the Poodle: Standard, Miniature, and Toy. The UKC also holds specialty shows.

Group Shows: In the AKC, these shows are limited to dogs belonging to one of the seven groups. For example, the Potomac Hound Group show features only breeds belonging to the hound group, such as Beagles, Afghan Hounds, Basset Hounds, and so on. The UKC also holds group shows.

MBDCA SHOWS

In a stunning new take on conformation, the MBDCA has its own shows. Their rules are a little different from those of the AKC. Dogs competing in MBDCA conformation trials must demonstrate physical soundness, good health, and a well-balanced and symmetrical appearance. For example, dogs must not be knock-kneed, have spinal problems, or have an excessive overbite or underbite; their coats and skin must be healthy; and they must not be overweight or underweight for their build. Dogs compete against other dogs of similar height. Also, unlike in the AKC and UKC, MBDCA dogs must be neutered.

The MBDCA is the only dog organization in the United States that requires a dog to complete an obedience title before he can complete his conformation championship. This ensures that the dog is not merely attractive but has also learned basic obedience.

The MBDCA allows not only mixed breeds to compete at its events but also purebred dogs who cannot be registered for whatever reason with the AKC, UKC, or the Canadian Kennel Club (CKC).

Requirements

Dogs
- gait easily beside the handlers
- good manners
- stack
- stand for examination

Handlers
- ability to groom for show
- ability to learn ring etiquette
- ability to stack their dog
- contain good eye for structure and movement
- patience

Conformation shows identify the best examples of a particular breed.

Equipment and Supplies

No special equipment is required, although almost everyone purchases a show lead for their dogs. This is not a glittering rhinestone-studded affair as you might imagine but a very thin nylon lead designed to be "invisible." You want the judge to look at your dog, not at the lead.

Exhibitors wear comfortable shoes and ordinary clothing that blends in or contrasts sharply with their dog's coat color—you don't want to clash. Women often wear a skirt or nice trousers, and men wear a sports coat. No one wears jeans, shorts, or tank tops.

Sponsoring Organizations

By far, the best-known conformation shows in the United States are held by the AKC. The UKC and MBDCA shows tend to be somewhat more casual than the AKC variety.

AMERICAN KENNEL CLUB (AKC)

The major goal in an AKC conformation event is for a dog to earn points toward attaining his championship. This means that he has to compete against others of his breed and prove himself to be a worthy example. To win a championship, a dog must accumulate 15 points under at least three different judges, which will necessitate winning in at least three shows—that's with the very best luck possible. It usually takes many more. The highest number of points possible to get in any one show is five. In addition, the number of points available at a particular show may differ from breed to breed; a show might offer five points to Collies but only one point to Yorkshire Terriers. It depends on the number of dogs entered and how many dogs of that breed are registered in the area. If three, four, or five points are offered, the show is considered a "major" for that breed. A dog must win at least two majors under two different judges to get a championship.

This point schedule may be different for males and females and may change with changing registration numbers.

Conformation shows offer several different classes for each breed, each awarding ribbons, depending on sex, age, background, and experience. Males and females are shown in separate classes, males first and then the females. They are shown separately because the male dogs in many breeds are considered more "impressive" than females. Examples of possible classes for dogs who have not earned their championship include:

- **Puppy:** Open to dogs between 6 and 12 months of age.
- **Twelve-to-Eighteen Months**: Open to dogs 12 to 18 months of age.
- **Novice**: For dogs six months of age and over who have not, prior to the date of the closing of entries, won three first prizes in the Novice Class; a first prize in Bred-by-Exhibitor, American-Bred, or Open Classes; or one or more points toward their championship.
- **Bred by Exhibitor:** For dogs who are exhibited by

97

Handlers must be able to stack their dogs.

their owner and breeder. In contrast to the Novice Class, many experienced exhibitors proudly enter this class because they are eager to show off the products of their breeding program.

- **American-Bred**: For dogs born in the United States from a mating that took place in the United States. This is sort of a leftover category from the days when many dogs were bred outside of the United States. It is designed to give home-grown dogs a chance. Today, this class is often selected by breeders who may be showing a different dog in the Open Class or for other strategic reasons.

- **Open:** For any dog of the breed who is at least 6 months of age. Entering this class shows that you are confident your dog can take on all comers!

You can decide which class you want to enter as long as you and your dog fulfill the qualifications for that class. For example, if your dog is two years old, he can't enter the Puppy Class. If your dog was bred in Canada, he can't enter the American-Bred Class, and so on. All dogs who have not yet won a championship, however, can enter the Open Class, which usually contains the toughest competition.

In each conformation class, four ribbons are awarded, but only the blue ribbon (first place) will allow the dog to move on to the next level: the Winners Class. Other ribbons, in order, are red, yellow, and white.

Dogs who won first place in their class compete again to see who is the best of the winners. In the Winners Classes, males and females still compete separately. In a big show, for example, the Winners Classes will include winners from the Puppy, Novice, American-Bred, Bred by Exhibitor, and Open Classes. The male who wins the Winners Class gets a purple ribbon and is called the Winners Dog, while the female winner gets a purple ribbon and is called Winners Bitch. Each receives points toward his or her championship.

The Winners Dog and Winners Bitch then compete with dogs who have previously attained their championships (called Specials) for the Best of Breed award. In some cases, more points can be earned by dogs who win Best of Breed. Dogs who are already champions don't get any extra points. They are entered simply for the glory of the thing.

Three awards are usually given at the Best of Breed Competition:

- **Best of Breed (BOB):** The dog judged as the best in his breed category. The BOB gets a purple and gold ribbon.
- **Best of Winners (BOW):** The dog judged as the better of the Winners Dog and Winners Bitch. The BOW gets a blue and white ribbon.
- **Best of Opposite Sex (BOS):** The best dog who is the opposite sex to

Fun Fact

The American Kennel Club (AKC) is a "club of clubs"; in other words, its members are not individuals but breed clubs. The member clubs can designate delegates who vote on bylaw and rule changes.

To do well in conformation, you must have a show-quality dog.

the Best of Breed winner. The BOS gets a red and white ribbon.

The Best of Breed dogs then compete against each other in their respective group: Herding, Hound, Non-Sporting, Sporting, Terrier, Toy, or Working.

- **Herding:** These dogs were bred to help shepherds and ranchers herd their livestock. Members include Collies, German Shepherd Dogs, and Old English Sheepdogs.
- **Hounds:** These breeds were bred for hunting other game by sight or scent. They include such dogs as Afghan Hounds, Basset Hounds, and Dachshunds.
- **Non-Sporting:** This group is made up of dogs who really don't fit into any other category. Examples include Bulldogs, Chow Chows, and Dalmatians.
- **Sporting:** These dogs were bred to hunt game birds both on land and in the water. Breeds include English Setters, German Wirehaired Pointers, and Labrador Retrievers.

- **Terrier:** Terriers were bred to rid property of vermin. This group includes Airedale Terriers, Cairn Terriers, and Parson Russell Terriers.
- **Toy:** These dogs were bred to be household companions and include Chihuahuas, Maltese, and Pekingese.
- **Working:** These dogs were bred to pull carts, guard property, and perform search-and-rescue services. Examples include Boxers, Doberman Pinschers, and Saint Bernards.

A Miscellaneous category also exists for breeds that have not yet been accepted for registration with the AKC. These breeds usually "move up" to one of the other classes after a time.

Four placements are awarded in each group, but only the first-place winner advances to the Best in Show competition, in which the group winners compete against each other for the top honor of all: Best in Show (BIS) and a red, white, and blue ribbon.

Eligibility Requirements: Dogs must be registered with the AKC and be intact—not altered. Puppies must be at least six months old for entrance in a regular show.

Titles: Dogs acquiring a total of 15 points through the procedure described earlier are awarded a Championship, with the right to have the "Ch." prefix placed next to their names. The number of points a dog can win at any one show ranges from one to five and is based on the number of entries in the class, which can vary by breed and region. The points must be won under three different judges.

Premier Events: For each breed, an annual National Specialty is held; however, the entrance requirements are no different than for any other show. The annual Westminster Dog Show is the biggest event and is held each February in New York City; it is restricted to dogs who are already champions, with a few places reserved for the "top" dogs in each breed. Other events include the AKC/Eukanuba National Championship, which awards prize money for the Best in Show winner.

MIXED BREED DOG CLUBS OF AMERICA (MBDCA)

The MBDCA is a registry for dogs of unknown or mixed parentage, as well as for those purebred dogs who are barred from competing in purebred breed shows because of a disqualifying trait (such as wrong coat type or eye color). It has local chapters in California, Oregon, Missouri/Illinois, and Washington. Classes are divided into Dog and Bitch and are further divided into three groups according to size: under 15 inches (38 cm) at the withers, 15 inches (38 cm) up to but not including 22 inches (56 cm), and 22 inches (56 cm) and over. Classes may also be divided into Junior (under six years) and Senior (six and over).

Eligibility Requirements: Dogs must be spayed or neutered and at least nine months of age.

Titles: The title of Mixed Breed Champion is awarded when a dog has won 30 points under at least three judges. The Mixed Breed Grand Champion (MBG-Ch) is awarded to dogs who have won ten or more Mixed Breed awards.

Premier Events: For the past few years, the MBDCA has sponsored an annual National Specialty.

UNITED KENNEL CLUB (UKC)

The UKC also holds conformation events, which are similar to those of the AKC. As with the AKC, dog shows may be held for one breed, several breeds, or all breeds, depending on the club managing the events. In general, UKC events are more relaxed and casual than those of the AKC, and professional handlers are not allowed. UKC shows usually

FROM THE EXPERT

Jean Di Fatta, an experienced handler and breeder of Gordon Setters, has some great advice for beginners: "It goes without saying that your dog should be groomed and structurally sound. Equally important, keep your dog happy. A happy dog presents himself better. But you need to prepare yourself, too. Psychologically, you must believe that your dog is the best-looking dog in the ring—and your job is to present him to the judge in that way. Be confident!"

typically draw 500 entries or fewer.

The UKC offers two levels of conformation titling: the Show Champion and the Grand Show Champion. To win a Championship, a dog must earn 100 points under three different judges. Depending on the breed, the dog may earn as many as 15 points by winning a class, with further points awarded for Winners Dog or Best of Winners. (No additional points are given for Best of Breed or Best in Show.) Male dogs are shown first until a Best Male and Reserve Best Male are chosen. The same procedure is followed for females. The Best Male and Best Female next compete against each other in a Best of Winners (BOW) class. The single Best of Winners is then eligible to continue forward into the Best of Breed (BOB) competition. After BOW, the Champions compete in their own class, and a Champions Winner and a Reserve are chosen. Then the Grand Show Champions compete in their own class and a winner is chosen. Finally, the BOW, the Champions winner, and the Grand Champions winner—just the three of them—compete against each other for the BOB award.

Eligibility Requirements: Dogs must be registered with the UKC, intact, and at least six months of age.

Titles: The UKC offers two levels of conformation titling: the Show Champion (U-Ch) and the Grand Show Champion (U-Gr.Ch).

Premier Events: Various shows are held throughout the United States.

How To Get Started

The first dog shows were charity events but soon became a venue for breeders to show off their stock and advertise their breeding program. If you don't have any stock (except for your pet) or a breeding program, a dog show is just a way to have fun exhibiting your dog, meet other dog fanciers, and have a good time.

OBTAIN A SHOW-QUALITY DOG

To do well, you need a show-quality dog. If your dog's breeder is involved in showing, she can probably discuss his chances with you. If the breeder is not involved in the

When showing your dog, wear something professional that complements your dog's coloring.

sport, it's likely that your dog is not show quality. (That doesn't mean that you don't have a great dog, just that he will probably not meet the high expectations of the dog show judges.)

Not only must a successful show dog be a good example of the breed, but he must also be well conditioned. A flabby, overweight, or skinny dog won't look good, nor will one who is not clean and groomed to perfection. "Coated" breeds (such as setters) usually require the services of a groomer-handler; most pet groomers are not sufficiently familiar with your breed's standard or show grooming style to provide the most advantageous cut—one that will emphasize your dog's best points.

JOIN A BREED CLUB

If you think that your dog can indeed make the cut, contact your nearest breed club or all-breed kennel club and join. Here you can find friends and possibly a mentor. Just as important, you can sign up for handling classes that will teach you the ins and outs of show-ring handling. Some clubs even have fun matches so that you can get some good practice. (Fun matches award no points and don't usually require advance registration.) Some people decide to hire a professional handler, but if your goal is to participate in the sport, you should definitely handle your own dog.

There's a great deal of strategy in deciding in which class to enter your dog, and that strategy varies from situation to situation (and from breed to breed). This is why having a mentor is very helpful. You can talk to your dog's breeder or make a friend of someone in your breed club, but in any case, don't go it alone.

TEACH YOUR DOG TO GAIT, STACK, AND BE HANDLED

Dogs don't have to learn any special tricks to participate in a conformation event, but well-trained show dogs gait properly around the ring, learn to stack (stand in a particular position that shows the body off to advantage), and allow themselves to be handled by the judge.

It is important to learn how to gait your dog around the ring to show him off. Most owners move their dogs too fast, which doesn't allow the judge to evaluate their reach and drive. Get someone to videotape you at several speeds to learn which one shows your dog to his best advantage. Keep the dog (not yourself) at the center of attention.

Show dogs stand in a rather unnatural but pleasing position called a "stack." This allows the judge to see the dog's basic structure. From the side, the judge should see only two legs, not four. The back feet are a little farther away from the front ones than is normal for a relaxed dog so that the dog looks stretched out in back. Start with teaching your dog to stand tall. When he is where you want him, give him a small treat. At first, don't worry about his front and back feet being "even"—that comes later. When you do move his foot, do it from the elbow, not lower down. (Pushing a dog's paw around is the sign of an amateur.) Keep another hand on the muzzle because that controls the dog. When the front feet are in place, move the back feet—again, not touching below

105

the hock joint. This is called "hand-stacking." A higher level of perfection, required in some breeds, is "free stacking." In free stacking, the back legs are "anchored," and the handler uses bait to lure the dog into moving his front feet forward.

The examination may also include having the teeth and testicles touched, so your dog must be calm and unflustered by personal attention. The judge is looking at his teeth to make sure that his bite is aligned correctly for his breed and that all teeth are present. She checks the testicles to make sure that both are properly descended. The best way to succeed here is to practice (and ask your friends to assist) doing these checks.

Strategies for Success

Success means, as always, having fun. If you get overwhelmed or angered by competition, learn to relax or pick another sport. Because showing dogs is totally subjective, you'll have to learn to live with a judge's opinion about your dog's quality. Be patient, too; one judge's opinion is not necessarily the same as another's.

CATER TO YOUR JUDGE

Experienced exhibitors generally know what the particular judge of the day likes and what she de-emphasizes, and they take advantage of it. Most judges pay attention to movement, so if your dog is a good mover, it's important for you to show off to the judge during the first pass around the ring. That's your first chance to make a good impression on the judge even before she looks at each dog singly. To do that, you need to have room. If your dog is fast, you'll need to trot him deeper into the corners so that he doesn't rush up on the dog in front. If he's slower, you can round corners to keep the pacing even. These are all tricks that people pick up after a time.

WEAR THE RIGHT CLOTHING

Dress professionally when you show your dog. Jeans are out, although you can wear sneakers. A dress or suit is best. Men should wear a sports jacket and dress pants. Wear clothing that complements your dog's color without overwhelming or matching it. (If you have a black dog and you wear black, for example, the danger is that your dog will "disappear" into you.)

VIEW YOUR DOG DISPASSIONATELY

It is not true (as is sometimes claimed) that an owner-handler has no chance against a professional because of "politics." Owner-handled dogs win over professionals all the time. However, the major advantage professionals have over owners is that they can look honestly at a dog. Many owners think that their dogs are perfect. No dog is perfect, and professional handlers have the ability to look at their charges dispassionately. To be successful, you have to do that as well. You will need to study the breed standard very carefully to learn your dog's weaker points—and how to compensate for them as much as you can. You can also ruin your dog's good conformation by misplacement of the legs or head. Practice stacking your dog in front of a mirror to see how to place his legs. If he has a shorter than desirable neck, for example, learn how to stretch it out by "baiting" him with a small flavorful treat.

ADDITIONAL ORGANIZATIONS

Canadian Kennel Club (CKC)
www.ckc.ca
International All Breed Canine Association, Inc. (IABCA)
www.iabca.com
The Kennel Club
www.thekennelclub.org.uk/activities/exhibiting.html
Kennel Club Plovdiv
www.fair.bg/en/events/CACIB08.htm
Mixed Breed Dog Clubs of America (MBDCA)
http://mbdca.tripod.com

Chapter 8

Coonhound Events

Definition

Coonhound events are competitions specifically geared to test the abilities of coonhounds. The events include bench shows, field trials, nite hunts, and water races.

History of Coon Hunting

Raccoon hunting is a part of the culture of some rural areas. As a contest, the modern formal coon hunt dates back only to 1948, when the first self-described "world championship" was held in Wickliffe, Kentucky. More than 20 dogs competed in this first championship, and the winner was a Redbone Coonhound named Dan. Unlike the competitions of today, no strict set of rules or point system governed the event. Dan was simply chosen by the judge as the dog thought to have performed best in the events.

Seeing that the subjectivity of these championship hunts was not exactly the best way to conduct business, a group of coon hunters set out to improve the rules that governed these events. Over the years, a new scoring system and scorecards were introduced, time limits imposed on events, and all of the kinks in the system were ironed out. As this happened, the sport continued to gain in popularity. By 1956, at the World Hunt in Oblong, Illinois, 137 hounds entered into the competition. A new era in coonhound competitions had begun.

The American Kennel Club (AKC) began offering coonhound events in 2005, and the United Kennel Club (UKC) has been holding events since the late 1800s.

Overview

Absolutely no firearms are permitted in coonhound events, and game is not taken. In fact, all game is left undisturbed, for the most part. Aggressive behavior and fighting between dogs is not tolerated and can lead to disqualification. The exact procedures and event rules may differ slightly among the varying organizations from the general overview presented here.

Hounds can earn points in four specific events: nite hunts, field trials, water races, and bench shows. Events are usually held every weekend throughout the year.

TREEING

"Treeing" means to cause the game animal (a raccoon in the case of a coonhound event) to ascend a tree and stay there.

NITE HUNTS

The most popular event is the nite hunt (it is always spelled "nite" by the AKC and UKC), which as the name suggests, occurs at night. It features groups of four coonhounds and their handlers, known as "casts." The hunt is led by a guide (who herself may be a cast member) and can last for several hours. (Hunts last longer on weekends.) The object of this event is to test the hound's ability to locate the trail of a raccoon, track it, and identify the tree in which it climbed to escape.

> ## TOP BREEDS
>
> As the name suggests, coonhound events are limited to coonhounds. The Treeing Walker Coonhound is probably the best at these events, but other coonhounds also excel, including the Black and Tan, Plott, Redbone, Bluetick, and English.

FIELD TRIALS

Another coonhound event is the field trial. In this event, a course is laid out with two sets of flag lines, and an artificial scent is dragged along the trail. At the end of the trail is a pole or "home tree" in which a caged raccoon is placed or an artificial lure is hung. Surrounding the tree is a circle that is 40 to 50 feet in diameter (12 to 15 m); this is a boundary marker, and dogs who get outside the boundary marker are disqualified. Competing hounds are drawn into heats; all dogs in the heat start simultaneously and must proceed between the flags. The object is for the hounds to follow the scent trail to the finish line and subsequently tree the lure or raccoon.

WATER RACES

In this event, a well-scented lure is placed on a float or suspended in a cage above the water in a pond at least 20 yards (18 m) from shore and marked with a circle 40 to 50 feet (12 to 15 m) in diameter. Boundary markers designate the entry and exit points and the swimming course, and the water is deep enough to ensure that the dogs must swim. The dogs are released simultaneously, and the handlers are taken around the pond by a marshal and not allowed to

In a water race, the dog must follow the scent of the lure to the home tree and indicate the lure by vocalizing.

encourage their dogs—or discourage anyone else's dogs.

The line winner is the first dog to correctly follow the scent to the home tree and indicate the lure by vocalizing. The tree winner is the first dog to enter the designated circle around the home tree and bark appropriately.

BENCH SHOWS

In bench shows, dogs are judged according to their conformation, just as in a regular dog show. In other words, it is a conformation show based on the written breed standards for each sponsoring organization.

Requirements

DOGS

- endurance
- fearlessness of water (for water races)
- loud bark
- powerful hunting instinct
- strong and accurate nose

HANDLERS
- ability to work at night (for nite hunts)
- good physical condition
- interest in hunting and tracking
- patience

Equipment and Supplies
- collar
- commercial scent
- headlamp/flashlight
- heavy-soled boots and waterproof chaps (for humans)
- leash

Collar: You don't need a collar for the actual coonhound event—dogs run free. However, many owners use a radio collar to keep track of their off-lead dogs.

Commercial Scent: You'll need a bottle of artificial raccoon scent with which to train your dog.

Headlamp/Flashlight: A good light is essential for night hunts. Many hunters wear headlamps on their caps to help them see when it's dark.

Heavy-Soled Boots (Muck Boots) and Waterproof Chaps: If it is going to be cold, you might want boots with a thermal underlay. Rubber is always a good choice because it's so easy to clean. Chaps will keep you warm and dry and allow you to stay out in the field longer.

Leash: You'll need a leash to get your dog to the site, although when participating in an event, he will be working off lead.

Sponsoring Organizations

AMERICAN KENNEL CLUB (AKC)

NITE HUNTS

Judges award plus and minus points to individual dogs; wandering off, for instance, results in a minus. When all hounds are treed, the handlers (or cast) then have eight minutes to find the raccoon by shining a light into the tree. If they succeed, a "+" is placed next to the dogs' scores. If not,

Water races are divided into Novice and Open Classes.

a "-" is entered. Minus points are then subtracted from plus points to determine each dog's total score. The hound with the most plus points is named the cast winner. Five cast wins earn the Nite Champion (CNC) title.

FIELD TRIALS

Points are awarded based on a dog's order of crossing the line and treeing. To qualify for a "line decision," the dog must pass the last set of flags and give signs of recognizing game within 15 minutes of the start time. To qualify for a "tree decision," the dog must be within the tree circle within five minutes after the first dog passes the last set of flags. To be a tree winner, the dog must show interest in the treed game, bark to the judge's satisfaction, and be within the tree circle. The dog may go out of the circle and return but not to the extent that there is doubt about his interest in treeing game. All First Line and First Tree Winners advance to Final Line and Final Tree Heats. Dogs must win Line and Tree in heat and finals at the same trial to earn the title of Field Champion (CFC), Grand Field Champion (CGF), or Supreme Grand Field Champion (CSGF).

WATER RACES

Points are awarded to First Line and First Tree dogs. This race is divided into Novice Class and Open Class. The Novice Class is open to all coonhounds, regardless of age, who have not won the Water Race Champion (CWC) title. No points are awarded in this class; however, it is a fun event for beginners. Water Race Champions may compete in the Open Race Class for credit toward the Grand Water Race Champion (CGW) title. Grand Water Race Champions may compete for the Supreme Grand Water Race Champion (CSGW) title.

BENCH SHOWS

All classes are divided by age and sex, as well as between dogs in the Open Class and Champion Class. Open Classes include Puppy (six months to one year old), Junior (one to two years old), and Senior (over two years of age). The winners compete for Best of Breed Male or Female. Those who attain the title Best of Breed then compete for Best in Show Male or Female. The Champion Classes are divided by sex and open to those dogs who have been awarded the title of Bench Show Champion. The winner is awarded the title of Male Champion of Champions or Female Champion of Champions.

Coonhounds have their own bench or conformation events because for a long time, the AKC refused to register coonhounds separately and regarded them merely as foxhounds. (They have the same ancestry.)

Eligibility Requirements: Coonhound breeds that are eligible to participate include the American English Coonhound, Black and Tan Coonhound, Bluetick Coonhound, Plott, Redbone Coonhound, and Treeing Walker Coonhound. Dogs must be six months of age or older and healthy. Spayed and neutered dogs or dogs altered in any way other than are dictated by breed standards are not eligible to participate. Bitches in season are not permitted to compete in any class. Dogs must be registered with the AKC or recorded with the

AKC Foundation Stock Service (FSS). Dogs with Indefinite Listing Privileges (ILP) are not permitted to compete in Licensed or Member events.

Titles: Because different events and different sponsoring organizations are associated with coonhounds, it makes sense that different titles are awarded. The AKC offers the following:

NITE HUNT TITLES

Nite Champion (CNC): To earn this title, a registered hound must win five casts with "plus" points. *Grand Nite Champion (CGN):* Nite Champion hounds wishing to earn this title must win five casts with "plus" points. *Supreme Grand Nite Champion (CSGN):* Grand Nite Champion dogs must win five casts with "plus" points.

FIELD TRIAL TITLES

Field Champion (CFC): To earn a Field Champion title, a hound must win one First Line and one First Tree in the Finals at least once in the same trial with competition. *Grand Field Champion (CGF):* To win the title of Grand Field Champion, a Field Champion hound must win three First Lines and/or three First Trees. These must be won in three Line or Tree Finals. *Supreme Grand Field Champion (CSGF):* To earn this title, a Grand Field Champion must win three First Lines and/or three First Trees in three Line or Tree Final events.

WATER RACE TITLES

Water Race Champion (CWC): To earn a Water Race Champion title, a hound must win one First Line and First Tree in the same Water Race with competition. The hound must earn a total of 200 Championship points. *Grand Water Race Champion (CGW):* To earn this title, a Water Race Champion hound must win First Lines and/or three First Trees in three Line or Tree Finals on separate dates. *Supreme Grand Water Race Champion (CSGW):* To earn the title of Supreme Grand Water Race Champion, a Grand Water Race Champion must win three First Lines and/or three First Trees in three Line or Tree Finals. These must be earned in three separate water races with competition.

FROM THE EXPERT

The experts at CoonDawgs.com recommend waiting until a dog is seven or eight months old before starting him on true coonhound training. In fact, coonhounds don't "grow up" until they are two years old. Until then, practice in basic obedience. Some suggest keeping a raccoon skin in the refrigerator and letting the dog get curious about the scent by having him drag it around the yard.

BENCH SHOW TITLES

Champion (CCH): Dogs must have a total of 100 points under two different judges, as well as one Best in Show win with competition, to become a Bench Show Champion.
Grand Champion (CGCH): To become a Grand Champion, a hound with a Champion title must win three Champion Classes (against all Champions).

Supreme Grand Champion (CSG): To earn the title of Supreme Grand Champion, a Grand Champion hound must win three Champion Classes (against all Champions).

Premier Events: The AKC World Hunt & Show Championship is the premier coonhound event sponsored by the AKC. The event lasts for nearly a week, and there is a cash prize for the winner.

UNITED KENNEL CLUB (UKC)

The UKC coonhound procedures are similar to those of the AKC.

Eligibility Requirements: Dogs must be registered with the UKC and be at least six months of age. Spayed and neutered dogs are permitted, except for the bench shows.

Titles: The UKC has its own offering of titles.

NITE HUNT TITLES

Nite Champion (NITECH): To be declared an official Nite Champion, a hound must have at least 100 UKC points recorded in the UKC Championship Office. The dog must also have at least one first-place win in a UKC Licensed Nite Hunt. A hound must have a total score consisting of plus points and must be a cast winner. *Grand Nite Champion*

Find a mentor to help you succeed in coonhound events.

(GRNITECH): This title is earned by winning five Champion of Nite Champions events. In this portion of the event, only Nite Champions are eligible to compete. The number of dogs awarded Nite Champion wins toward their Grand Nite Champion title will be based on the number of Nite Champions entered in the event per night. Placements will only be given to those hounds who are cast winners.

FIELD TRIAL TITLES

Field Champion (FCH): To earn this title, hounds must earn 100 Championship points that must include one First Tree and First Line win in the Grand Finals. They must earn at least one on the same date in the same trial. *Grand Field Champion (GRFCH):* A Field Champion must win five Champion category events or heats, including at least one Grand Line and one Grand Tree Final on the same date in the same trial to earn this title.

WATER RACE TITLES

Water Race Champion (WCH): To earn this title, a hound must earn 100 Championship points, which include one First Line and First Tree win in the Grand Finals. This must be done on the same day at the same race. *Grand Water Race Champion (GRWCH):* A Champion must win five Champion category events or heats, including at least one Grand Line and one Grand Tree Final on the same day in the same race to earn this title.

BENCH SHOW TITLES

Show Champion (CH): To earn this title, a hound must have earned a minimum of 100 UKC Championship points under two different judges and one win for Best Male/ Female of Show. The hound must have competition in the Class, Breed, or Show level in which they earned this win. *Grand Show Champion (GRCH):* A hound may earn this title after winning five Champion of Champions Show Classes in at least five different UKC Licensed Bench Shows under three different judges. In this event, only Show Champions may compete against one another. Males and females will compete separately, and a Championship win will be awarded to the best of each class.

Premier Events: The premier UKC coonhound event is the Autumn Oaks, founded in 1960.

How to Get Started

This is a sport for those interested in hunting (or at least pretending to hunt). You need to be an outdoor enthusiast, something of a night owl, and have a real passion for hearing a lot of canine vocalization. People or dogs afraid of the dark need not apply.

EVALUATE YOUR COONHOUND

The ideal dog for coonhound events is athletic and well muscled. He has a high prey drive, well-padded feet, and a passion for exercise and hunting. A proper hound must also have a very loud and distinctive voice—whether it is high or low or sweet or obnoxious is your choice. The important thing is that he be heard. It is not uncommon for the

FUN FACT

Freedom Hills, located in northwestern Alabama, is the world's only coondog cemetery. The first occupant was Troop, buried on September 4, 1937. He and his owner, Key Underwood, hunted together for 15 years. Troop was "half redbone and half birdsong" and was famous for being able to follow a cold scent until it turned fresh. Today, more than 185 coonhounds are buried there. On the markers are listed such tributes as: "A joy to hunt with" and "He wasn't the best, but he was the best I ever had."

combined yelps of coonhounds to reach over 100 decibels during an event. Remember that coonhound competitors will work approximately five to six hours per night, so your dog should have some stamina as well.

FIND A MENTOR

A mentor is absolutely required to become involved in this esoteric sport, as it is impossible to learn on one's own; many people hire a professional trainer. It is best to contact the AKC or UKC to find out where trials are being held. There you can meet the handlers and learn how you (and your dog) can become involved in coonhound events. Many people also elect to have their dogs professionally trained.

TRAIN YOUR COONHOUND

Many people get started by having their dog chase a live raccoon in a roll cage. However, check with local officials first. Not all jurisdictions allow people to keep raccoons. Other people maintain that a true coonhound does not have to see a raccoon to maintain interest—after all, this is a scenthound.

Although coonhounds have the instinct to trail and tree raccoons, it must be honed with proper training. Coonhounds are very sensitive animals who do not respond well to rough training. They mature slowly, not reaching full maturity until they are at least two years old. If you don't have the time to train your dog properly, you may wish to consult a professional trainer, but be sure to pick one

who uses humane methods. Good training is not just about
results—the journey matters.

Strategies for Success

The following tips will help you succeed in coonhound
events.

TRAIN WITH ONE DOG

It is best to practice with just one dog. If you try to train
with a pack, the pack-minded hound won't develop the
independence he needs to find game by himself.

DON'T DISCOURAGE BARKING

Don't discourage your coonhound from barking. These are
very loud (really loud) dogs, but they win events by letting
hunters know in the dark of night where a raccoon is hiding.
They were bred to be high-decibel dogs, which is why most
coonhounds live in rural areas among tolerant neighbors.

VARY PRACTICE TIMES

Vary your practice times—let your dog experience "hunting"
at various times of the day or night. This will help make him
more versatile. In the same way, let him experience different
kinds of terrain: mudflats, hills, open fields, and any kind of
variety that will expand his horizons.

ADDITIONAL ORGANIZATIONS

American Coon Hunters Association, Inc. (ACHA)
www.acha-wcchr.com

Chapter 9

Dock Diving

Definition

Dock diving (also known as dock jumping) is a sport in which competitors take a running jump from a dock (real or simulated) in an effort to achieve the longest distance or highest leap. This sport is the ultimate pier pressure—a competition in which dogs really take a flying leap!

In dock diving, competitors take a running jump from a dock to achieve the longest distance or highest leap.

History of Dock Diving

Legend has it that dock diving originated when a couple of duck hunters, bored between hunts, argued about which of their dogs could jump farther. In 1997, Purina added the sport to its "Incredible Dog Challenge" program. Cable network ESPN got into the act in 1999, when it sought to develop a new dog sport for its "Great Outdoor Games" (GOG) concept.

The first formal dock diving event was orchestrated by Shadd Field, the president of DockDogs, who had contacted CNN in 1998. The sport proved unexpectedly popular. In the wake (pardon the pun) of the event's success, the sport's sanctioning body, DockDogs, was created in 2001 to book events, develop rules, and keep records. Beginning in February 2008, the United Kennel

Club (UKC) added dock jumping events to its roster of dog sports.

Overview

This is a thrilling event for both dogs and spectators—dogs don't jump unless they love it. If your canine friend is the type who loves to splash around in large puddles of water or can't seem to refrain from leaping into the family pool once the back door is opened, then dock diving just might be the perfect sport for both of you!

DockDogs®

DockDogs offers three major events: Big Air, Extreme Vertical, and Speed Retrieve.

Big Air®

Big Air is a long jump in the water. The distance is measured to the base of the dog's tail so that long-tailed dogs are not penalized. Handlers may position their dog anywhere on the dock, in front of the 40-foot (12-m) starting line. The dog's tail may rest over the line, but the remainder of his body must rest in front of it. A floatable chase object (toy) may be used to entice the dog into the water. The handler may choose to release the dog at any time, regardless of when she releases the chase object. (The dog is not required to retrieve the object to receive a score. If he doesn't, someone will fish it out of the tank or pond.) Each team gets 90 seconds on the dock from the time the dog sets foot on the dock until he is in motion. Big Air has three divisions so that dogs with different jumping abilities can all have fun and participate.

Extreme Vertical®

From time to time, DockDogs also holds Extreme Vertical competitions, consisting of up to 12 dogs per division, of which there are two—Cadet and Top Gun—jumping for height. The dogs jump after a designated retrievable object, called a bumper, that is suspended 8 feet (2.5 m) out from the edge of the dock, over the water. The starting heights are 5 feet (1.5 m) for the Cadets and 6 feet (2 m) for the Top Gun Division. During Extreme Vertical competition, the bumper moves up in 2-inch (5-cm) increments after each of the dogs either knocks down or grabs the retrievable. These are elimination competitions that result in a winner within each division.

SPEED RETRIEVE™

This is a relatively new sport in which an entrant runs to the water, leaps in, and swims to retrieve a toy held on a pole 38 feet (11.5 m) past the end of the dock. The timer starts at the 20-foot (6-m) mark on the dock and ends when the dog snatches the toy from the pole.

UNITED KENNEL CLUB (UKC)

The UKC offers Ultimate Air or Distance Jumping and Ultimate Vertical events.

ULTIMATE AIR OR DISTANCE JUMPING

The rules are similar to DockDogs Big Air competition, described above.

ULTIMATE VERTICAL

Ultimate Vertical (high jumping) began as a training tool to get more distance out of dogs. A training bumper with strings at both ends is held 8 feet (2.5 m) out over the water by an extender. The object is for the dog to catch and pull down the bumper. The height is measured from the surface of the dock to the bumper. A starting height is set, and dogs must bring the bumper down (by either a knock or a catch) for the height to count. Then the bumper is moved up 2 inches (5 cm) and the dog progresses to the next round. This process is repeated until only one dog remains in competition: the winner.

Requirements

DOGS

- ability to jump far and/or high
- fearlessness about jumping into water
- strong retrieve or chase instinct
- strong swimming skills

TOP BREEDS

The most successful dock diving breeds have been Labrador Retrievers, and to a lesser extent, Chesapeake Bay Retrievers. However, the current world record holder is a Greyhound mix named Country, with a huge jump of 28 feet 10 inches (9 m). Even small dogs, such as Jack Russell Terriers, have jumped more than 20 feet (6 m)! In general, the successful competitor is a passionate dog who loves water, loves to show off, and has a tremendous willingness to put it all out there.

HANDLERS
- ability to swim (you never know if you might have to rescue your dog)
- good sense of timing
- strong throwing arm

Equipment and Supplies
- body of water
- collar
- dock
- fetch toy or bumper
- leash
- life vest
- rubber matting
- towels

Body of Water: For the UKC and DockDogs competitions, the pool or natural body of water must be at least 4 feet (1 m) deep, clean, and free of debris and algae. In the case of a pool, it must have a safe exit ramp or steps for the dog to exit the water.

Collar: For the UKC, only ordinary collars are permitted; the judge must approve type and fit. Chain collars, fancy collars (like sequined or studded collars), "pinch" or "prong" collars, head harnesses, or any type of special training collars are prohibited in the competition area. Collar tags or other items hanging from the collar are prohibited in the competition area. It is also not permissible for a dog to wear a scarf or bandanna, caps, or sunglasses. DockDogs also

You may want to get a doggy life vest while training your dog to dock dive.

forbids any kind of collar other than a flat buckle collar.

Dock: For the UKC, the dock used for dock jumping competitions must be of sturdy construction with some sort of surface, such as Astroturf, outdoor carpet, or rubber matting, to make for better traction and to prevent slipping. The dock must be a minimum of 35 feet (10.5 m) and a maximum of 40 feet (12 m) long. For distance jumping, it must sit 2 feet (0.5 m) off the surface of the water. It may sit lower for Ultimate Vertical. For DockDogs, the dock must be 40 feet long (12 m) and 8 feet (2.5 m) wide. It must be covered by rubber, stiff carpeting, or a similar nonslip surface.

Fetch Toy or Bumper: The toy must be throwable, inedible, nondissolvable, and floatable.

Leash: A leash is used only to bring the dog to the dock—it is not used in the event. Retractable or long-line leads are not allowed by either organization. DockDogs requires that dogs be kept on a lead no longer than 4 feet

(1 m) when outside of the dock area.

Life Vest: You may want to get a doggy life vest for your dog while training for the event. Dog vests are permitted in the dock diving events but are not required.

Towels: Bring an old towel from the spare bathroom to dry your dog after competition—or yourself after he shakes water all over you.

Sponsoring Organizations

DockDogs®

DockDogs is the independent governing and sanctioning body for regional, national, and international dock jumping performance sports for dogs. They established the rules and standards of the sport and also keep track of and record event results.

Depending on how far your dog jumps, he can be classed as a Junior Jumper, a Senior Jumper, or a Master Jumper. Dogs under 17 inches (43 cm) tall at the withers compete in the Lap Dog Division, while all others are grouped into the general class.

Within each class—called Waves—of competition during any sanctioned DockDogs event, a Team (consisting of one dog and one handler) can secure one leg toward a title based on their overall score. A title is earned by accumulating five legs within one division. Once a Team has earned a Division Title, it can only earn ribbons in that Division or a higher Division.

Eligibility Requirements: Dock diving is open to dogs of any size and breed, including mixed breeds. Dogs must be at least six months old, and handlers must be at least seven years of age.

Titles: DockDogs awards titles such as Junior, Senior, and Master Jumper, depending on just how far a dog can jump in competition.

Premier Events: When ESPN discontinued its GOG series, DockDogs stepped up to offer its World Championships, modeled after the old GOG plan. There are also National Championships—any team of handler and dog that holds any National DockDogs title automatically

FUN FACT

The world record for "big air" dock jumping is 28 feet 10 inches (9 m)—just short of the human record of 29 feet 4.5 inches (9 m) set by Mike Powell in 1991. One of the latest DockDogs champions (November 2007) is Pico, the amazing Belgian Tervuren out of New York who won the Super Elite Division with a jump of 25 feet 7 inches (8 m). Weighing only 48 pounds (22 kg), she is continually flying to new heights and is the top-jumping female dog in the history of the sport.

qualifies for the Nationals. DockDogs also offers a High Points Championship Chase.

UNITED KENNEL CLUB (UKC)

The UKC has distance jumping divisions of Novice, Junior, Senior, Master, and Ultimate, depending on how far a dog can jump. Several rounds of competition are held, called, appropriately enough, "splashes." At the end of the day, the top five dogs in each division jump in the finals.

Eligibility Requirements: A dog must be registered with the UKC and be at least six months of age; any breed or mix is allowed.

Titles: The UKC offers a multitude of titles in its Ultimate Air and Ultimate Vertical events, including United Ultimate Jumper (UUJ), United Ultimate Jumper Champion (UUJCH), Grand Ultimate Jumper Champion (GUJCH), United Radical Ultimate Vertical (URUV), and United Grand Radical Ultimate Vertical Champion (GRUVCH).

Premier Events: The most noted UKC event is probably held at the annual Premier, which includes other dog events as well.

How to Get Started

Most dogs are not born dock divers, so it's up to you to gently nudge yours in the right direction—that is, toward the water.

GET YOUR DOG A CHECKUP

While dock diving is a low-injury sport, you'll want to

make sure that your dog's heart and lungs are strong enough for the event and that he has no muscle problems or arthritis that could hinder his participation. In addition, he'll be around other dogs, so you'll need to keep his vaccinations current.

CONDITION YOUR DOG

Conditioning is an absolute must. Many dock diving events take place in cold water, to which you may have to accustom your dog. Plenty of healthy running and playing is a great way to accomplish this. Successful dock diving dogs already love to run, jump, and swim, so the key is not to take the edge off their enjoyment. Dogs probably have only two or three "great jumps" a day, so you will need to save your dog's strength.

Training on dry land is a great way to condition your dog and increase his jumping strength. In fact, having him retrieve as he runs uphill is a fantastic way to build up muscle strength in his hind legs. When your dog has built up his endurance and confidence, you can progress to

Conditioning your dog to dock dive is a must.

When training your dog to dive, begin in an area with reduced stimuli to keep him focused.

having him jump long distances into the water. If practicing jumping on land, DockDogs recommends that you not begin until the dog is 12 to 18 months old. Just leaping into water to get him accustomed to it can begin much earlier.

TRAIN YOUR DOG TO DIVE AND RETRIEVE

Successful dogs are well versed in basic obedience work and can reliably sit and stay until released by their handler. So before you train him to dive and retrieve, he must know basic commands.

Start the retrieving work on dry land, but keep the toy in your hand at first. Gradually hold it higher and higher so that eventually he has to jump up for it, and praise him for jumping. Retrieving and love of water often go hand in hand; most water-loving dogs are natural retrievers. (If your dog is not good at retrieving or at least running after a stick, this may not be his sport.)

Make sure that your dog is sufficiently and gradually

warmed up before training him to dive into water after a toy. Begin with low-level activity in an area with reduced stimuli—not somewhere where he can see other dogs leaping off the dock. Always (even when you are at a familiar site) check the area for underwater hazards and other obstacles. You never know what may have been thrown in the lake since you were there last. In the case of rivers and streams, make sure that your dog is able to navigate them, and never train in the presence of fast-moving currents. Always use common sense. If it doesn't seem safe at first glance, it probably isn't.

After you've done this, move to the shoreline and wade in a few inches (cm). Call your dog and let him play at leaping for the ball and splashing around. This splashing is extremely important! You want him to associate splashing in the water with fun and not fear. Don't try to correct him at all during this play period. Next, ask your dog to sit several feet (m) away from the water while you wade in. Then call him to you and repeat the same fun exercise.

Finally, it is time to move to the dock. Get your dog to sit at the edge of the dock, and toss the toy in quite close. If he does not jump in, you may have to wade into the water and lure him in. As you progress, ask him to sit a bit farther back on the dock, and throw the toy farther every time. If he doesn't leap in right away, be patient. He will get the idea sooner or later, and if he doesn't, he probably doesn't have the chops or desire to be a dock diver. Perhaps a different sport would be more up his alley.

BUILD A BOND OF TRUST

One of the most important aspects of the sport is building a strong bond of trust between you and your dog. After all, you are asking him to plunge into deep water—it is more natural, even for water-loving dogs, to wade rather than jump in.

Some people without ready access to water get their dogs jumping off onto the ground, but this is hard on the joints and should be avoided, especially with young dogs. Get your dog really "driven" for the chase object—once that happens, he'll follow it to the ends of the earth, or at least over the end of a dock. You can start him off level to the water and gradually build up your "training dock" a few inches (cm) at a time. In competition, the dock is about 2 feet (0.5 m) off the platform.

LEARN FROM THE PROS
Currently few training clubs exist, but more and more are being established all the time. There are also camps and seminars. Mostly, however, you'll be on your own unless you can find a mentor. Most dock diving events have plenty of practice time, and there are lots of friendly people standing around anxious to help beginners.

Strategies for Success
As always, patience is important to success; however, this is one sport that should come naturally to your dog. If he is afraid of water or doesn't like to chase, select another activity.

TAKE CARE OF YOUR DOG
It's especially important to take good care of your dog when he's participating in dock diving. Remember that water dogs need special attention paid to their ears, which can fill with water and easily become infected. Clean and

dry the ears thoroughly, using a good commercial cleaner and drying powder after each practice. Keep any excess hair on the inside of the ears clipped short to help prevent infection.

Rinse your dog off after his adventures in the water. Algae and other organisms in the water can cause skin rashes and itching. The quicker your dog dries off, the more likely hot spots will be prevented from developing.

A common affliction of water dogs is a syndrome called "dead tail" or "cold water tail," a usually temporary condition in which the tail seems dead and lifeless. No one knows exactly why it happens, although there are plenty of guesses. It is certain that some damage occurs to the tail muscles after being in cold water. The condition is painful, but dogs usually recover on their own.

FORM A STRATEGY

Some participants have the best luck with the so-called "place and send" strategy, in which the handler walks the dog to the end of the dock, throws the toy, and lets the dog mark it (observe where it falls). Then the person walks the dog to the back of the dock and releases him. Usually this method requires a large, easily observable toy. This method works best with people who are not good throwers and for dogs who can work with a stationary target.

A more common strategy is the "chase." The handler asks her dog to sit/stay on a preferred starting point, then walks to the end of the dock, releases the dog, and throws the toy as the dog runs toward her. The point is to try to get the dog to launch and chase the toy into the air. This method is more difficult to get right than the first because timing is critical, but it can often produce better results.

Practice both methods to see which works best for you and your dog.

Chapter 10

Earthdog

Definition

Earthdog trials are competitive events that are intended to simulate the work of terriers in controlling vermin (rat hunting). The emphasis is on prey that burrows underground, hence the name "earthdog." The events are designed to test a dog's natural searching and hunting abilities.

History of Earthdog

Terriers, who compose most of the earthdog breeds, are indigenous to the British Isles. (Dachshunds hail from Germany but have many terrier-like qualities.) When the Romans invaded Britain in 55 BCE, Roman historian Pliny the Elder recorded, "They found much to their surprise, small dogs that would follow their quarry to the ground." Earthdogs were used by hunters and farmers even before that time to help hunt game and eliminate vermin. Because of their small size, as well as their courage and mental abilities, terriers were perfect for trailing vermin like rats and mice into their lairs and then killing them.

Competitive earthdog trials in the United States did not gain in popularity until 1971, when the American Working Terrier Association (AWTA) began initiating artificial den trials. Prior to this, however, many local terrier clubs held "go-to-ground" programs. Today, the AWTA holds many events (both earthdog and aboveground hunting) all around the country. The American Kennel Club (AKC) got involved in the sport in 1988, when a group of enthusiasts met to discuss the development of a program that might be accepted by the AKC. It wasn't until 1993 that the plan was finalized, complete with a new set of rules and regulations to govern the sport. Finally, on October 1, 1994, the first AKC-sanctioned earthdog test was held in Portland, Oregon.

One difference between AKC trials and AWTA trials is that in some of the latter's events (such as the Hunting Certificate), the prey animal *may* be injured or killed. In AKC trials, the prey animal is always protected.

TOP BREEDS

Most terriers and Dachshunds (who share many terrier characteristics) are enthusiastic earthdog participants because of their heritage, temperament, and to a lesser degree, their body type. If you have a Maltese who loves digging and hunting, you're out of luck because sponsoring organizations limit eligibility to terriers or terrier crosses.

In earthdog, the dog must enter a tunnel and "work" a caged rat or other designated quarry.

Overview

In the sport of earthdog, a dog must enter a tunnel and "work" a caged rat or other designated quarry (prey). "Working the quarry" is defined on the judge's score sheet as barking, growling, whining, digging, biting at the cage, lunging at the cage, and/or a frozen and focused stare. In most events, the prey animal is not harmed.

Earthdog trials are conducted in dens whose exact configuration (including number of turns) varies according to the sponsoring organization and event. Bars at the end of each tunnel protect the caged quarry from direct contact with the dog. At the start of each test, the dog is released into the den from no higher than the waist of the owner. Throwing the dog in the direction of the den entrance is not permitted and may result in disqualification. Once the dog is released, the owner must stand quietly until the judge instructs otherwise.

This is a sport that calls for a good deal of courage on the part of a dog—to enter a dark, unknown den in pursuit of who knows what! Claustrophobic dogs need not apply.

> ## Fun Fact
>
> The word "terrier" comes from the Latin word *terra,* meaning "earth." The term "earthdog" was invented to differentiate these dogs from those in other hunting test programs. It's not a word recognized outside of these events.

American Kennel Club (AKC)

In the AKC, dogs are judged on searching ability, obedience to commands, endurance, patience, adaptability, independence, and cooperation (demonstrated when a dog works harmoniously with others). However, the encounter is controlled, and neither the prey nor the dog are in danger of being injured during the event.

Three types of earthdog tests are recognized by the AKC: member, licensed, and sanctioned. Member earthdog tests are those in which qualifications for titles are awarded and given by a club or association that is a member of the AKC. Licensed earthdog tests are basically the same as member tests, except the club or association holding the test is not a member of the AKC. They have, however, been licensed by the AKC to hold the test. The third type, the sanctioned test, is a bit different. These tests are sanctioned by the AKC, but they do not award titles to participating dogs. They are more like practice events. These tests are usually held by clubs and associations to qualify for approval to hold a licensed or member event in the future.

American Working Terrier Association (AWTA)

In AWTA earthdog tests, dogs are judged on how long it takes them to reach the quarry (two mature, caged rats) as well as the total time (without a break) the dog has worked the animal. The AWTA offers one "earth" (the technical term for the whole den setup) for the Novice Classes and one for the Open and Certificate Classes. Earths are to be dug in the actual ground. The Novice earth is about 10 feet (3 m) long with one right-angle (90-degree) turn. The Open and Certificate earth, when fully constructed, is about 30

feet (9 m) long with three right-angle (90-degree) turns.
The Certificate Class earth may also include obstacles, blind
tunnels, and false entrances.

Requirements

Dogs
- curiosity
- fearlessness
- independence
- obedience to basic commands
- perseverance
- strong prey drive

Handlers
- ability to read dog's body language
- ability to work with rodents
- patience
- trust in dog

Equipment and Supplies
- collar
- lead
- practice den access
- practice den supplies (varies depending on method
  of training)
- quarry
- tunnel/chute

Collar: A flat, sturdy collar is desirable for bringing the
dog to the test. However, earthdogs work without collars or
leads in the actual test.

Lead: You'll need a solid leather or webbed 4- to 6-foot (1-
to 2-m) lead for the event and a longer slip lead (8 to 12 feet
[2.5 to 3.5 m]) for practice and training.

Practice Den Access: For best results, you will need
access to a training den much like those you will be using in
an actual event.

Practice Den Supplies: The supplies you need for a
practice den will vary depending on your method of training.
You will need at the very minimum a rat (you can get one in

a pet store—do not try to capture a wild rat) in a cage (about 8 by 8 by 6 inches [20.5 by 20.5 by 15 cm]) to pique the dog's interest.

Quarry: The quarry is a rat, or more commonly, rats—two are usually used.

Tunnel/Chute: Chutes have two sides and a top. Junior earthdog tests use straight, 30-foot-long (9-m-long) liners, but you can use several smaller pieces, joined with hinges, which can be taken apart for portability. You'll also need to make a trap door in the roof of the liner so that the cage can be removed.

Sponsoring Organizations

AMERICAN KENNEL CLUB (AKC)

The AKC has been offering earthdog trials since October 1994 and both licenses and sanctions events at clubs and associations around the United States.

Four classes exist in earthdog trials: Introduction to Quarry, Junior Earthdog, Senior Earthdog, and Master Earthdog.

INTRODUCTION TO QUARRY TEST

In this test, the den is approximately 10 feet (3 m) long and incorporates one 90-degree turn. The dog must reach the quarry within two minutes from the time he enters the earth and continuously work the quarry for 30 seconds. This is the only test in which the judge may assist the dog by tapping or scratching the quarry cage to pique the dog's interest.

JUNIOR EARTHDOG TEST

The Junior Test den consists of a 30-foot (9-m) tunnel with three 90-degree turns. The owner must release the dog 10 feet (3 m) from the entrance to the den and may give a short command without penalty. The dog must reach the quarry within 30 seconds. Once the quarry has been reached, the dog may remain with it for a maximum of 30 seconds before beginning to work. The dog must work the quarry continuously for 60 seconds. He must complete these requirements twice under two different judges to be awarded the title of Junior Earthdog (JE).

One of the things a judge looks for in an earthdog is the ability to search for the quarry independently, with limited distractibility.

SENIOR EARTHDOG TEST

This test consists of a den that is 30 feet (9 m) long with at least three 90-degree turns. The dog is released 20 feet (6 m) from the entrance to the den. To enhance difficulty, distractions such as a false, unscented exit and unscented rat bedding at the end are added. The dog has 90 seconds to reach the quarry and must begin working the rats within 15 seconds of coming into contact with them. He must continually work the rats for 90 seconds. The rats are then removed from the den, and the dog has 90 seconds to make his way back out of the den and return to his owner. During this time, the owner is allowed to approach the entrance to the den and call or whistle for the dog. Once the dog has completed these requirements in three different tests under two different judges, he is awarded the title of Senior Earthdog (SE).

MASTER EARTHDOG TEST

In a Master Earthdog test, two dogs (bracemates) are worked at the same time. The object of this test is to simulate natural hunting conditions and to gauge the ability of the dogs

WORKING THE QUARRY

"Working the quarry" is earthdog talk for attacking the caged prey by barking, digging, growling, lunging, or biting at the protective bars. In other words, he is making an effort to "get at" the prey.

to work with an unfamiliar bracemate. The den is constructed in the same way as in the Senior Test, except that modifications are incorporated to enhance difficulty. A 20-foot (6 m) scent line leads to the entrance of the den, and a false den entrance is located midway along the scent line. In addition, an 18-inch (45.5-cm) section of the tunnel constricts to a 6-inch (15-cm) passage, and an obstacle consisting of a 6-inch (15-cm) diameter section of PVC pipe is suspended crossways with 9 inches (23 cm) on either side for the dog to maneuver around.

The owners and their dogs join the judge at the release point. A steward stands at the entrance to the den, which is blocked, to deal with overly aggressive dogs. The dogs are released into the den from a distance of 300 feet (91.5 m). The owners and judge proceed at a normal walking pace toward the entrance to the den, and the owners are permitted to give direction to their dogs by voice or whistle. The dogs may inspect the false den but are disqualified if they bark. Both dogs must identify the real den entrance. When both have identified the entrance, one of the dogs stake out quietly while his bracemate works the den. The working dog has 90 seconds to reach the quarry and must work it for 90 seconds. Once this is accomplished, the owner removes the dog within 15 seconds so that the other dog may work the den.

Once the dog has completed these requirements four times under three different judges, he will receive the title of Master Earthdog (ME) and will be allowed to continue competing in all three levels of earthdog.

Eligibility Requirements: The following breeds are eligible to participate in AKC earthdog trials: Dachshund and terrier breeds, including Australian, Bedlington, Border, Cairn, Cesky, Dandie Dinmont, Fox (smooth and wire), Glen of Imaal, Lakeland, Manchester, Miniature Bull, Miniature

Schnauzers, Norfolk, Norwich, Parson Russell, Rat, Russell, Scottish, Sealyham, Silky, Skye, Welsh, and Welsh Highland White.

All dogs must be at least six months of age, and all must be registered with the AKC or recorded with the Foundation Stock Service (FSS). Dogs who have been spayed and neutered, those with Indefinite Listing Privileges (ILP), and those with Limited Registration are all eligible to participate.

Titles: Titles include Junior Earthdog (JE), Senior Earthdog (SE), and Master Earthdog (ME).

Premier Events: Earthdog events are held all around the United States.

AMERICAN WORKING TERRIER ASSOCIATION (AWTA)

The AWTA has members throughout the United States and Canada. The Canadian Kennel Club (CKC) recognizes the AWTA Certificate of Gameness and will record it on a CKC pedigree.

In an AWTA den trial, two separate dens are constructed: one for Novice Classes and one for Open Classes. In the Novice Classes, points are deducted for the level of encouragement the dog receives from his owner. The Novice A Class is open to dogs and bitches under 12 months of age who have not earned 100 percent in the Novice Class. The Novice B Class is open to dogs and bitches over 12 months of age who have not earned 100 percent in the Novice Class. The Open Class is open to dogs and bitches who have scored 100 percent in the Novice Class or who have worked in a similar artificial or natural earth environment. A Certificate Class is also available.

NOVICE CLASSES (A AND B)

The Novice Den is approximately 10 feet (3 m) long with one 90-degree turn. The 9-by-9-inch (23-by-23-cm) dens are constructed in the earth and marked from entrance to end with rat scent. The area directly over the quarry must be covered. Prior to judging, the quarry is placed inside the den behind bars that prevent the dog from coming into contact with it.

In an AWTA class, the handler must carry her dog to the starting point.

At the beginning of the trial, the judge calls the dog to be judged from the holding area. The owner then removes the dog's collar and leash at the entrance to the trial area and carries him to the starting point, which is approximately 10 feet (3 m) from the entrance to the den. Verbal communication is acceptable during this time. The judge goes over what the handler must do and then gives the okay to release the dog. The owner should release the dog gently from the waist or by placing him on the ground. Throwing the dog toward the entrance will result in disqualification. A brief command to the dog is permitted, but the owner must remain silent throughout the rest of the trial.

Points are given based upon the time it takes to reach the quarry and how long it takes the dog to work the quarry. Fifty points are awarded if the dog reaches the quarry within one minute and 25 points if he reaches it within two minutes. After two minutes, no points will be awarded. Once the dog has reached the quarry, to encourage him, the judge may disturb the cage by shaking, tapping, rattling, or scratching it. The dog must work the quarry continuously for 30 seconds by barking, whining, digging, growling, biting, or other means. If he succeeds, 50 points are awarded. Once the trial is over, the owner retrieves the dog and removes him from the judging area.

OPEN CLASSES

With the exceptions of timing, scoring, and den size, the rules for an Open Class trial are basically the same. The Open Class den is approximately 30 feet (9 m) long and contains three 90-degree turns. The dog must reach the quarry within 30 seconds and work the quarry continuously for 60 seconds. If he fails to achieve the time limit in either portion of the trial, no score will be given. Also, unlike in the Novice Class, the judge and handler may give no help during the trial. The dog must rely on his own instincts to complete the trial.

The owner may give one command upon release, then wait quietly at the release point while the dog seeks out the quarry. The dog may enter, exit, and then re-enter as long as he has not traveled the full distance to the quarry. In addition, the dog will not be penalized as long as he reaches the quarry within 30 seconds from the time of release. Once he finally reaches the quarry, he must not leave it. If he does, no points will be awarded. However, if he reaches the quarry within 30 seconds and continues to work the quarry for a full minute, he will earn his Certificate of Gameness (CG).

CERTIFICATE CLASS

This class is provided for dogs who live in areas where natural quarry is limited or nonexistent. The trial for the Certificate Class is judged in the same way as the Open Class but may include challenges such as simple obstacles, blind tunnels, and false entrances.

Eligibility Requirements: The AWTA recognizes the following breeds: Dachshunds and terriers, including Australian, Bedlington, Border, Cairn, Cesky, Dandie Dinmont, Fell, Wire Fox, Smooth Fox, Glen of Imaal, Jack Russell, Jagdterrier, Lakeland, Norwich, Norfolk, Patterdale, Scottish, Sealyham, Skye, Welsh, and West Highland White. In addition, any Dachshund or terrier breed (including some cross breeds) not listed may also be entered as long as the dog is of suitable size to fit into a 9-inch (23-cm) hole.

Titles and Awards: *Certificate of Gameness (CG):* When a dog scores 100 percent in the Open Class, he is awarded the Certificate of Gameness. Once he has earned this, he will then be eligible for the Certificate Class and will no longer be able to participate in any other class. *Certificate:* Open to dogs and bitches who have earned the Certificate of Gameness. *Working Certificate (WC):* This certificate is awarded by application to dogs whose owners are AWTA members in good standing. Dogs must enter natural earth structures (drains and other man-made

FROM THE EXPERT

Pam Dyer, earthdog organizer and judge, notes several common misconceptions related to earthdog:

Doing earthdog will make my dog aggressive: "Not true. It will bring out the dog's innate instincts but in a safe, appropriate, and controlled manner. The earthdog experience is a form of release for these pent-up instincts. Having an appropriate place to channel this energy may well relieve the dog and settle some problems at home."

A dog needs to be aggressive to do earthdog: "Not true. Some of the best earthdogs are very laid back and easygoing when not working. The ability to work harmoniously off leash in the presence of another dog is a requirement for the Master Earthdog Test. Good working ability is a trait just like good shoulders, good movement, or good temperament—it must be bred for and nurtured."

My dog is a great ratter and should do well at earthdog: "Not necessarily. Although rats are generally used to represent the quarry, earthdog tests are not about ratting. They are about the instinct to go to ground and work the quarry—they must mark its presence. Some dogs who are good ratters are also good earthdogs but not all. Many ratters faced with a rat or mouse they cannot reach will stare and wait for it to come out or move. This is inappropriate behavior for a dog in the earth."

structures do not count) after a quarry such as woodchucks (i.e., groundhogs), foxes, raccoons, badgers, or aggressive possums. The owner is not allowed to assist the dog except in the case of removing a restriction impeding entrance, such as a root or large stone. The dog must travel far enough to be completely out of sight and locate the quarry on his own, although simple and quiet verbal commands from the owner are permitted. The dog must then work down to the quarry and cause it to bolt or "draw it" from the earth. A positive visual identification of the quarry is required and must be witnessed by another AWTA member. There is to be no doubt that the dog is right up to the quarry. If the handler does not dig to the dog, the dog must show evidence of a face-to-face encounter with bites or quarry fur in his mouth. The baying must be continuous for at least three minutes. Note: This is a blood sport. It is quite possible that one or both of the animals (prey and/or dog) may be injured or killed.

Hunting Certificate (HC): This certificate is awarded (by application) to dogs whose owners are AWTA members in good standing. It is issued to dogs regularly used for hunting game or for flushing and/or retrieving upland birds. It can be earned for hunting above ground and/or drawing out the quarry and is awarded for either specific quarry or multiple quarries (rabbits, squirrels, opossums, rats, raccoons, muskrats, mongooses, or feral pigs). It can also be earned for retrieving upland birds, for dogs used to draw quarry at the end of a dig in connection with earthwork, and for working quarry below ground that otherwise do not qualify for a Working Certificate. Like the Working Certificate, this is a blood sport.

The dog must seek out and find the game. "Draw dogs" must draw the quarry from an opening at the end of a dig and bring the quarry into the open. The game must be killed by the dog or taken using another legal method of hunting. The dog must have hunted for a full season before being issued the certificate. Also, another AWTA member must observe the dog hunting on at least six different occasions and confirm that he is regularly used for hunting. *Veteran Earthdog Award:* Awarded to dogs who have earned ten

Working Certificates and/or Hunting Certificates. The work must have included at least three different quarries and have been observed by at least three different witnesses.

Earthworker Award: This is awarded to members who have accumulated ten Working Certificates on ten different earthdogs.

Premier Events: Trials are held all over the United States.

How to Get Started

Most dogs, especially "earthdog breeds," are already born with the instinct to track unusual scents in their environment— just watch your dog the next time you are out walking him and see how often he will put his nose to the ground or sniff out an unfamiliar tree or shrub!

GET YOUR DOG A CHECKUP

Before getting started in earthdog, take your dog to the vet to ensure that he is in good health, up to date on vaccinations, and can withstand tough physical activity.

TAKE YOUR DOG TO THE PARK

To introduce your dog to tracking rodents and other small quarry, take him to a local park or field that you know to be teeming with squirrels or rabbits and encourage him to put his nose to the ground by patting the scent line. (Because you can lay the scent yourself using store-bought commercial scent, you'll know exactly where it is.) This will not only teach him how to pick up the scent, but it will also help him trust that you are his hunting partner and will assist him in his task.

Once he picks up the scent, the rest is mostly up to his basic instinct. But to qualify in an earthdog test, your dog must be willing to track the scent of the quarry below ground into dark and unfamiliar territory. You can teach your dog to have an interest in vermin by buying some from a local pet store and presenting them to him in a cage. Encourage any interest he shows. If he seems cautious, give him plenty of time to examine the cage on his own. Show interest in it yourself— ultimately, you want him to aggressively attack the cage (although he's not physically hurting the rat). Never force an interest because that will only frighten your dog. As he shows

Take your dog to an earthdog event; many clubs hold practices after the main event is over, which is a great way to introduce him to the real thing.

interest, use a cue phrase such as "Get the rat! Get the rat!" to further motivate him.

TRAIN YOUR DOG TO GO TO GROUND

Simulating a den is relatively easy. You can simulate the tunnel by installing a series of wooden liners, cardboard boxes, or even PVC pipe large enough for your dog to maneuver through. Make sure that they are big enough not to restrict him. Whether you build a standard earthdog den or improvise is entirely up to you. The point is to get your dog used to tracking the scent of the quarry into a dark, confined space. Go slowly, and be quiet so as not to distract him. After he is used to going in straight lines, add an "elbow" to the den to get him used to turns.

Next, scent the trail he is to follow into the tunnel. You can usually purchase rats or other small rodents at your local pet store. If handling these furry little creatures is not your idea of fun, another alternative will work just as

151

well: Most pet shops will not mind handing over their used rodent bedding to an eager customer and will understand completely when you explain what you plan to use it for.

Once you have acquired the source of the scent, you should do one of two things. First, place a toy in a jar with a portion of the bedding and seal it for a few days. This will allow the toy to absorb the scent, and presto! You have a perfectly acceptable rodent stunt double.

Next, make a scent trail that your dog can follow. You can do this by soaking the remainder of the bedding in water, straining it into a spray bottle or other container, and marking the scent trail. It's that easy.

TAKE YOUR DOG TO AN EARTHDOG EVENT

Training should not be confined to your backyard. Whether he is completely ready or just starting out, consider taking your dog to a real earthdog event. Many clubs hold practices after the main event is over, which is a great way to introduce him to the real thing.

Even more exciting, enter him in an AKC Introduction to Quarry Class. This will help in two ways: It will introduce him to working real, live quarry (if you have not already done so), and it lets you know if he is even willing to work quarry at all. In addition, this is a great way to meet many other earthdog enthusiasts who are usually willing to share training tips and tricks.

LEARN THE SCORING CRITERIA

Judges base their scores on a number of key criteria. The skills most often looked for in an earthdog are the following:

- *Searching ability:* The ability to search for the quarry independently with limited distractibility, as well as an eagerness to explore.
- *Obedience:* The attentiveness and responsiveness to his owner or handler and his ability to remain under the handler's control at all times.
- *Endurance:* The ability to continue with the task at hand as long as needed to be successful.
- *Patience:* The willingness of the dog to remain focused on the task regardless of what obstacles he

may encounter, and a desire to finish to the end.

- *Adaptability:* The ability to adjust to changes in conditions of the trail, as well as the ability to work cooperatively with additional running mates if they are introduced.

- *Independence:* The confidence to work on his own, disregarding any distractions from any additional dogs with whom he may be working.

- *Cooperation:* The ability to work harmoniously with others and not be a hindrance to any additional dogs with whom he may be working.

Strategies for Success

Always remember that as you participate in earthdog, your dog's skills will build as he progresses to each level. However, regardless of whether you decide to compete for earthdog titles or not, the most important thing is to have fun and build a trusting bond between you and your dog.

PAY ATTENTION TO YOUR DOG'S INSTINCTS

Pay attention to your dog's instincts and continue to build on them during everyday activities. If he picks up a scent while you are out for a walk, allow him to follow the trail. When indoors, play games that allow him to seek out an object by following its scent and crawling into darkened spaces and under furniture. The important thing is that he enjoys what he is doing and feels a sense of accomplishment when he has succeeded in his task.

KEEP YOUR DOG FOCUSED

Once at an earthdog event, keep your dog focused and away from other dogs. Terriers are not always the most sociable of dogs under the best of circumstances, and you don't want a fight to break out. You want your dog's attention on the game at hand.

ADDITIONAL ORGANIZATIONS

Canadian Kennel Club (CKC)
www.ckc.ca

Chapter 11
Field Trials, Basset Hounds

Definition

A field trial is a competitive event that tests a dog's ability to locate the quarry that he was bred to hunt. In the case of the Basset Hound, this is the rabbit or hare. In general, the procedures and rules governing Basset Hound trials are identical to those of Beagle trials, although the hunting methods vary somewhat. Dogs compete against one another.

Although many people think of Basset Hounds as "couch potatoes," they were actually bred to hunt rabbits.

History of Basset Hound Field Trials

The Basset Hound is a French breed, and the first Bassets came to the United States from France—a gift from the Marquis Lafayette to George Washington. (The first field trials were actually held for pointing breeds and began in Britain in 1866; the United States followed soon after. The first recorded field trial was held in 1874 near Memphis, Tennessee.) Basset Hounds have been participating in American Kennel Club (AKC) field trials since 1937.

Overview

Although many people think of Basset Hounds as lazy couch potatoes, they were bred to hunt rabbits, and field trials demonstrate what they can actually do. (The dogs never actually catch rabbits. They're not allowed to—that's the hunter's job.) All phases of the tracking should be approached eagerly and willingly; however, the dog's movements should be efficient and deliberate rather than impulsive or haphazard.

Dogs are judged on their overall ability to find a rabbit and solve the problems presented in its pursuance. The Basset is to work entirely by scent, and visualizing the rabbit and then chasing it does not count. (This is just one issue that makes this sport different from real rabbit hunting.) Following a scent trail is difficult because rabbits don't crawl along like a groundhog or opossum; instead, they hop and change direction frequently, resulting in a discontinuous scent line. The point is not for the dog to actually catch a rabbit but to move it toward the hunter, who can then shoot it. However, field trials do not involve the actual killing of game or firing of guns. The rabbits are quite safe and very well cared for.

Just as in conformation events, there exists a written standard for judging performance in the field. AKC judges look for the following skills in field trial hounds:

- *Searching ability:* Ability to recognize and willingness to explore promising cover.
- *Pursuing ability:* Proficiency in keeping control of the trail while making good progress.
- *Accuracy in trailing:* Ability to keep to the trail with a minimum of weaving around; also the ability to know the direction in which the game is traveling.
- *Proper use of voice:* The loud proclamation to the immediate world that a rabbit has been identified and is being pursued. A clear, sweet tone is always an added bonus.
- *Endurance:* The ability to compete throughout the hunt and continue as long as necessary.
- *Adaptability:* The ability to adjust quickly to a variety of different environments and running mates.
Patience: A willingness to stay with the scent in a workmanlike manner and not go off on a gambol or "wild rabbit chase."
- *Determination:* Imperturbability in the face of obstacles and other problems, a similar quality to patience.

- *Independence:* Self-reliance and the ability to ignore other hounds when they make an error. Although pack animals, each hound is expected to be sensible and use his own judgment as well.
- *Cooperation:* The ability to work harmoniously with other hounds.
- *Competitive spirit:* The desire to outdo other hounds in the pack. This is a quality that should be present to a moderate degree only. Overly competitive dogs are not successful because are unable to honor other hounds in their pack.
- *Intelligence:* The ability to learn from experience and make the most of opportunities presented.

Faulty actions include:

- *Quitting:* Lack of desire to hunt, a most serious fault.
- *Backtracking:* Following the trail in the wrong direction.
- *Ghost trailing:* "Pretending" to follow a trail that does not in fact exist—at least, one that no one is aware of.
- *Pottering:* Hesitating, lack of forward motion, listlessness.
- *Babbling:* Excessive or unnecessary use of voice.
- *Swinging:* Casting out too far from the last point of contact; "gamboling" with the scent.
- *Skirting:* Purposely leaving the trail to avoid strenuous work or tough obstacles.
- *Leaving checks:* Failure to stay in the vicinity of a loss and charging off looking for a new scent before it is reasonable to do so.

FUN FACT

Did you know that William Shakespeare makes mention of the Basset Hound in his play *A Midsummer Night's Dream*?

"Their heads are hung with ears that sweep away the morning dew,

Crook-knee'd, and dew-lapped like Thessalian bulls; slow in pursuit, but match'd in mouth like bells."

Field trial handlers must be in good physical condition and able to navigate the terrain.

- *Running mute:* Failure to give voice or "tongue" when on the trail.
- *Tightness of mouth:* Failure to give voice sufficiently.
- *Racing:* Attempting to outrun the other hounds, often resulting in overshooting the trail.
  Running hit or miss: Attempting to make progress without carefully and continuously following the scent.
- *Lack of independence:* Watching other hounds and allowing them to determine the course of action.
- *Bounding off:* Simply taking off when game is scented without attempting to determine its direction.

159

Field trial events include Brace, Small Pack, Large Pack, and Gundog Brace.

BRACE TRIALS

The oldest events are the Brace Trials, in which two (or more rarely, three) dogs are run as a brace. They are judged on how accurately they can track a rabbit. During the trial, each brace is taken separately to be "put on rabbit" in the order in which they are drawn. The spectators (gallery) and handlers line up out of the way as directed by the marshal. The entire group "beats the bushes" as they walk across a section of the ground, hoping to scare up a rabbit. The first person to see a rabbit actually yells out "Tally-ho!" just like in the books. The gallery then halts, and the hounds and handlers come out to track the rabbit. The main criterion is accuracy, and the Basset is expected to handle the checks (rabbit misdirection) with aplomb. While on the trail, the Basset will bay, or "give tongue." If he does so when he has lost the trail, however, he loses points. After each brace is run, the first series is

In Gundog Brace, a pair of Bassets is cast to find a rabbit.

FROM THE EXPERT

Marge Skolnick, who has been field trialing Bassets for many years, writes:

"So how do you begin to train your Basset to learn the game of trailing rabbit? You will have to start with finding a place where you know there are rabbits and it is safe to trail him. There are places like this at grounds rented by people who are members of Beagle clubs or (if you are lucky) who will let you join the club. These grounds are nearly always surrounded with a fence and have quite a few or many rabbits kept and bred there.

"Some of the Beagle grounds also have an acre or two with "starting pens" to find two or a few rabbits. Sometimes people have their own property with rabbits, and some have starting pens. Using a starting pen offers the opportunity to try a hound often and in a smaller area.

"Remember that the rabbits are cared for and are not killed—the dogs do not catch them!"

declared over. The half dozen or so dogs judged best in the series are called back for a second series. This can be repeated until the judges have decided the placements.

SMALL PACK TRIALS

In the Small Pack Trials, dogs are run in packs of seven; they are expected to follow the rabbit's trail with enthusiasm while at the same time keeping track of the rabbit.

LARGE PACK TRIALS

The Large Pack Trial is run on hares (not rabbits) in packs of up to 25 dogs. These dogs are expected to run for at least several hours in the Open Class—the one that counts for winning points for a field championship.

GUNDOG BRACE

In the Gundog Trials, a pair of Bassets is "cast" (let free) to find a rabbit. They are judged on how well they search. In this trial, a gun is fired close by to test the dogs for gun-shyness.

The good field trial dog will work independently of his bracemate when the scent is lost but will immediately join him when the other dog signals a find.

Requirements

Dogs
- accurate nose
- good physical condition
- obedience off lead is a plus but cannot be expected in hounds
- perseverance
- sociability
- strong prey drive, specifically directed toward rabbits

Handlers
- ability to navigate brushy fields, even in the rain
- good physical condition

Equipment and Supplies
- muck boots

Muck Boots: These are waterproof hunting boots you'll need to go slogging around after your dog. Make sure that you can walk in them!

Sponsoring Organizations

AMERICAN KENNEL CLUB (AKC)

The main classes are Derbies, All Age Dogs, All Age Bitches, and Champion Stakes. However, as frequently happens, if there are fewer than ten entries in one of the classes, they are combined if possible and run with both sexes in a single class. A Derby Class is a nonregular class offered for dogs who have not reached their second birthday on the day the class is scheduled. In regular Open All Age classes, dogs earn points toward a Field Championship.

Eligibility Requirements: Only registered Basset Hounds are eligible to participate. Dogs may not be spayed or neutered.

Titles: A field championship is hard to earn and shows serious achievement on the part of your hound. To become a Field Champion, a Basset must have placed in Open All Age Classes at four or more trials, have placed first in at least one of them, and have won a total of 60 championship points. The top winner of the day is termed the Absolute Champion. A newly introduced honor is the title of Grand Field Champion (GFC), awarded by the Basset Hound Club of America (BHCA) to Bassets winning a total of 20 points from the Field Champion Class. The title Dual Champion (DC) designates a Basset who has fulfilled both AKC requirements for a Field Champion and Bench Champion. As of this writing, only eight Bassets have achieved the honor of winning a Dual Championship.

Premier Events: Basset field trials are held all around the United States. The most prestigious event may be the trials held annually at the Basset Hound National Specialty every year.

How to Get Started

Bassets are always on the snoop for rabbits, so the best thing you can do is get your dog out where they are—which is almost everywhere!

ENSURE THAT YOUR BASSET IS SUITABLE

The Basset Hound must be endowed with a keen nose, a sound body, and an intelligent mind, and he must have an intense enthusiasm for hunting. He must also be determined and a good problem solver. The good field trial dog will work independently of his bracemate when the scent is lost but will immediately join him (harking) when the other dog signals a find. The dogs compete with each other to see who can first find the trail, but the competition should not hinder the forward progress of the hunt. He should be competitive with his bracemate but not so jealous that he interferes with the steady progress of the chase. The "prize" does not necessarily go to the fastest dog; concentration and control are more important.

You will know if your Basset is not suitable if he is not sound or shows absolutely no interest in rabbits. Some dogs are like that. If he walks by a rabbit sitting in the yard without appearing to notice, find another sport.

GET YOUR DOG A CHECKUP

Your Basset Hound should be healthy and limber, as he'll be covering a good deal of ground. Because he'll be around other

Your Basset should be healthy and limber to participate in a field trial.

dogs, it's especially important to make sure that he is current on all of his vaccinations.

FIND A MENTOR

Unlike many retrievers and pointing dogs, your Basset Hound will probably not need a professional trainer to compete in field trials. Bassets hunt rabbits naturally, but you'll need the help of a mentor to get started in the sport. Find a club near you, and start making friends!

TRAIN YOUR DOG

Most people wait until their pups are six months old before they start training; you want a dog with some degree of maturity and mental acuity. Field trial dogs under two are still considered very youthful. Some people start their dogs on tame rabbits, believing that they have a stronger scent than wild ones, although this is speculation. Some people actually walk around with the tame rabbit on a lead, then put him back in the hutch. Then they see if the dog can follow the scent. In the wild, look for honeysuckle—rabbits both live in it and eat it.

Strategies for Success

One of the best strategies for success involves being patient and letting your dog find the rabbit for himself.

BE PATIENT

In field trialing, your job is to be as patient as your dog. Rabbits are warier than they seem and don't always appear on cue; hunting by scent is slow work, but sure. Your hound's breeding took centuries to develop his super-sensitive nose, so have faith in him.

DON'T SHOW YOUR DOG THE RABBIT

The trick to rabbit finding is to remember that rabbits hop. This may not seem like such a big deal, but when a rabbit hops, his scent disappears. Because your dog is hunting by scent only, when he comes to a "bare spot," he has to smell around carefully until he picks up the scent again. Don't try to "show" your dog the rabbit—let him find it by smell.

Chapter 12

Field Trials, Beagles

Definition

A Beagle field trial evaluates the breed's prowess in finding and tracking rabbits or hares. No animals are hurt, and no firearms are used (except in the Gundog Brace Trials, in which case guns are fired into the air to test the dog's reaction to the sound). Dogs compete against one another.

The successful field trial Beagle needs a good nose.

History of Beagle Field Trials

Beagles have been participating in American Kennel Club
(AKC) field trials for more 100 years. It all began with this
announcement in the Sunday *Boston Herald* on October
26, 1890: "A group of Beagle Owners would hold a Beagle
field trial in Hyannis, Massachusetts, in a fortnight." This
group called itself the National Beagle Club of America, and
the advertised trial was held on November 4, 1890, with 18
entries. The United Kennel Club (UKC) calls its Beagling
events "Hunting Beagle" and "Performance Pack," but for all
intents and purposes, they are the same as a field trial. The
UKC held its first licensed event in 1990 in Maryland.

Overview

The Beagle may be the world's most ancient gundog, one
who was specifically bred to follow rabbits and hares.
However, Beagles are among the many breeds in which a
split has occurred between show dogs ("bench Beagles")
and field trial dogs, and almost no Beagles are "dual

champions," winning championships in both classes. To make things more complicated, the most common type of field trialing Beagle, the Brace Beagle, isn't of much use on a real rabbit, either, because he is too specialized at slow tracking.

During a field trial, the Beagle's job is to find a rabbit and follow it, tonguing (vocalizing) as he goes. This lets the hunter know where he is. An experienced Beagler can pick out the sound of her dog's voice among many others and can also often tell how close the dog is to the rabbit.

The successful field trial Beagle is expected to be eager and willing to stay with the game trail. He needs a good nose, a sound body, and a highly intelligent mind. Actions should appear deliberate and efficient—not haphazard or impulsive. Rabbits tend to hop around, and the Beagle needs to move carefully over the area to pick up the scent. Judges look for the following skills:

- *Searching ability:* The ability to recognize and willingness to explore promising cover.
- *Pursuing ability:* Proficiency in keeping control of the trail while making good progress.
- *Accuracy in trailing:* The ability to keep to the trail with a minimum of weaving around; also the ability to know the direction in which the game is traveling.
- *Proper use of voice:* The loud proclamation to the immediate world that a rabbit has been identified and is being pursued. A clear, sweet tone is always an added bonus.
- *Endurance:* The ability to compete throughout the hunt and continue as long as necessary.
- *Adaptability:* The ability to adjust quickly to a variety of different environments and running mates.
- *Patience:* A willingness to stay with the scent in a workmanlike manner and not go off on a gambol or "wild rabbit chase."
- *Determination:* Imperturbability in the face of obstacles and other problems, a similar quality to patience.

- *Independence:* Self-reliance and the ability to ignore other hounds when they make an error. Although pack animals, a hound is expected to be sensible and use his own judgment as well.
- *Cooperation:* The ability to work harmoniously with other hounds.
- *Competitive spirit:* The desire to outdo other hounds in the pack. This is a quality that should be present to a moderate degree only. Overly competitive dogs are not successful because they must be able to work together with a pack.
- *Intelligence:* The ability to learn from experience and make the most of opportunities presented.

Faulty actions include:

- *Quitting:* Lack of desire to hunt, a most serious fault.
- *Backtracking:* Following the trail in the wrong direction.
- *Ghost trailing:* "Pretending" to follow a trail that does not in fact exist—at least, that no one is aware of.
- *Pottering:* Hesitating, lack of forward motion, listlessness.
- *Babbling:* Excessive or unnecessary use of voice.
- *Swinging:* Casting out too far from the last point of contact; "gamboling" with the scent.
- *Skirting:* Purposely leaving the trail to avoid strenuous work or tough obstacles.
- *Leaving checks:* Failure to stay in the vicinity of a loss and charging off looking for a new scent before it is reasonable to do so.
- *Running mute:* Failure to give voice or "tongue" when on the trail.
- *Tightness of mouth:* Failure to give voice sufficiently.
- *Racing:* Attempting to outrun the other hounds, often resulting in overshooting the trail.
- *Running hit or miss:* Attempting to make progress without carefully and continuously following the scent.
- *Lack of independence:* Watching other hounds and

FUN FACT

In the early days (the 1890s), the American Kennel Club (AKC) was solely interested in conformation shows, not field trials, and when the National Beagle Club (NBC) applied for entrance to the AKC, the latter organization strongly objected to the Beaglers' active participation in both shows and field trials. The Beaglers stood firm, however, and wrote a stiff note back to the AKC that read, in part, "This club was formed for improvement in the field and on the bench of the Beagle hound in America and will enter the AKC with its constitution unchanged, if it enters at all." The AKC buckled. To this day, however, the Beagle field trial is a sport found only in the United States and Canada.

---

allowing them to determine the course of action.

- *Bounding off:* Simply taking off when game is scented without attempting to determine its direction.

AMERICAN KENNEL CLUB (AKC)

Event options include Brace, Small Pack, Small Pack Option, Large Pack, and Gundog Brace Trials. A Beagle may become a Field Champion (FC) by winning points in any combination of these trials. If you are less than fiercely competitive, your Beagle can participate in Hunt Tests for Two Couple Packs

BRACE

The oldest of the events are Brace Trials, in which two or three Beagles work at the same time. They are judged on how accurately they track a rabbit. This event evolved to accommodate Beaglers who could not (and cannot) afford to own and care for a whole pack of Beagles. Pack hunting at one time was more common, but the sport was limited to the affluent. (A few large Beagle packs still exist, with their liveried huntsmen and whippers-in, but this is a rare sight nowadays.) Most people who participate in trials do so with a single dog (often referred to by pack-oriented Beaglers as "singles"). Because most such trials are done on rabbits that are kept in an enclosure rather than on rabbits that have

In a Brace Trial, two or three Beagles work at the same time.

the run of the free world, the emphasis in Brace Trials is on style rather than speed. This is especially important because there is no shooting of game; the dog must give evidence of his quality by the way he moves and searches. Brace Beagles are known for their slowness. They're so slow that real rabbit hunters won't use them—they breed their own hunting Beagles.

SMALL PACK OPTION
In Small Pack Option, trials are run with dogs in a group of seven. They are expected to follow the rabbit "with enthusiasm" yet maintain control of the rabbit's trail.

LARGE PACK
In the Large Pack, Beagles chase hares, not rabbits. This sport is most common in the northern states. It's about 30 dogs against one hare, so the odds are not really good for the hare, even though they are faster than rabbits. The dogs are

expected to run for at least three hours in the Open Class, the class in which the dogs are able to win points for a Field Championship (FC).

GUNDOG BRACE

In the Gundog Brace Trials, pairs of Beagles are set loose to hunt down their own rabbit. They are judged on how well they search. During the hunt, a gun is fired into the air to test the dogs for gun-shyness.

HUNT TESTS

In the AKC Hunt Test for Two Couple Packs, the hounds are placed in groups of four. They are cast (set loose) to find a rabbit and judged on how well they search. Generally, each pack is run for at least 20 minutes. At some time during the run, the Beagles are tested for gun-shyness. Once a dog has completed his title in the Hunt Test, he may use the initials MH, for Master Hunter, after his name.

These Hunts Tests are not head-to-head competitions—the dogs compete against a written standard rather than each other. A dog either meets the criteria for the class or fails. There is no "placement," so all of the ribbons look the same. All of the dogs can qualify.

UNITED KENNEL CLUB (UKC)

The UKC offers Hunting Beagle and Performance Pack events.

HUNTING BEAGLE

Hunting Beagle events allow participants to take part in each cast as an active handler. Both the handler and her dog work as a team while attempting to outscore the three other handlers and dogs in the cast.

PERFORMANCE PACK

In Performance Pack events, dogs are drawn to five-dog casts and sent to the field with a judge, who stays with the dogs as they run a track. Judges evaluate each dog in the pack on their ability to accurately run a rabbit. In the end, the judge tabulates the scores she has accumulated on each dog and a winner is announced.

Requirements

Dogs

- accurate nose
- endurance
- good physical condition
- obedience off lead is a plus but cannot be expected in hounds
- perseverance
- sociability
- strong prey drive, specifically directed toward rabbits and hares

Handlers

- ability to plod around brushy fields, even in the rain
- good physical condition

Equipment and Supplies

- harness
- muck boots

Harness: Any type of tracking harness or plain dog collar may be used. Remember, your dog is working off lead, and Beagles, being hounds, tend to get "lost." Be sure that your dog is microchipped and/or tattooed as well for his protection. And a radio collar isn't a bad idea either.

THE AMERICAN RABBIT HOUND ASSOCIATION (ARHA)

The ARHA is a registry that is less than 15 years old but already has 170 clubs nationwide. It registers only Beagles, Basset Hounds, and Harriers. The Association holds both field trials and conformation shows. If your Beagle is not registered with another registry but meets the ARHA standard, you can register him and enter him into its many competitions. This group holds Little Pack and Big Pack Trials for fast dogs, Progressive Pack for medium-speed Beagles, and Gundog Pack and Gundog Brace for tighter, line-control hounds. It also has bench competitions.

Muck Boots: Waterproof boots will keep you warm and dry while trudging around after your Beagle.

Sponsoring Organizations

AMERICAN KENNEL CLUB (AKC)

Regular AKC classes are Open Dogs not exceeding 13 inches (33 cm) in height; Open Bitches not exceeding 13 inches (33 cm) in height; Open Dogs over 13 inches (33 cm), but not exceeding 15 inches (38 cm); and Open Bitches over 13 inches (33 cm), but not exceeding 15 inches (38 cm) in height. Judges may combine classes if fewer than six hounds of a sex are eligible to compete in any class. No dog may be entered in more than one of these classes at any field trial.

For less competitive souls, the AKC offers a Beagle Hunt Test, listed separately, which is open to altered animals (unlike the field trial). Beagles under the age of two can compete in Derby Trials for beginners.

Eligibility Requirements: Unaltered Beagles are eligible to participate. Beagles recorded with the Purebred Alternative Listing Program/Indefinite Listing Privilege (PAL/ILP) or dogs with conditional registration are *not* eligible to participate.

Titles: The title of Field Champion (FC) is earned by compiling 120 points, including three first-place wins in classes with not less than six starters, at licensed or member field trials. A Beagle may earn his Field Champion (FC) by earning points in any combination of the following trials: National Brace Championship Field Trial, National Small Pack Option Championship Field Trial, and National Large Pack Championship Field Trial. The letters "SPO" before the FC title are used to designate that the hound earned all of his title points under the Small Pack Option format. "LPH" before a dog's name indicates that he earned all of his title points under the Large Pack on hare trials.

Premier Events: The AKC holds a National Brace Championship Field Trial, a National Small Pack Option Championship Field Trial, and a National Large Pack Championship Field Trial every year. The winners of each class at a national championship receive credit for a win and

Successful field trial dogs usually come from a long line of field trial dogs.

the points available in accordance with requirements for a Beagle Field Trial Champion.

UNITED KENNEL CLUB (UKC)

The UKC holds more field trials than any other registry. In UKC field trials, classes must be split according to size, with the sizes being hounds 13 inches (33 cm) and under and hounds over 13 inches (33 cm) but not over 15 inches (38 cm). Classes may further be split according to sex at the option of the club holding the trial.

The UKC offers a Show Championship too, with separate classes for Puppies (6 to 12 months); Juniors (between the age of 1 and 2 years); Seniors (2 to 3 years); and Veterans (over 3 years old). Males and females are judged separately except in Best of Winners, Champion, and Grand Champion Classes.

Eligibility Requirements: There is no age limit for Beagles to participate.

Titles: *Hunting Beagle Champion (HBCH):* This is awarded to a dog acquiring 100 points with at least one win in a UKC hunt. Fifteen points are awarded for first place, ten points for second, and so on. *Grand Hunting Beagle Champion (GRHBCH):* This is achieved by winning five Hunting Beagle Champion events at a UKC-licensed hunt. In this portion of the event, only HB Champions compete against HB Champions. Titles for dogs participating in Large and Small Pack are: *Field Champion (FCH):* The dog must acquire 120 points and three first places. They are awarded for each class at licensed Large Pack and Small Pack trials. The dog must have at least three first-place wins in licensed UKC Large Pack or Small Pack events. *Grand Field Champion (GRFCH):* To be declared an official UKC Grand Field Champion, a dog must win at least three trials after earning his FCH degree. Champions are run and judged against open competition. Grand Field Champions may continue to be run in open competition.

Premier Events: Beagle field trials are held all around the United States.

How to Get Started

One really great way to begin your adventure in Beagling is to try the hunt test; it is noncompetitive and geared to beginners. It's also a good chance to meet up with fellow Beaglers.

GET YOUR DOG A CHECKUP

Beagling is hard work, and even though the dogs don't move especially fast, they are subject to lots of environmental stresses—not the least of which are ticks! Make sure that your dog is healthy, vaccinated, and most important of all, on a good anti-tick medication.

FIND A MENTOR

As always, the best advice is to find a mentor and start having fun! Many "old-timers" out there will be happy to share their love and knowledge of Beagling with you. All you need do is ask—and listen.

FROM THE EXPERT

In his online article "Getting the Beagles Back In," Beagler Jeff Hirst found that his Labradors responded very well to a whistle. He then decided to try out the whistle on his Beagles and found that they responded to it much better than to voice commands. It probably helps that he used hotdogs as a reward. However, he admits that even a whistle won't call back a Beagle when he is on game. Nothing will.

ENSURE THAT YOUR BEAGLE IS SUITABLE

The more experience your dog has running rabbits, the better he will get at it. Strive for an all-around dog who can work alone and in a brace, in a small pack, or even in a large pack if you can find one. You should also let your dog work in all kinds of cover and terrain, all weathers, and all seasons.

USE TAME RABBITS TO START

Rabbit tracking comes naturally to Beagles, and they love it. Many people start teaching their dog to trail rabbits by using tame rabbits, which are slow and apparently leave a strong scent. The next step is your local Beagling club, where dogs can get some good experience in smallish "starting pens" that are well stocked with rabbits.

Strategies for Success

To be successful in Beagle field trials, you need the right dog. Successful field trial dogs usually come from a long line of field trial dogs. Hunting Beagles tend to be too fast, and bench types have no nose. This is something that is almost totally inherited. (Even though the Beagle is probably the world's oldest gundog, not all of them have this naturally endowed ability.)

USE TREATS

One way to see if your Beagle is a natural is to start hiding bits of hotdog or other yummy edibles around the house—get him used to seeking the elusive goody with his nose. You can also tie a hotdog on a string and then drag it around in the grass. Every few feet (m), leave a bit of hotdog as a treat to encourage your pup to keep following the scent trail. Then try the same thing with commercial rabbit scent and a bit of rabbit. (Yes, many people keep frozen rabbit meat just for this purpose.) Then progress to large, slow, heavy-scented tame rabbits, who hop slowly along while the puppy follows in a good-natured way.

FOLLOW YOUR BEAGLE

The trickiest thing about working with Beagles over open terrain is that many of them simply keeping going. Hounds are bred to follow their noses, not their owners. *You* are supposed to follow *them*. After all, they know where the rabbit is—not you. Beagles are famous for running off, and there are stories of people having to leave their old, smelly clothes around so that their dog will return to the spot. It is not possible to teach a Beagle to recall on command once he is in pursuit of game, which is why field trials are held in fenced areas—and also why the proper ID is so important.

TAKE YOUR TIME

Remember, this is not a race—a dog who starts off too fast in the wrong direction may never recover. Take the time to make sure that your dog "has the scent" before you release him. Don't get pressured to release him too early.

ADDITIONAL ORGANIZATIONS

American Rabbit Hound Association (ARHA)
www.arha.com
Canadian Kennel Club (CKC)
www.cka.ca
United Beagle Gundog Federation, Inc. (UBGF)
www.ubgf.org

Chapter 13

Field Trials, Dachshunds

Definition

Dachshund field trials are an adaptation of the brace Beagle field trial, in which a brace (pair) of dogs tracks a rabbit. No rabbits are killed, and trials are almost always held in fenced areas where dogs are not in danger of becoming lost or hit by cars. This is not a lure-coursing event, where dogs hunt by sight, but a scenthound event. The Dachshund is supposed to use his nose follow the track of the rabbit and is required to problem solve as he follows the meandering path of the rabbit. (Rabbits tend to hop and change direction a lot, so the scent is not continuous.) Dogs compete against one another.

In a Dachshund field trial, a brace (pair) of dogs tracks a rabbit.

History of Dachshund Field Trials

The short-lived US Dachshund Field Trial Club held the first organized field trial for Dachshunds in the early 1930s to test the "aboveground" ability of the breed. In those days, the hounds were put to ground in artificial rabbit burrows and were judged by rules imported from Germany. Although this organization did not last long, the idea caught on. In 1935, the Dachshund Club of America (DCA) held its first trial in Lamington, New Jersey, under rules tailored for American competition. It remained the only club holding field trials for Dachshunds until the Dachshund Club of New Jersey held its first trial in 1966. Today, 28 clubs hold 53 field trials each year across the United States.

Overview

In Dachshund field trials, braces of dogs are put on the scent line of a rabbit or hare and judged on the quality of their work on that line. The field marshal directs the handlers and the gallery (audience and observers) to the starting point. The beaters (volunteers from the gallery) line up in a straight line to flush out the rabbits. They use sticks: broomsticks, polo mallets, or whatever is handy for this purpose. When a rabbit appears, the beater calls out "Tally ho!" in time-honored fashion. She may add "Running straight for the maple tree," or "north-by-northwest," or whatever other description may be called for by the judge. At this point, the handlers take their dogs near to the spot where was rabbit was sighted. The dogs are released, and the handler must remain quiet. She can follow her dog, but she must stay behind the judges at all times. In fact, everyone is supposed to be very quiet and allow the dog to work. It is important to observe the running path of the rabbit once flushed out—this becomes the scent line that the Dachshund is expected to follow. When the judges are certain of the rabbit's direction and path, they "request the brace" (in other words, bring on the first pair) and the hunt is on! Field trials are usually held during the cooler weather of spring and fall; rabbits are hard to "jump" in hot weather.

Dogs are expected to work in a "sensible and efficient" way and show intense enthusiasm for their task. However, unlike in Basset Hound and Beagle field trials, dogs are to be credited with their accomplishments—finding the game—and not with the style of their work. It is simply assumed that form follows function.

Local terrain and quarry type make a difference with working Dachshunds. The most common object of the trial in the eastern parts of the United States is the cottontail rabbit, which runs around in circles. In the west, however, jackrabbits (which are really hares and not

rabbits), with their long strides and straight-running paths, abound.

The judge will observe the proceedings for a period and then ask the handler to pick up her dog and tuck him neatly under one arm. (This is something that doesn't happen in other field trials—Bassets and Labradors do not tuck up neatly.) At this point, the run is discussed, and the judges call for the next brace. The end of the first series is marked when all of the braces have been run. The judges will decide which dogs are worthy of the callback, or second series, and continue with the trial. This will continue until all of the dogs have been judged and the winner determined.

Judges look for the following skills:

- *Searching ability:* The ability to recognize and a willingness to explore promising cover.
- *Pursuing ability:* Proficiency in keeping control of the trail while making good progress.
- *Accuracy in trailing:* The ability to keep to the trail with a minimum of weaving around; also the ability to know the direction the game is traveling.
- *Proper use of voice:* The loud proclamation to the immediate world that a rabbit has been identified and is being pursued. A clear, sweet tone is always an added bonus.
- *Endurance:* The ability to compete throughout the hunt and continue as long as necessary.
- *Adaptability:* The ability to adjust quickly to a variety of different environments and running mates.
- *Patience:* A willingness to stay with the scent in a workmanlike manner and not go off on a gambol or "wild rabbit chase."
- *Determination:* Imperturbability in the face of obstacles and other problems, a similar quality to patience.
- *Independence:* Self-reliance and the ability to ignore other hounds when they make an error. Although pack animals, a hound is expected to be sensible and use his own judgment as well.
- *Cooperation:* The ability to work harmoniously

FUN FACT

Like other scenthounds, Dachshunds are expected to vocalize ("give tongue") as they trail the rabbit. This is called "open trailing" and is obviously important for the hunter so that she knows where her dog is. However, unlike Basset Hounds and Beagles, most Dachshunds tend to run "mute" unless the trail is extremely hot or the quarry is in sight.

with other hounds.

- *Competitive spirit:* The desire to outdo other hounds in the pack. This is a quality that should be present to a moderate degree only. Overly competitive dogs are not successful because they must work together with a pack.
- *Intelligence:* The ability to learn from experience and make the most of opportunities presented.

Faulty actions include:

- *Quitting:* Lack of desire to hunt, a most serious fault.
- *Backtracking:* Following the trail in the wrong direction.
- *Ghost trailing:* "Pretending" to follow a trail that does not in fact exist—at least one that no one is aware of.
- *Pottering:* Hesitating, lack of forward motion, listlessness.
- *Babbling:* Excessive or unnecessary use of voice.
- *Swinging:* Casting out too far from the last point of contact; "gamboling" with the scent.
- *Skirting:* Purposely leaving the trail to avoid strenuous work or tough obstacles.
- *Leaving checks:* Failure to stay in the vicinity of a loss and charging off looking for a new scent before it is reasonable to do so.
- *Running mute:* Failure to give voice or tongue when on the trail.
- *Tightness of mouth:* Failure to give voice sufficiently.

185

- *Racing:* Attempting to outrun the other hounds, often resulting in overshooting the trail.
- *Running hit or miss:* Attempting to make progress without carefully and continuously following the scent.
- *Lack of independence:* Watching other hounds and allowing them to determine the course of action.
- *Bounding off:* Simply taking off when game is scented without attempting to determine its direction.

According to official AKC records, 119 Dachshunds have acquired the coveted Dual Champion designation, showing that the same dog can successfully compete in both conformation and field trialing.

Requirements

Dogs

- good physical condition
- perseverance
- powerful nose

Field trial Dachshunds must have a strong prey drive, specifically directed toward rabbits.

FROM THE EXPERT

According to the American Kennel Club (AKC), when training, your dog may not understand right away what you want, but just keep him moving along the track where you sighted the rabbit. Once he picks up the scent, step back and let him work. If he gets confused, retrain him gently and show him where the track went. The minute he is moving in the right direction, stop interfering.

- sociability
- strong prey drive, specifically directed toward rabbits

HANDLERS
- good physical condition

Equipment and Supplies
- collar
- comfortable clothing (handler)
- field
- slip lead

Collar: Although not required, you may want your dog to wear a buckle collar. There should be no dangling tags attached to the collar, and your dog's ID should be embossed right on the collar itself for safety.

Comfortable Clothing: The handler needs comfortable walking footgear and seasonable clothing. Long pants and sleeves are suggested even in warm weather because bushes abound with thorns and ticks. Brush chaps are advisable in some areas of the country. Bring raingear if it looks cloudy—field trials are conducted in all weathers.

Field: During the event, you will be trialing in a rabbit-inhabited, preferably fenced, field. Most fields are a couple hundred acres in size.

Slip Lead: Your dog needs a lightweight 8- to 12-foot (2.5- to 3.5-m) slip lead. He will be working off lead during the trial, but you must be able to leash him quickly when asked by the judge at the end of his run.

Sponsoring Organizations

AMERICAN KENNEL CLUB (AKC)

AKC classes include Open All-Age Dogs (OAAD), Open All-Age Bitches (OAAB), and Field Champions. Points toward AKC Field Championship titles are earned in the Open stakes (classes). The Field Champion Stake is for dogs and bitches who have completed the requirements for an AKC Field Championship. The Field Champion Stake may be divided by sex (the premium list will specify if the Field Champion Stake is divided).

Eligibility Requirements: The AKC allows all AKC-registered Dachshunds of all sizes and coat types on an equal eligibility basis. Dogs who have done well in obedience are often the same dogs who do well in Dachshund field trials.

Titles: A Dachshund may earn the title of Field Champion (FC). Points toward a field championship are earned in the Open All-Age (OAA) stake. A Dachshund must accumulate at least 35 points, with a minimum of three placements, including one first place, to earn a field championship. The top Dachshund of any field trial is named the Absolute Winner.

Premier Events: The DCA holds an annual National Field Trial.

How to Get Started

When getting started in Dachshund field trials, make sure that your dog is socialized. Although Dachshunds are sometimes not thrilled about other dogs, they will hunt in braces in field trials and are expected to react to the scent of rabbits—not to other dogs.

CONDITION YOUR DACHSHUND

Before you think about field trialing your dog, your Dachshund should be sociable with other dogs and people, in good condition, and reasonably obedient. He should also be used to getting picked up and carried, as this is the norm in Dachshund field trials.

Also, get your Dachshund checked out by a vet to

Before you think about field trialing your Dachshund, he should be sociable with other dogs and people.

make sure that he is in condition and up to date on his vaccinations.

GO TO A BEAGLE FIELD TRIAL

Dachshund field trials are not as common as Beagle field trials, so the best way to learn about them is to attend a Beagle trial. Your local Beagle club can point you in the right direction. Dachshunds and Beagles don't hunt in precisely the same way, but the similarities are more important than the differences.

TRAIN YOUR DACHSHUND TO HUNT RABBITS

Some people train with tame live rabbits, but that isn't practical for most people. Instead, buy some commercial rabbit scent at hunting or sporting goods stores; this is a great tool for letting your dog get a whiff of what is he supposed to be looking for. If he is still not sure about your intentions, try using a bunny-scented lure as a tug-of-war toy

In a Dachshund field trial, it is important for your dog to work independently and ahead of you.

to get his attention focused on it. Soon, he will transfer his interest to the scent.

It is also important for your dog to work independently and ahead of you. Play hide-and-seek games or use other methods to encourage his native ability to work on his own. You can start this with a puppy under a year old. The next thing is to get your dog into open fields where he can work some real rabbits. The best time to begin this part of the training is when a Dachshund is between 6 and 12 months old.

To find rabbits, set out at dusk, when they tend to feed. The most likely spots have both bushes for cover and open grassy terrain where the rabbits feed. You may have to rely on your own eyesight in the beginning. If you spot the quarry, lead your Dachshund to the place where you saw it and then release him verbally (but keep him leashed) with an appropriate phrase such as "Find it!" His nose will take over. Not every Dachshund gets it right away, but be patient, and allow plenty of time for him to find the scent. A good dog cannot be hurried. If you have a Dachshund who does not "open trail," you might want to pair him with a dog who does. To some extent, this trait is genetic.

Dachshunds are slow developers, so don't worry if your dog doesn't seem to acquire the rabbit-tracking knack all at once. Some of the best field trialing dogs in the country got off to a late start! The more practice your dog gets, the better.

Strategies for Success

Some of the best strategies for success include limiting your dog's meals directly prior to a trial and keeping him away from the rabbits until it's his turn on the field.

LIMIT MEALS BEFORE TRIAL

Some experts recommend not feeding a dog for 12 hours before the trial. It gives them a keener edge, and you don't have to worrying about embarrassing elimination on the field when the dog is supposed to be trailing game. However, talk to your vet before fasting your dog.

KEEP YOUR DACHSIE AWAY FROM THE RABBITS

Don't let your Dachsie see the rabbits before he's actually called up—just the sight of them is enough to put most Dachshunds in a frenzy, and you run the risk of tiring your dog out. Curiously, you don't want your Dachshund to exhibit too much energy before the actual run; the judge may not think that such a dog is "steady."

Chapter 14

Field Trials, Pointing Breeds

Definition

A field trial is a competition for pointers and setters in which they are judged against other dogs on their ability and style in finding and/or retrieving game. Although pointers and setters may work a bit differently in the field, as far as most organizations are concerned, both are members of the "pointing" type of sporting dog rather than retrievers or flushers.

In field trials for pointing breeds, pointers and setters are judged on their ability and style in finding and/or retrieving game.

History of Pointing Breed Field Trials

The first field trials were held in Britain in 1876, and the United States was not far behind, having its first trials in 1884 in Memphis, Tennessee. (The first winner was an English Setter named Knight.) These early trials were for "bird dogs," meaning in those days pointers and setters only. (Spaniels and Retrievers are bird dogs too, of course, but they hunt differently.)

The first American Kennel Club (AKC) field trial was held in Medford, New Jersey, by the English Setter Club of America (ESCA) in 1924. The next one wasn't held until 1931—a joint effort by the Gordon Setter Club of America (GSCA) and the Irish Setter Club of America (ISCA), also in New Jersey. Some scattered field trials were held during the 1930s and 1940s, but things didn't really pick up until after World War II, when a number of European pointing breeds became popular in the United States. The German Shorthaired Pointer Club of America (GSPCA) held the first National Championship in 1953. In 1965, the first meeting of the Pointing Breed Advisory Committee was held; its task was to recommend rules for AKC field trials. Although the first field trials were held on foot, by 1966, an agreement was reached to allow handlers, judges, and spectators to follow on horseback. This popular idea soon doubled the number of field trials being held. The United Kennel Club's (UKC) first licensed field trial was held in 2004.

Overview

Field trialing is a highly competitive event that participants take very seriously. As for the competing dogs, some are deadly serious, others gaily insouciant. But all are dedicated to their work (or play), which is the very wellspring of their life. For sheer poetry in motion, little can match and nothing exceeds the beauty of a pointer or setter afield.

AMERICAN KENNEL CLUB (AKC)

In AKC field trial events, spectators are called the "gallery," and spectators, handlers, and judges may be on horseback in AKC events. The job of the Field Trial Marshals is to regulate and control the gallery and assist the judges.

In this extremely competitive sport, all dogs compete against each head to head. This means that untitled dogs must go against champions to garner those all-important points. Untitled dogs need the points to achieve their championships; those who already hold championship titles need them to qualify for the prestigious national championship trials. In most entry fields, about half of the competing dogs are already champions, so the competition is tough.

Pointing dogs run in braces (pairs), which are randomly selected by drawing. If one dog finds and points a bird, the other dog is supposed to "honor" the first dog by ceasing his own activity and pointing in the same direction; however, he should not interfere with the first dog. Shooting the bird is then permitted upon direction by the judge. Only clean, sportsman-like shooting while the bird is in flight is permitted. Each class, called a "stake," is judged by at least two judges; if the brace dogs part ways during the stake, one judge follows each dog and handler.

The numbers and types of birds in a field trial can vary, but the course layouts for each stake must be specified. All courses contain sufficient acreage and cover to make it a real test of the dog's ability. A real gun is used in field trials, and birds are killed. Electronic collars are not permitted for the event, although they are frequently used in training.

Both professionals and amateurs can compete in field trials. To qualify as an amateur, the handler is not to have been paid for training a hunting dog or for handling a dog in a field trial for a specified period of time preceding the event. A title of Amateur Field Champion (AFC) (awarded to the dog) is highly regarded and sought after.

Points are achieved by placing ahead of other dogs. The more dogs a participant bests, the more points awarded.

UNITED KENNEL CLUB (UKC)

The UKC has its own field trials in which all participants (handlers and spectators) must be on foot, as this is the way real bird hunters hunt. The trials must be advertised as one of two types: Type W (wild bird trial) and Type L (liberated bird trial). A placement in both types of trials is required to earn the UKC title of Champion of the Field (CHF), assuring that a dog is a dependable retriever of downed game and has the ability to handle wild birds.

TYPE L

In Type L shot bird trials in the Gun Dog Class, the dog must retrieve to hand or within 15 feet (4.5 m) of the handler to secure a pass or better score. Liberated birds come from stock raised in a pen.

TYPE W

In a Type W trial, the game consists of wild upland game birds of various species that are known to naturally inhabit the area where a field trial is held. No game is shot in this type of trial.

Requirements

DOGS

- obedience to commands
- pointing ability

HUNT TESTS

For a less competitive but still exhilarating experience, the American Kennel Club (AKC) offers hunting tests for pointing breeds (see Chapter 20), and the United Kennel Club (UKC) offers a program called the Natural Ability Test (TAN), which evaluates dogs on (1) hunting instinct; (2) pointing instinct; and (3) reaction to gunfire.

- reliable off lead (to a certain extent)
- retrieving ability
- steady to wing and shot (dog does not react adversely when bird flushes and shots are fired)
- top physical condition

HANDLERS
- firearms proficiency (for training)
- interest in hunting and tracking

Equipment and Supplies
- bird launcher
- blanks pistol
- collars
- leash
- walking shoes/hiking boots
- whistle

Bird Launcher: Bird launchers may be used in training only to teach dogs to "steady to wing and shot," help develop a steady point, or even as a correction tool when a dog starts crowding birds. Some trainers may even put several in one area to simulate a covey of birds flying out from the bushes.

Blanks Pistol: Most field trials and hunting tests require the handler to carry a blanks pistol while her dog is on the course. A blanks pistol is one that has been manufactured specifically for firing only blank cartridges and has a solid barrel. Blanks pistols come in two calibers: .22 and .32. These pistols can be hard to get and are fairly pricey. The purpose of the pistol is to make a sound that simulates the sound of a shotgun. The judges observe to see if the dog is gun-shy.

197

FUN FACT

Setters get their name from the way they "set" their hindquarters down a bit while pointing. This posture became common in Britain when shooting became popular. Dogs were trained to "drop" to the sight of a bird a-wing or at the sound of a gunshot. This kept the dog out of danger of being injured. (English game birds are low flying because their cover is low growing.) In addition, the first guns used for the purpose were single-shot shotguns that took a while to reload; any dog who took off immediately could flush other birds from the brush before the hunter was ready to shoot again. Thus, this "setting" action was sought after. Nowadays, many hunters prefer a dog who stands tall, and the "setting" has been bred out of many setters.

Collars: Tracking collars (radio or GPS) are allowed unless the host club specifies on the premium list that they are not allowed. *Note:* A battle is raging within the AKC about the use of GPS tracking collars at pointing field trials. As of this writing, rules limit the use of tracking collars to devices weighing under 5 ounces (141.5 g), excluding the strap itself. The AKC ruled in December 2008 that the GPS collars are not allowed in pointing breed field trials or pointing breed hunt tests at present.

Leash: Field trial rules require that you unleash your dog, but most handlers use a short (3- or 4-foot [1-m]) lead to bring their dog into the field and to allow him to walk comfortably by their sides.

Walking Shoes/Hiking Boots: It's best to get something sturdy with traction soles—you'll be doing a great deal of walking. If you are riding, you may choose riding boots, of course. Don't forget the extra socks.

Whistle: Don't count on being loud enough for your dog to hear you—you need a whistle. The whistle can be made of any material except metal. Metal tends to freeze to your mouth when it's really cold and can get hot enough to burn in the direct sunlight of summer. The important thing is that it has a good loud sound that will travel over distance. It's a plus if the whistle can make different sounds;

with luck, you and your dog can recall what each of them means. It's even better if the whistle is distinct enough so that your dog can distinguish its sound from the whistles other handlers will be blowing.

Sponsoring Organizations

AMERICAN KENNEL CLUB (AKC)

The AKC offers both Field and Amateur Field Championship programs. (Professional handlers are not eligible for Amateur trials.) The main stakes are as follows:

- *Puppy Stake (Open and/or Amateur Walking):* Dogs must be between 6 and 15 months old, and the Amateur Walking Puppy Stakes do not allow handlers to work from horseback. Puppies are judged on boldness, desire to hunt, covering ground, and searching cover. They must show reasonable obedience to their handlers.
- *Derby Stake (Open and/or Amateur Walking):* Open to dogs six months old and under two years of age. No horseback handling is allowed in

Field trial courses contain sufficient acreage and cover to make it a real test of the dog's ability.

Pointing dogs must largely be reliable off lead.

Amateur Walking Derby Stakes. Derby dogs must show stronger hunting qualities than puppies, find game, and point, and a shot must be fired if within range.

- *Gun Dog Stake (Open and/or Amateur):* Open to dogs six months and older. Judges look for a finished performance, with the dog under handler control at all times. The dog is expected to handle "kindly" and must hunt at all times in range of a handler on foot. The dog must locate game, point, and remain steady to wing and shot. Dogs must demonstrate intelligent use of the wind and terrain, an accurate nose, and style.
- *Limited Gun Dog Stake (Open and/or Amateur):* Dogs six months or older who have placed first through fourth in any Gun Dog Stake. Judging is similar to that for Gun Dog Stakes.
- *All-Age Stake (Open and/or Amateur):* For dogs six months and older. Dogs are judged on a finished

performance and reasonable handler control. Judges look for intensity and "purpose."

- *Limited All-Age Stake (Open and/or Amateur):* For dogs six months or older who have placed first through fourth in any All-Age Stake. Judging is similar to that for All-Age Stakes.

Eligibility Requirements: Participation is limited to pointing and setting dogs bred to hunt upland game birds such as quails, pheasants, prairie chickens, grouses, woodcocks, chukars, and Hungarian partridges. Pointing breeds include the Brittany, German Shorthaired Pointer, German Wirehaired Pointer, English Setter, Gordon Setter, Irish Setter, Pointer, Spinone Italiano, Vizsla, Weimaraner, and Wirehaired Pointing Griffon.

Participating dogs must be registered with the AKC and may be spayed or neutered. Dogs must be at least six months old.

Titles: A dog can win a championship by winning ten points in at least three recognized field trials, with at least three of those points won in an Open All-Age, Open Gun Dog, Open Limited All-Age, or Open Limited Gun Dog Stake worth (because of the number of dogs entered) three points or more. No more than four of the ten points can come from Amateur Stakes wins, and no more than two points each can come from Open or Amateur Puppy or Derby Stakes. Titles that can be won by field trial dogs include *Field Champion (FC):* Must win ten points in regular stakes in at least three field trials. (The rules are slightly different for Brittanys, German Shorthaired Pointers, German Wirehaired Pointers, Vizslas, and Weimaraners.) *National Amateur Field Champion (NAFC):* Must win first place in a stake that has been designated a National Amateur Championship stake. *National Amateur Gundog Champion (NAGDC):* The dog must win first place in a National Amateur Gun Dog Stake at a national championship field trial event for pointing breeds. *Gun Dog Stake Champion (GDSC):* Must win first place in a stake that has been designated an Open Gun Dog Championship stake. *National Field Champion (NFC):* Must win first place in a stake that has been designated a National

Open Championship stake. *National Gundog Champion (NGDC):* Must win first place in a stake that has been designated a National Open Gun Dog Championship stake.

Premier Events: The Pointing Breed Gun Dog Championship is the AKC's premier event for pointing dogs. Two championships are available, one for retrieving dogs and one for nonretrievers. In the Gun Dog Retrieving Championship, dogs are expected to show good hunting and pointing skills, as well as prompt retrieves. In the Non-Retrieving Championship, dogs are expected to run and hunt for one hour. They are judged on their pointing ability, style of hunting, and ease of handling.

UNITED KENNEL CLUB (UKC)

In the UKC Pointing Dog Program, owners are not permitted to utilize professional handlers to run their dogs in licensed field trials. Professional handlers may run their own dogs, and owners may have someone else (other than a professional) handle their dogs.

Bird dogs have to find, point (shown here), and retrieve game.

FROM THE EXPERT

George Hickox, trainer of upland hunting dogs, in his online article "Field Training Tips" suggests alternating bird "plants" to the left and right of the direction the dog is traveling. This prevents him from taking off too fast straight down the field and will encourage him to look around. In fact, he will be rewarded for running a left and right pattern.

Field Trials are divided by age and ability, with puppies eligible for the Puppy Stake and Derby Stakes. The ages can overlap between the two, so some dogs run in both events.

Gun Dog Stakes and All-Age Stakes are for pointing dogs and further divided by the dog's previous achievements. Dogs can be handled by an amateur or a professional. Dogs must be steady to wing and shot; some breeds (like German Shorthaired Pointers, Vizslas, and Weimaraners) are also expected to retrieve. Braces may be run in either division at the club's discretion. The field trial rules are specifically devised to reflect real hunting conditions, with the hunter on foot, not horseback.

The Gun Dog Class is designed for beginning- and intermediate-level dogs and handlers. It is open to dogs six months or older who have not earned a title in the Open Dog Class. (In the Gun Dog Class, the steadiness factor is turned up a notch above that required for a HUNT title because dogs must be steady to wing and flush.)

In the Open Class, a dog may pass, but not place, if he stands steady to flush; he does not have to be steady to wing. Dogs who receive three passes may earn a HUNT title, which is the first-level field trial title. However, a dog must stand steady to wing (that is, through the flush and all the way up to the point at which a gun is fired) to earn a placement in this class. This class is open to dogs of at least one year of age and is designed for dogs who are finished gundogs.

Eligibility Requirements: All purebred gundogs and Airedale Terriers are eligible. The UKC has events for additional breeds as well, such as Small Munsterlanders.

Dogs who participate in field trials must be in top physical condition.

Altered dogs are permitted to participate in UKC field trials. All dogs entered must be of a breed designated as a pointing breed and must be registered with the UKC.

Titles: *GUN Degree:* The GUN degree is earned when a dog earns three passes in the Gun Dog Class, including one first place or two reserve placements. Dogs may break at the shot and still earn a placement, but steadiness can be a deciding issue in placing dogs in the Gun Dog Class. Just because a dog meets the minimum requirements for steadiness is not a guarantee that he will earn the necessary first or reserve placement required for the GUN title. *Trialer (TR), Champion of the Field (CHF):* Must achieve three wins. *Grand Champion of the Field (GRCHF):* The dog must win a total of five field trials, with at least two of those wins being in field trials run in braces. Dogs earning a GRCHF must demonstrate that they can win in both single and braces competitions in Type W (wild) and Type L (liberated) bird trials.

Premier Events: The UKC Pointing Breed Gun Dog Championships are held annually, and the UKC also offers annual National Level Field Trials. Various breed clubs also hold trials at their respective national specialty shows.

How to Get Started

Bird dogs have to do it all: find, point, and sometimes retrieve. For some dogs, this comes naturally, while others have to learn the finer points—especially the "steady to wing and shot" part, which means that the dog must be calm and still while the birds fly and the hunter is shooting. Dogs must be in top condition, and a successful outcome depends not only on natural ability but also on careful training. Many people choose their field trial prospects from carefully selected "field lines" as opposed to "bench" or show lines. Field trial dogs may indeed look rather different from their conformation brethren.

CONDITION YOUR DOG—AND YOURSELF

Both you and your dog must be in top physical condition before undertaking the rigors of a field trial. You both will be running (or riding), probably over difficult terrain. Be sure you visit your respective medical personnel before embarking on this fairly strenuous endeavor.

Also, dogs need good nutrition to perform well. Eating on the morning of the test is not a good idea, but providing extra food for a couple of days before the trial will get your dog successfully through the day. Be sure to carry water during the trial, especially if little is available on the course itself.

OBEDIENCE TRAIN YOUR DOG

As with every other sport, the foundation of field work is always good obedience training. A good field trial dog shows a delicate balance between independence and responsiveness, and you'll want to reward both. If your dog is not responsive to you in the backyard, it's a good bet he won't be any better when he has a hundred acres in which to run.

Because field trials are so competitive, many people hire a professional trainer.

CONSIDER A PROFESSIONAL TRAINER

Because this sport is so fiercely competitive, many people elect to hire a professional trainer. Not only do these people have the time to dedicate to training a dog, but they also have access to the extensive and expensive facilities and equipment needed, such as bird-release traps and remote launchers. However, such people are not cheap, and for many, the fun is in training one's own dog.

Most professional trainers nowadays resort to the use of electronic "correction" collars, which bring quicker results, but which, many say, ruin the spirit and artificially spark mediocre performance, with an ultimate loss of ability. They can cause extreme pain to a dog and should be avoided.

If you choose to go with a professional trainer, try to find one who is familiar with your particular breed and his way of hunting.

Strategies for Success

To succeed in pointing field trials, consider entering the UKC's TAN program and desensitize your dog to gunfire.

ENTER THE UKC TAN PROGRAM

The best beginning is to enter your dog in the UKC TAN program to see if he has the natural abilities to cut the mustard. Along the way, you'll meet people who are interested in helping you train your bird dog.

DESENSITIZE YOUR DOG TO GUNFIRE

It is absolutely critical that your dog is not gun-shy, so this is something to practice thoroughly. Don't start blasting away with a rifle next to your dog's sensitive ears, though. Let his first experience be with shots fired at a distance while you act happy and unconcerned. Gradually, the noise can get closer and louder.

ADDITIONAL ORGANIZATIONS

American Hunting Dog Club (AHDC)
www.ahdc.org
Canadian Kennel Club (CKC)
www.ckc.ca
The Kennel Club
www.thekennelclub.org.uk
National Bird Dog Challenge Association (NBDCA)
www.nbdca.com
National Shoot to Retrieve Association® (NSTRA)
www.nstra.org
North American Versatile Hunting Dog Association (NAVHDA)
www.navhda.org

Chapter 15

Field Trials, Retrievers

Definition

A retriever field trial is a competitive event designed to evaluate a dog's ability to retrieve game over both land and water. Dogs are not expected to find the game on their own, simply to bring it down when the hunter shoots it. Dogs compete against one another.

History of Retriever Field Trials

Retriever field trials originated in England in the late 1800s as a means of determining the best hunting stock. The trials were imported to the United States in the late 1920s and early 1930s. Very early trials were all marked retrieves. Blind retrieves and hand signals came along later.

The first formal American Retriever field trial was held on December 21, 1931, by the new Labrador Retriever Club on Robert Goelet's 8,000-acre estate, Glenmere Court, in Chester, New York. The event was actually conducted under British rules, even though it was promoted as an American Kennel Club (AKC) competition. Even the Labradors were imported from England. Early trials were simple by today's standards, rarely covering more than 100 yards (91.5 m) in distance; today, trials can be three times that distance. Early trials were very small, whereas today, as many as 90 dogs may be entered in an elimination contest.

Overview

Field trials have been called the "major leagues" for working retrievers. In retriever field trials, dogs retrieve over longer distances and with a more complex path than in a retriever hunt test. Dogs are tested equally on land and water. Spectators are welcome. Although it is not possible to keep the conditions precisely the same for every dog, every attempt is made to keep them equal. (Judges can retest dogs if they feel that it is called for.)

Retriever trials are supposed to approximate real hunting conditions but are generally more rigorous than what a dog is likely to encounter in any one day of hunting. This is intentional because the purpose of the event is to find the best dog among the contenders. In general, therefore, more demands are made of a field trial dog than of a regular hunting dog or a dog in hunt tests, which measure dogs against a standard and not against each other. As is the case in many sporting breeds, the ideal field trial dog and the ideal hunting dog are not the same. Field trial dogs are often tough, high-energy, and even hyperactive animals who can undergo continuous training without

RETRIEVER FIELD TRIAL DIFFICULTY

Some people believe that current field trials have gone "too far," and the difficulty level is far above what many dogs could attain—at least without a professional trainer and the heavy use of electronic shock collars. This is the reason why hunt tests were developed and became popular. (See Chapter 21: Hunting Tests, Retrievers.)

getting bored. Good hunting dogs tend to be calmer, more cooperative, and softer. They are actually easier to train.

In a retriever field trial, gunners and throwers (the people who throw the dead birds at a signal from the judge) position shot birds for the dogs to retrieve. In all stakes except Derby, which is for beginners, dogs and handlers then perform an "honor exercise" in which the dog is required to hold steady at the line for another dog's retrieve. The handler is not allowed to touch the dog or continue to give him repeated commands. According to AKC rules, the job of a "nonslip retriever" (a dog who is steady to shot and fall and therefore does not require a slip lead) is to seek and retrieve fallen game on command. He should sit quietly on line or in the blind (the hunter's hideout), walk at heel, or assume any station designated by his handler until sent to retrieve. When ordered, the dog should retrieve the quarry quickly, without disturbing too much ground (which causes loss of other game). He should deliver the game "tenderly" to hand (hold the game softly). He should then await further orders. A nonslip retriever is not expected to find or flush new game.

Two kinds of retrieves are used: the marked retrieve and the blind retrieve. In a marked retrieve, the dog watches the bird fall and must demonstrate the ability to efficiently find and retrieve it. Accurate marking (seeing where the bird falls) is critical. The judges are looking for a dog who marks the fall of a bird, uses the wind, and follows a strong cripple (an injured bird that still has some power of flight). In a blind retrieve, the dog doesn't see the bird fall; he must take direction from his handler.

Retriever field trials include a water portion.

Each field trail stake, or class, is judged by two judges, who not only judge the dogs but also set up the tests they must pass. Challenges in these trials almost always involve multiple marking tests consisting of double, triple, and quadruple marks with one or more gun stations hidden from the dogs' sight. Single and multiple blinds may also be involved. The tests are planned so that it is difficult for a dog to negotiate the area near the bird fall unless he can both remember where it happened and has the perseverance to negotiate the pathway to it. Natural obstacles may include ditches, brush, logs, and rolling terrain and boulders. The water part of the test may include irregular shorelines, sandbars, winding creeks, and islands. Although the dog's native ability is a primary consideration, wind direction and strength and terrain type are also influential.

Serious faults include (but are not limited to): repeated evidence of "poor nose"; refusal to enter rough cover, water, ice, mud, or other unpleasant conditions; returning to the handler without the bird (unless under certain conditions); stopping the hunt or ignoring the bird; switching birds; dog out of control; extreme freezing (refusal to release a bird on delivery); retrieving a decoy; hardness of mouth; and failure to go when sent on a blind retrieve.

Requirements

Dogs
- excellent retrieving skills
- fearlessness in water
- fearlessness of gunshots
- obedience off lead

Handlers
- firearms proficiency (for training)
- good physical condition
- interest in hunting and tracking

Equipment and Supplies
- bird launcher
- bumper
- chaps
- neoprene vest/doggy wetsuit

Bird Launcher: A bird launcher springs the dead birds into the air farther than a human arm can possibly throw; it is used to get a "flyer effect" on the bird. With a bird launcher, you can control the direction and the timing of the flush. A launcher can be manual or automatic and triggered by remote radio control.

Bumper: This is a stuffed canvas retriever toy that's oblong in shape and used in training.

Fun Fact

One reason why retrievers make such excellent obedience dogs and are so trustworthy off lead is because they were bred to this behavior. Contrast this with the behavior of hounds, who were bred to find game on their own. Such dogs are by nature more independent and less reliant on a handler than a retriever is.

Chaps: Chaps will keep you warm and dry when out in the field.

Neoprene Vest/Doggy Wetsuit: For cold water or winter work, wetsuits are good for retaining your dog's body heat.

Sponsoring Organizations

AMERICAN KENNEL CLUB (AKC)
The main stakes offered are the All-Age Stakes, Amateur All-Age Stake, and Minor Stakes.

THE MAJOR STAKES
All-Age Stakes: The All-Age Stakes might be Open All-Age, Limited All-Age, Special All-Age, or Restricted All-Age. They are offered to both amateurs and professionals. Championship points are awarded in the Open All-Age Stake, which is open to all retrievers eligible for an AKC-licensed retriever field trial. Tests in this stake consist of triple or quadruple marks and blinds with and without retired guns (hidden after the bird is shot) and single, double, or triple blind retrieves. Only the highest-level dogs can hope to succeed. The stake usually begins with a marking test on land followed by a land test with at least one blind retrieve. Dogs must be steady and under control at all times. Those who are called back after the land tests must then successfully perform a blind retrieve on the water, followed by a marking test on the water.

Amateur All-Age Stake: The other major stake, offered to amateurs only, is either Amateur All-Age or Owner/Handler Amateur All-Age. Points won accumulate toward an Amateur Field Championship (AFC). In addition, points earned each year count toward an invitation to both the National Open Retriever Championship and the National Amateur Field Championship.

THE MINOR STAKES
In the minor stakes, judges evaluate natural abilities more than attributes acquired through training. The two minor stakes held at field trials include a Qualifying Stake (similar to an All-Age Stake but not as difficult) and a Derby, offered

to dogs between the ages of six months and two years.

Derby Stakes: These involve marked retrieves only. Points awarded for this stake count toward a yearly Derby Championship offered by the Retriever Field Trial News (RFTN), a publishing corporation owned by the National Retriever and Amateur Retrieve Clubs.

Qualifying Stake: This is open to all dogs who have not previously won two Qualifying Stakes, have not received a Judges Award of Merit in the Open All-Age Stake, and have not received a placement in the Amateur All-Age Stake. The Qualifying Stakes are similar to the All-Age Stakes but not as difficult.

Eligibility Requirements: Eligible breeds include AKC-registered Chesapeake Bay Retrievers, Curly-Coated Retrievers, Flat-Coated Retrievers, Golden Retrievers, Irish Water Spaniels, Labrador Retrievers, Nova Scotia Duck Tolling Retrievers, and Standard Poodles. Dogs must be at least six months old. Spayed and neutered dogs are eligible.

Titles: Earning a Field Championship is a tremendous feat because the dog must defeat Field Champions and dogs from all of the retriever breeds. To attain the title of Field Champion (FC), a dog must earn ten points in the Open All-Age Stake, of which five points must be for a first place. If the dog is handled by an amateur handler in the Open All-Age Stake, that dog also attains the title of Amateur Field Champion (AFC) with points earned in the Open All-Age Stake. To attain the title of Amateur Field Champion with points earned in the Amateur All-Age, a retriever must

---

FROM THE EXPERT

According to an online article, "A Simple Answer to a Tough Question," by Joe Pilar of the American Kennel Club (AKC), two major physical factors that determine performance are wind (its strength and direction) and terrain (the amount and type of cover, presence of water, and contours of the land itself). Getting your dog out for plenty of exposure to the elements and noting his reaction to them will help him develop confidence and versatility.

Make sure that your dog can handle a retrieve on land before you start him in water.

earn 15 points, of which 5 must be for a first place. Open All-Age points combined with Amateur All-Age points also count toward the 15 points required for the Amateur Field Championship.

Each year, the dog winning the most Derby points is designated the "High-Point Derby Dog." Even though this title is not an official AKC title, it is a prestigious award administered by the Retriever Field Trial News and is recognized by the whole retriever field trial fancy. Other honors include the "Top Ten Derby Dogs" (ranking in the top ten dogs in the country for Derby points earned) and the "Derby List" (dogs who accumulate ten or more Derby points).

The very prestigious High-Point Amateur Dog Award is awarded each year to the dog earning the most points in the Amateur All-Age Stake at AKC-licensed field trials for that year.

Premier Events: The National Amateur Championship is held in June every year, and the National Open Championship is held in November every year. The site of the National Championships are rotated to each of the four time zones every four years. To qualify for the National Open Retriever Championship or the National Amateur Retriever Championship, a dog must have a five-point win plus two other points during the preceding year. Points earned toward qualification for the National Open must be earned in the Open All-Age Stake. Points earned toward qualification for the National Amateur must be earned in the Amateur All-Age Stake or the Open All-Age Stake if the dog is handled by an amateur handler.

How to Get Started

One of the best ways to get started in field trials of any type is to first enter the hunt tests for the relevant breed. Hunting tests are specifically designed to be an easy entry into the sport of field trialing. (See Chapter 21.)

GET YOUR DOG A CHECKUP

Retrieving is hard work, and your dog must be in top condition to go plunging into cold water after downed waterfowl. Get him checked out by your vet before you embark on this pursuit. It is especially important to get his hips evaluated, as retrievers are prone to hip dysplasia.

POSITIVELY TRAIN YOUR DOG

Forget coercive punishment and electronic collars; dogs learn better and remember longer through positive reinforcement. Every dog is an individual, so take the time to know your dog and find the kind of positive rewards that encourage his very best behavior.

Obviously, your dog needs to love retrieving; he should be a natural at it. After practicing easy retrieves, you can gradually start making them more difficult—longer distances, adding obstacles, hiding the bumper, and so on. But don't go too fast or make it too difficult; you want

Start training your field trial dog in shallow water first, like a stream.

your puppy to retain his zest for retrieving. That's more important than anything else.

Make sure that your dog can handle a good long retrieve on land before you start him in water. And of course, start him in shallow water. Not all dogs realize right away that they can swim. Never rush, push, or throw a dog into water. Give him a reason to get in, either because he wants to retrieve or because he wants to follow you. (Yes, you must be willing to get wet.) Many people try to expose their dog to a stream first because most will play happily in it. Start throwing bumpers into shallow enough water where your dog can still keep his feet on the ground while retrieving. The swimming part will come later.

In any training, always know when to quit, and practice a variety of skills. Drilling one skill at a time tends to diminish performance in other areas. Don't let your dog get tired of training.

CONSIDER A PROFESSIONAL TRAINER

If you decide to use a professional trainer, spend some time with her before you commit your dog to her care. (Professional trainers often require the dog to stay with them for six months!) Does she treat her dogs the way you want yours to be treated? Does she achieve the results you are looking for? Check over the facilities carefully. Good trainers have clean indoor/outdoor runs and fresh water always available.

Strategies for Success

Strategies for success with your field trial retriever include training your dog while he's young and remaining patient. Start by seeking an AKC Junior Hunter (JH) title. It takes at least one year of consistent training to make a good field trial dog but only three to five months for the hunt title.

START TRAINING YOUNG

Start young. Although older dogs can be trained, it generally takes an expert. A younger dog is easier to train.

BE PATIENT

Don't introduce your dog into a hunting or field trial situation until he has completed basic training and is reliably obedient. An uncontrolled dog ruins everybody's day. Don't be tempted to use harsh or coercive training methods; a quicker "result" can ruin your relationship with your dog.

ADDITIONAL ORGANIZATIONS

Canadian Kennel Club (CKC)
www.ckc.ca
The Kennel Club
www.thekennelclub.org.uk

Chapter 16
Field Trials, Spaniels

Definition

Field trials for spaniels are a competitive sport involving both the dog and his handler. Spaniels are judged on both their natural and trained ability to hunt, flush, and retrieve game on land and in water. The purpose of the sport is to demonstrate the dog's hunting ability against the ability of other dogs. The trials are similar to what a dog may experience in the field but are more rigorous.

History of Spaniel Field Trials

Spaniel field trials were first held in England around the turn of the 20th century. In the United States, the first such trials, for Cocker Spaniels, were held in 1924 in Verbank, New York, under the auspices of the Hunting Cocker Spaniel Field Trial Club of America. Later, the name of the club was changed to the Cocker Spaniel Field Trial Club of America. Later that same year, the English Springer Spaniel fancy followed suit. The Great Depression and World War II saw a decline in the number of field trials held, but the post-war year saw a rebirth of the sport, at least until 1962, when it declined at the national level. This downturn occurred largely because the most common spaniel, the Cocker, had become largely a pet and show dog, not the hunting dog he was meant to be. The hunting instinct in the Cocker was almost, but not quite, destroyed. In 1998, to demonstrate a rekindled interest in the Cocker's original abilities, a national trial open to both American and English Cocker Spaniels was held.

Overview

Spaniels are "generalists" in the dog world; they hunt doves, grouse, woodcocks, pheasants, and even waterfowl. They are especially good for single birds that tend to hide in dense cover.

Spaniel field trials are designed to display hunting ability and training, and dogs are expected to behave in a manner that will be of maximum use to a hunter. First, the dog "quarters," meaning that he zigzags, or ranges from 30 degrees to the left to 30 degrees to the right of the hunter, while looking for birds. He is supposed to keep within gunshot range, about 30 or so yards

FIELD VERSUS SHOW SPANIELS

It should be noted that in many breeds, "field-type" dogs look quite different from their show or "bench-type" counterparts. If your dog is a bench-type spaniel, he may be an excellent pet, but chances are he will fail at field trials.

Although spaniels are mainly land dogs, they must be able to work in water when required.

(approximately 27.5 m), of the hunter and not run around chasing birds that are too far away to shoot. When he finds a bird, the dog must flush it (drive it out of cover and into the air). After flushing the bird, the dog should "hup" (sit) and continue to hup without moving while the bird is in the air and is shot (or at least shot at). This is called being "steady at wing and shot." After the bird drops, the dog must retrieve the fallen bird and bring it briskly back to the hunter without inflicting further damage on the prey.

The terrain hunted with spaniels is often marshy, so the dog needs to be able to move in and retrieve from some water, although not as much as a dog hunting ducks is expected to do. Field trials are run seasonally in the spring and fall, when the cover is conducive to the effective planting of the birds, usually pheasants but sometimes chukars.

Each dog is expected to find all of the birds on his section of the course. He must honor the flushes on the opposite course by hupping when he sees a bird fly up or when he hears the gun. He must then wait for instructions

A good field trial spaniel must adhere to basic obedience commands.

from his handler. Major faults include being out of control, breaking instead of remaining steady, failing to honor the other dog when working in a brace, failing a retrieve, passing a bird, poaching (taking a bird from the other course), pointing, or having a hard mouth (injuring the body of the bird).

Trials range in size from a minimum of 10 entries to as many as 70 entries in each All-Age Stake. An All-Age Stake usually consists of three land series and may, at the discretion of the host club, include a water series. (Although spaniels are mainly land dogs, they are expected to be able to work through water when required.) In the first two series, two handler/dog teams run in braces, one team running on each side of the shared center line of parallel courses. One judge presides over each course. Dogs are judged on control; scenting ability and use of wind; manner of covering ground and briskness of questing; perseverance in facing cover; steadiness to flush, shot, and command; aptitude in marking the fall of game and ability to find it; ability and willingness to take hand signals; promptness and style of retrieve and delivery; and tender mouth. Selected dogs are called back for a second series, and the top dogs come back for a third series.

> ## FUN FACT
>
> Interestingly, when the English Springer Spaniel Field Trial Association (ESSFTA) joined the American Kennel Club (AKC) in 1926, it was the only AKC breed parent club to carry a reference to field trials in its name. To its great credit, the ESSFTA has kept the name.

Requirements

Dogs
- flushing ability
- hunting ability
- obedience to basic commands
- retrieving ability
- steady to wing and shot (dog does not react adversely when bird flushes and shots are fired)

Handlers
- firearms proficiency (for training)
- good physical condition
- interest in hunting and tracking

Equipment and Supplies
- bird launcher
- collar and leash
- dummy

- shotgun and .22 training revolver
- whistle

Bird Launcher: This is a training tool that flushing dog owners often use to help in lengthening marks (making a longer distance than you can get by just throwing the birds by hand) for their dogs on both land and water. It is also a good tool to help teach a flushing dog to honor another dog's flush.

Collar and Leash: You will need a leash and collar to take your dog to the starting line to begin the trial. He will work off lead, however.

Dummy: This training tool is a stuffed "bird" made of canvas to help the dog learn to retrieve. Dummies can be purchased at any sporting goods store.

Shotgun: A shotgun will help your dog get used to the noise that he'll hear at an actual trial. (However, during a trial, designated gunners do the shooting.) You can also use a blank .22 training revolver.

Whistle: Your whistle, which carries farther than a voice, should have different sounds that command your dog to do different things.

Sponsoring Organizations

AMERICAN KENNEL CLUB (AKC)

Classes include Puppy, Novice, Limit, Open All-Age, Qualified Open All-Age, and Amateur All-Age.

Puppy Stakes are frequently only one series and are open to dogs between the ages of six months and two years. Here dogs run unbraced and usually on pigeons. The Novice Stake is for dogs who have never won first, second, third, or fourth at an Open All-Age Stake, a Qualified All-Age Stake, or an Amateur All-Age Stake or first in any other regular stakes except Puppy Stake. The Limit Stake is for dogs who have never won first place in an Open All-Age Stake or firsts in any regular official stake except Puppy Stake. A Qualified All-Age and Open All-Age Stake are for dogs over six months of age. The Qualified is for dogs who have placed first, second, third, or fourth in any stake except Puppy Stake. The Open is the "big" stake, in which

FROM THE EXPERT

According to Jason Givens in the March 2004 edition of the *Spaniel Journal,* the delivery of the game is extremely important—you should not have to play tug-of-war with your dog to get it. He should come to you quickly, give you the bird, and then wait for the next command. You should then take the bird and quickly hand it to the judge so that she can examine it. This is the last impression the judge will have of your dog, so make it a good one.

dogs who place first, second, third, or fourth earn points toward a Field Championship. An Amateur All-Age Stake is for dogs over six months of age who are handled by amateurs.

Puppy Stakes are frequently only one series and are open to dogs between the ages of six months and two years. Here dogs run unbraced and usually on pigeons. Puppies are judged using the same criteria as all-age competitors, including the requirement that they be steady. Puppy Stake placements do not count toward championship titles. Puppies may also be entered in an All-Age Stake at the same trial.

Eligibility Requirements: Spaniel field trials are available only for registered Cocker Spaniels, English Cocker Spaniels, and English Springer Spaniels. Spayed and neutered dogs are eligible to participate.

Titles: The judges may award a first, second, third, and fourth place in each stake. Dogs who earn enough points in either Open or Amateur Stakes will be given a title of either Field Champion (FC) for points earned in the Open Stake or Amateur Field Champion (AFC) for points earned in the Amateur Stake. Each category requires the dog to have two wins and a water test or a win plus 10 points and a water test to earn the respective title.

Premier Events: All dogs who have placed in the Open Stake during the year qualify to compete in the National Open Field Trial, usually held in late November or early December. Dogs who place in the Amateur Stake qualify for

The most important quality for a successful spaniel is strong bird-finding ability.

the National Amateur Field Trial. A National Trial consists of five land series (four series are braced) and one water series. The dogs winning these trials become National Field Champions (NFC) and National Amateur Field Champions (NAFC), respectively, as well as automatically earning their FC or AFC if they do not already have that title.

How to Get Started

The most important quality for a successful spaniel is strong bird-finding ability. Spaniel field trials differ somewhat depending on which breed you are entering, but all share common characteristics. It should be noted at the start that these trials involve the actual hunting and killing of birds. If this isn't an activity in which you wish to participate, look elsewhere for something to do with your dog. About the only difference between regular hunting and a field trial is that birds are placed in the test area so that they can be readily found, while a hunter in the field must take his chances on actually finding any game.

CONDITION YOUR DOG—AND YOURSELF

Before you embark on this sport, take your dog to the vet
to make sure that he is up to date on all vaccinations and
healthy enough to participate. You might want to consider a
health checkup for yourself as well.

CONSIDER A PROFESSIONAL TRAINER

The actual training of a gundog, spaniel, pointer, setter, or
retriever is quite complicated, and most hunters leave it
to professionals. Some hunters, however, enjoy working
with their dogs and undertake the training themselves. We
will go over some of the principles here, but more detailed
instruction or the help of an experienced trainer will be
needed to fully train your spaniel. Each dog requires a
different approach, and part of a professional's skill is being
able to read a dog and tell what technique is apt to work
best for him.

Some dogs are born to hunt and some aren't. Training
improves on what nature provides. Practice can make your
dog good but won't make him great; a truly great hunting
dog must exhibit the hunting instinct as a puppy. If it's plain
that your puppy doesn't have the needed skills, consider
selecting a different sport.

TRAIN THE BASICS

Basically, using a spaniel to hunt involves retrieving,
steadiness, and hunting. It is usually easiest to start with
retrieving, then progress to steadiness, and finally hunting.
Start with retrieving on bare ground; lots of retrieving
games come naturally to a dog. Begin with objects like
balls or other favorite toys, then progress to dead birds. At
the same time, work with your puppy on basic obedience
commands, especially *heel*, *come*, *stay*, and *down*, using
both voice and whistle commands. He should change
directions on command and must reliably come when he
is called, no matter what he is doing. Gun-shy dogs will not
succeed, so you must accustom your dog to guns and their
noises from an early age by regular exposure. Gun-shyness
is easy to prevent but extremely difficult to cure.

Once your dog is used to working on bare ground, start

Be patient when training for field trials—it can take at least a year to prepare a dog.

his training in low cover and practice quartering (hunting in a zigzag pattern) by having him change directions on command as he ranges ahead of you in the field. Leave a few bird-scented objects in the grass for him to find. Gradually add in a few hups, then start throwing bird-like objects for him to retrieve. Eventually, you can start shooting during these exercises. He needs to be steady during shooting and not break his hup until he is told to. Not every hup should end with a retrieve because you don't want it to be automatic; your dog must respond to your commands. Each step may have to be repeated until he responds appropriately every time.

Start working with birds by placing a dead bird for your spaniel to find during quartering practice. Then shoot and throw a dead bird for him to retrieve. He must be able to stay in a *sit* during the shot before he retrieves the bird. Then use a live pigeon (a "fly-away" bird) to simulate a missed shot and allow it to fly away without your dog chasing it. He must learn that he should only go after birds that have been shot and not to chase after just any bird he encounters. A command of "no bird" may be used to tell him that he isn't to chase this one. Gradually build up to actual hunting.

Strategies for Success

When training for field trials, be patient! It generally takes at least a year—more often two—for a dog to succeed in the sport. Practice makes perfect.

BEGIN WITH A WORKING-STOCK PUPPY

As with all field trials, you must start with a puppy. An older dog, especially one not from field trial or hunting stock, is simply not going to succeed. It is very important to use a dog who comes from working stock. Most show- and pet-quality spaniels have had the urge to hunt bred out of them. Genetics count for a lot. If your young dog shows no interest in birds, find another sport.

START WITH THE HUNT TEST

Most people begin with the hunting test, which the AKC has been offering since 1988. Hunting tests are noncompetitive and are designed to see if a dog has the natural ability to succeed as a hunter. Hunt tests have lower expectations than field trials, a more relaxed atmosphere, and graduated levels of performance. These trials offer opportunities for those spaniel breeds that are currently ineligible for field trials.

KEEP BIRDS ON HAND

Keep a supply of dead birds handy. It's always a good technique to plant dead birds around so that when your puppy finds one and picks it up, you can praise him. If your instinct says instead, "Akh! Put that nasty thing down!" consider a different sport.

There is an old saying that birds make the bird dog, and there is nothing like raising your own birds to make a successful bird dog. Of course, this is not an option for everybody, which is why the next best solution is to join a spaniel club and get cozy with someone who does raise her own birds. You'll gain a mentor and a friend at the same time.

Chapter 17

Flyball

Definition

Flyball is a lightning-paced team sport in which dogs race over hurdles side by side, relay style, to fetch a tennis ball.

History of Flyball

Flyball was created in California in the late 1970s, when a group of dog trainers began working with scent discrimination hurdle racing. The tennis balls now so characteristic of the sport were originally used as a reward! Herbert Wagner is credited with developing the first flyball launching box, and he did a flyball demonstration on the *Tonight Show* with Johnny Carson, bringing the sport into the national spotlight.

The sport really expanded during the 1980s, when the first flyball organization, the North American Flyball Association, Inc., (NAFA) was established; its first flyball tournament was held in 1983. Today, the NAFA has more than 400 active clubs and 6,500 competing dogs. More recently, a second organization, the United Flyball League International (U-FLI), was founded in November 2004.

Overview

In flyball, teams usually consist of four dogs with a maximum of two alternates who may be substituted for team members at the end of a heat. The course consists of four jumps.

The jump height is determined by the smallest dog on his team; this dog, called the "height dog," is measured at the withers. That number is rounded down to the nearest 1 inch (2.5 cm), and another 4 inches (10 cm) is subtracted to determine the jump height, with a minimum of 7 inches (18 cm) and a maximum of 14 inches (35.5 cm). Thus, smaller dogs on a mixed team are especially prized because the hurdles are set to suit their heights, making the race easier for the bigger dogs.

TOP BREEDS

Herding breeds, such as Shetland Sheepdogs, Border Collies, and Australian Shepherd Dogs, and terriers (especially Parson/Jack Russell Terriers), with their relentless speed and energy, dominate, but every dog has an equal chance.

Dogs race one another down the course to the flybox, which automatically releases a tennis ball when a dog presses the spring-loaded

During competition, a dog races to the flybox, an automatic tennis ball launcher.

pad (electronic releases are not allowed). The dog then retrieves the ball (usually he will catch it as it pops out of the box) and brings it back to the handler. Each dog must return his ball all the way across the start line before the next dog begins his run. The handler must stay behind the start/finish line.

This continues until all four dogs have completed their runs over the same course. The first team to finish without error wins the heat. Penalties are applied to teams if the ball is dropped or if the next relay dog is released early. Amazingly enough, many teams can run all four dogs through the hurdles in under 20 seconds; the record is under 16 seconds.

Flyball tournaments are usually organized in a double-elimination or round-robin format. Titles are earned via a point system that is based on the time it takes a dog's team to complete each heat race.

Requirements

Dogs
- accuracy
- obedience to basic commands
- retrieving ability
- socialization skills
- speed

Handlers
- competitive
- dog savvy

Equipment and Supplies
- floor mat
- flybox
- judging system
- jumps
- shagger

To participate in flyball, a dog must have speed and good retrieving ability.

- tennis balls
- wrap and leg guards

Floor Mat: This is a running mat usually made of rubber so that the dogs do not slip.

Flybox: The flybox is an automatic tennis ball launcher (usually made of plywood) that was invented in 1970s by Herbert Wagner. These slanted, spring-loaded boxes can vary in design, but all work the same way: They release a ball when the dog applies pressure to a nonelectronic mechanism on the box. Often each team is required to supply its own flyball box. These boxes must meet specific size requirements.

Judging System: When the sport was just beginning, there were no start lights or passing lights—all starts and passes were called by the line judges, who also timed the events with handheld stopwatches. More recently, the NAFA has developed an Electronic Judging System (EJS), which uses lights and infrared timing sensors so that competitors can track their starts, passes, finishes, and individual dogs' times to the thousandth of a second. The U-FLI also has an electronic system, called the Digital Scoring System (DSS).

Jumps: For practice, jumps need not be fancy and can be bought ready made or are easy to make yourself. They must not be wider than 24 inches (61 cm), with standards between 24 and 36 inches high (61 and 91.5 cm). The U-FLI requires that the cross board be 5 inches (12.5 cm) tall, while the NAFA requires that the cross board be 7 inches (18 cm) tall. Both require solid white slats, which are used to raise the jump height accordingly.

Shagger: This is a ball cage that is taken back to the box for reloading. During racing and practice, teams often designate an individual to shag balls and keep them off the course while the dogs are running.

Tennis Balls: These can be regular tennis balls of any color, size, or substance. Select something your dog can carry easily and that will bounce. (This is a requirement.)

Wrap and Leg Guards: These will protect your canine athlete's legs.

Flyball is a vigorous, fast-paced sport, so your dog must be in tip-top shape to compete.

Sponsoring Organizations

NORTH AMERICAN FLYBALL ASSOCIATION (NAFA)

The NAFA recognizes five classes: Regular, Multibreed, Open, Veteran's, and Non-Regular. The Regular class includes teams made up of any breed, and this class must be offered at every competition. The Multibreed Class must consist of four to six different breeds recognized by the AKC, UKC, Canadian Kennel Club (CKC), Mexican Kennel Club, American Rare Breed Association (ARBA), Herding Breed Association, or a dog of mixed breeding. The Open Class is for dogs who switch clubs—it eliminates the normal 87-day waiting period. The Veterans Class is for dogs seven years of age and over. A Non-Regular Class is any class other than those already listed.

Eligibility Requirements: All dogs, including mixed breeds, can compete and earn titles. NAFA currently has more than 700 registered clubs with more than 16,000 registered dogs. The only requirement is a desire to have fun.

Titles: NAFA tournaments are divided into divisions, ensuring that teams compete against other teams of equal abilities. Each time a team races in an NAFA-sanctioned flyball tournament, each team dog racing in that heat earns points toward a flyball title. Titles are earned via a point system based on the time it takes a dog's team to complete each heat race. A dog earns the title of Flyball Dog (FD) when he has earned 20 points; Flyball Dog Excellent (FDX) when he has earned 100 points; Flyball Dog Champion (FDCh) with 500 points; Flyball Master (FM) with 5,000 points; Flyball Master Excellent (FMX) with 10,000 points; Flyball Master Excellent Champion (FMCh) with 15,000 points; and Flyball Grand Champion (FDCh-30) with 30,000 points.

Premier Events: The NAFA holds 21 regional tournaments around the United States throughout the year. The NAFA racing year begins on October 1st and extends through September 30th of the following calendar year. The organization also holds the World Cynosport Flyball Championship each year.

UNITED FLYBALL LEAGUE INTERNATIONAL (U-FLI)

The U-FLI offers standard classes open to any breed or mix of dog, as well as special classes that include variety teams, pairs teams, single teams, and exhibition teams.

Eligibility Requirements: Any dogs of any size and any breed can participate. The U-FLI even encourages creative teams, such as an all Miniature Schnauzer Team and All-Spotted Team—if you can imagine it, you can do it.

Titles: Titles include Top Flight Executive (TFE), Top Flight Premier (TFP), Top Flight First Class (TFFC), Top Flight World Class (TFWC), Top Flight Extreme (TFX), and Top Flight Ultimate (TFU).

Premier Events: The U-FLI offers an annual World Championship that is open to all levels of competition.

How to Get Started

A good flyball prospect is an intense, fast, self-reliant, focused dog who can get off to a quick start and jump well. Some

Mike Randall wrote the first NAFA rule book in 1985 and was the first NAFA Executive Director. He is also the author of *On Your Mark,* an electronic book freely available on the Internet. He writes, "With six dogs on a team, there are 240 possible combinations—depending which dogs race and the order they race. Depending on the circumstances, I always have in mind three or four combinations that have worked well in practice or in other tournaments. During the excitement of the competition it is difficult enough to make a decision, let alone the right one . . . . I like to run dogs with the least experience last—thus giving them a clear run back. I prefer to race the best dog first—hoping to take an early lead.

I have also observed that the dogs and handlers develop a certain rhythm as they race. Therefore, unless absolutely necessary, I will stay with the same four dogs in any given set of races. I might even stay with a slower dog in the third and final heat rather than introduce a new dog that might upset the rhythm the first dogs established in heats 1 and 2."

dogs are so ball crazy that they need little incentive to participate in the sport!

CONDITION YOUR DOG

Flyball is a vigorous, fast-paced sport, and your dog must be in tip-top shape to compete. Get him checked by your vet before starting training.

A puppy needs plenty of running/fetching games to get him in shape before the start of actual flyball training. Remember, however, that your puppy is still growing; don't allow him to overexert himself. Once his training has advanced enough, try to hold full practice sessions, simulating an actual competition, once or twice a week. Have vigorous exercise sessions on the other days. Your dog should run after a ball or other retrievable object, not just go for a walk. Don't forget to allow him some slow stretching time before a vigorous workout, whether it's practice or an actual tournament. He won't be ready to run his best when he gets out of a crate, and he is more apt to injure himself as well.

TRAIN THE BASICS

Flyball dogs must know basic obedience skills, including *come*, *sit*, *stay*, *lie down*, and *leave it*. They must also be smart enough to learn to trigger the box and catch the ball. Although many of these skills are inborn, some can be taught, and all are improved upon with practice sessions. Playing retrieve and other games will help your dog develop the skills needed.

Begin with teaching your dog to catch a ball. Gradually make the tosses harder and a little to the side to make him reach for it. Then teach him to retrieve the ball quickly to you. He must also learn to pick up the ball from the ground for those times when he might miss it as it pops from the box.

Once he reliably retrieves, get him used to the flybox. First, let him sniff it while it is unloaded; then get him used

When training for flyball, your dog must learn to catch a ball and bring it to you.

Your dog's flyball skills can be improved with practice sessions.

to stepping on the pedal. Just let it snap at first, without releasing a ball. Then start tossing him a ball when he steps on the pedal, and finally, after he is used to that, let the machine toss the ball to him. Gradually get him used to running the jumps and catching the ball; eventually, he will start doing it at speed.

More efficient running of the course is accomplished by using a U-turn similar to that used by human swimmers during a race. To teach this, place an obstacle in front of the flybox, making your dog approach it from one side. In this way, he will already be at an angle when he retrieves the ball, allowing him to complete his turn with a minimum of hesitation.

You will also need to work on passing, which is the precise timing needed to release the next dog as nearly as possible to when the first dog crosses the finish line. This takes a lot of practice. A common problem includes aggression during passing, when one dog finishes his run and the next is just starting his. This is especially true in terrier breeds, which tend to be a bit more dog aggressive.

FIND A TEAM

To get started in flyball, you need to find a team. Visit both the NAFA and U-FLI's websites for more information.

Strategies for Success

Some of the best strategies for flyball success include keeping a specific goal in mind and preventing your dog from dropping the ball.

HAVE A GOAL

For every training session, have a goal. What are you looking for? Faster retrieves? More speed? Better turns? Devise your training schedule to work on that particular skill, and keep a record of your progress.

KEEP YOUR DOG FROM DROPPING THE BALL

Dropping the ball is one of the most common mistakes flyball dogs make. To keep that from happening, never take a retrieved article unless it is dropped right in your hand. Teach this in the following way: If your dog brings you the ball but drops it, ignore him and refuse to play with him. Soon he'll start begging to play, and he'll get the idea that if you are gong to throw the ball for him, he must bring it directly to your hand. Sometimes you'll have to turn away from your dog, which will encourage him to hold onto his prize until you take it from him.

ADDITIONAL ORGANIZATIONS

Australian Flyball Association, Inc. (AFA)
www.flyball.org.au
British Flyball Association (BFA)
www.flyball.org.uk
The Kennel Club
www.thekennelclub.org.uk
South African Flyball Dog Association (SAFDA)
www.safda.netfirms.com

Chapter 18

Flying Disc

Definition

Flying disc is a sport in which dogs and their human partners play Frisbee! These human-canine teams compete in various events such as long-distance and "freestyle catching," which involves choreographed, stylish moves. This sport is growing "by leaps and bounds."

History of Flying Disc

Flying disc began in the 1970s as the human-oriented game of Frisbee was developing. The sport received an unintentional spotlight in 1974, when a college student named Alex Stein and his dog Ashley Whippet leaped the fence at a Dodgers/Reds game. He began throwing flying discs to the dog, who darted and leapt and caught them with style. The game was stopped, and Joe Garagiola even announced the goings-on—at least until Alex and the dog were escorted off the field by the authorities. Stein and Ashley were separated during the fracas, but a Long Beach boy took the dog in and returned him to Stein three days later.

The idea of dogs and flying discs had been born—although it had not yet come of age. Stein and a colleague, Eldon McIntire, began to work to create a nationwide flying disc competition, the Frisbee Dog World Championship, which is still held today.

Overview

Flying disc is a game that many owners happily play with their dogs in their own backyards, with no thought of competition. In fact, it is estimated that about 1 million dogs currently play flying disc in the United States.

A flying disc team consists of a handler and dog who play "catch" on a grassy area (or at least one where the ground is soft). This is a high-spirited sport that dogs really seem to enjoy playing with their handlers.

SKYHOUNDZ

DISCDOGATHON

The most exciting event is the DiscDogathon, which combines several events in one.

This marathon event includes:

Boomerang: Exhibitors have three attempts to catch the disc; the goal is to keep the disc in the air for the longest amount of time.

Bullseye: Exhibitors may use two discs to throw in any direction; they have one minute to score as many points as they can.

Top Breeds

The ideal flying disc dog is a medium-sized animal (30 to 60 pounds [13.5 to 27 kg]) with a lean build and a strong prey/retrieve drive. He should be fit, athletic, and trainable. This sport seems especially suitable for energetic, highly active dogs who need a "job" to keep them happy. Very large dogs may be too heavy-boned and clumsy. Retrievers and herding breeds usually excel, and repeated world champions feature Border Collies and Australian Shepherds, although mixes, Labrador Retrievers, and Vizslas have also won big.

Distance/Accuracy: Teams complete as many catches as possible within various scoring zones within the time allotted.

Freestyle: Teams get two minutes per round; the team with the highest combined scores in the Athleticism and Wow!Factor categories wins. (In addition, a Snapshot round is held, with each team taking turns; they get ten seconds to demonstrate their best trick or collection of tricks.)

Spot Landing: In this event, circular landing zones are laid out in different locations on the field. Competitors receive various point values for catches in which the dog lands with all paws inside a scoring zone. Competitors have one minute to score as many points as possible.

DISTANCE/ACCURACY

These events stress speed and accuracy. Only one disc is used. Teams (one dog/one handler) are given 60 seconds to get as many catches as possible on a field marked with increasingly longer distances. Dogs earn points based on the distance of the catch, and more points are awarded if the dog is airborne for the catch. Generally, the field is a rectangle laid out with lines representing distances from the throwing line, very much like a football field, with the throwing line being the end zone. This is the easiest event for beginners.

In distance/accuracy events, teams are given 60 seconds to get as many catches as possible on a field marked with increasingly longer distances.

FREESTYLE

Teams (one dog/one handler) have 60 to 90 seconds per round (120 seconds at the World Championship) and use up to five discs to show off their innovation, variety, and style.

PAIRS FREESTYLE

Pairs Freestyle is the same as freestyle except that two throwers and one dog compete as a team.

TIMETRIAL

Each competitor or team tries to complete two 20-yard (18.5-m) throws to a dog in the shortest amount of time possible. A maximum time of one minute is permitted.

XTREME DISTANCE CHALLENGE

In this event, the teams try to record the longest throws. All teams compete in two 90-second rounds, making as many throws as possible within that timeframe.

US Disc Dog Nationals (USDDN)

In the USDDN, all classes have Junior and Pro Divisions.

Freestyle

Teams have 120 seconds and may use up to ten discs; they are encouraged to show off their best tricks. Innovation is rewarded.

Toss & Fetch

Teams have 90 seconds and an unlimited number of attempts with one disc. The best five throws count toward the score.

Requirements

Dogs

- accuracy
- jumping, twisting ability
- obedience to basic commands
- retrieving ability
- speed
- top-notch physical condition

Handlers

- ability to handle the disc, starting with a basic forehand (sidearm) toss
- accuracy
- creativity for freestyle
- good throwing arm

Fun Fact

Ashley Whippet, the dog who started it all, is still considered the premier flying disc dog. He went on to perform at the White House, do a routine at Superbowl XII, and star in *Floating Free*, a short documentary nominated for an Academy Award. He also served as spokesdog for the Gaines dog food company and, upon his death, received a tribute from *Sports Illustrated*. Although Ashley has gone to his reward, the sport he helped create lives on. And in case you are wondering, Ashley Whippet was indeed a Whippet!

Equipment and Supplies

- cones
- flying disc
- grassy playing area
- measuring tape
- protective clothing

Cones: Buy some orange cones to help you mark off the scoring distances. You can find them at sporting goods stores.

Flying Disc: For competition, check with the hosting organization to see which flying discs are approved. These competition discs are slower-flying than normal discs. The best flying discs are light, thin, and made of rigid yet soft material. A disc should weigh no more than 0.5 ounces (11 g). To keep the disc in good order, clean it regularly in the dishwasher. You can also use sandpaper or a flexible sanding block to smooth it out—even the best disc gets a little bumpy with a dog chewing on it.

Grassy Playing Area: A large, grassy area is sufficient—there is no size requirement.

Measuring Tape: Best is a 30-yard (27.5-m) crank-type plastic (better than retractable metal) measuring tape. You can purchase one at most hardware stores.

Protective Clothing: You may want to have a heavy

FROM THE EXPERT

Expert flying disc handler Chuck Middleton writes: "No dog I know was born a natural Frisbee player. By examining the basic dynamics of how your dog learned to play simple throw and catch, you'll be much better prepared to teach your dog more advanced Frisbee moves and tricks." He suggests breaking the activity down into individual pieces "like links in a chain, and many dogs with some natural or encouraged desire can be taught to 1) chase, 2) catch, and 3) retrieve. There you have the basic pieces of canine Frisbee. Eliminate any one of those links and the game quickly becomes an exercise in stress management instead of a fun activity for you and your dog."

jacket or neoprene vest to protect you when your dog comes crashing down on your back. Some experts recommend a neoprene diving vest for this purpose. Thigh wraps, a waist pad, and safety goggles are also a good idea.

Sponsoring Organizations

SKYHOUNDZ
Although competitive classes vary from division to division, some that apply to regional, open, and international qualifiers include Expert (open to all), Masters (open to dogs nine years and older), Novice (a dog and thrower team that have never finished higher than fourth place in certain divisions), Youth (open to handlers 14 years and younger); and Team (male/female throwers alternate throws).

Eligibility Requirements: No special registration or membership is required. Spayed and neutered dogs are eligible. There are no age requirements.

Titles: Skyhoundz offers championships in each of its divisions, including a world championship in each.

Premier Events: Skyhoundz offers local championships, regional qualifiers, open qualifiers, international qualifiers, and a world championship. In 2000, Skyhoundz took over the World Canine Frisbee Disc Championship event for one year; since then, it has run its own championship event, the Hyperflite Skyhoundz World Canine Disc Championship. It also offers the Hyperflite DiscDogathons, which are staged by dog and disc clubs and similar volunteer organizations, as well as Hyperflite Xtreme Distance Challenge events.

US DISC DOG NATIONALS (USDDN)
The USDNN offers Div II Freestyle, National and International Freestyle, Pro Toss & Fetch, Novice Toss & Fetch, and Junior Toss & Fetch Divisions.

Eligibility Requirements: Any breed can participate; dogs can be spayed and neutered. Dogs must be 18 months old to participate in a national Qualifier Division.

Titles: A multitude of national championships are available.

Premier Events: The USDDN organizes events in the United States, Japan, the Netherlands, Germany, Poland,

In flying disc freestyle, dogs and handlers can show off their innovation, variety, and style.

Canada, and Australia. It holds a US Disc Dog Nationals Championships Series featuring the US Disc Dog Nationals Championships Weekend and also holds a championship series known as the USDDN Finals and US Disc Dog International Finals.

How to Get Started

Before getting started in flying disc, your dog should be in superb condition, with good hips and a solid social temperament because he will be off lead around other dogs. He should also be obedience trained.

GET YOUR DOG A CHECKUP

Get your dog thoroughly checked out by a vet before you start and regularly thereafter. This sport is *extremely* tough on a dog's anatomy, especially the spine, because the moves involved are not "natural." Hip dysplasia is of particular concern; the sport can exacerbate the disease in predisposed dogs. Dogs should not be leaping until they are at least 14 months old and physically mature.

LEARN TO THROW THE DISC CORRECTLY

Nothing is more important than throwing the disc correctly. As far as the dog is concerned, that means getting it up there with enough air time (which is largely a result of enough spin on the disc) so that he can mark it and catch it. When he does, he'll feel a rush of success that is as important as any praise you can give!

Here is the basic grip: Your middle finger should be straight and flat against the inside rim. The outside rim of the disc should make contact with the web between your thumb and index finger. Your grip should be firm. (If you're not used to it, it may be a bit uncomfortable.) Stand with your feet about shoulder width apart. While throwing, the main idea is to keep the outer tip of the disc down. The whiplash effect of the swing should culminate in a "snap" that gives spin to the disc, and it's the spin that contributes to the stability of the disc (like a top). When you are just starting, make only short throws, and keep the disc's flight as flat as possible.

TRAIN THE BASICS

Trainers often begin teaching their dog to catch the disc by rolling it on the ground rather than throwing it in the air and risking the dog getting hit. A bad experience at an early age can terrify a dog. (Of course, never throw the disc directly at your dog.) Soon he will become accustomed to chasing the object. Trainers also advise using the disc only when you are present. It should be a "special toy" whose use means fun times.

To teach your dog a basic retrieve, attach a 30-foot (9-m) length or rope to his collar or harness. When he catches the disc, recall him.

NYLABONE

To keep your dog revved up for this sport, don't let him play with the disc unless you are there to play with him.

(Don't hold onto the lead when he's racing after the ball, though!) If he drops the disc on the way back, just go get it yourself in an excited way and play with it. Soon he'll get the idea that the disc is an object of tremendous value and interest and will bring it back to you.

At this point, he will need to know a reliable *drop* command or you will be chasing him around the field all day. (Don't ever chase your dog—he'll make a game of it. The key is to get him to bring the item to you.) One popular way to teach the *drop* command is to offer a treat or other high-value item in exchange for the disc. Offer plenty of praise at the same time. After a while you can give the exchange item intermittently, but keep the praise. Soon you will be able to omit the treat altogether.

Always have water available for your dog while training.

Strategies for Success

If there is one sport where joy is the key, flying disc is it! A great disc dog is a happy dog. Convince your dog that you are playing (and you are), and you'll be well on the road to success.

Make the Disc a Special Toy

Keep the flying disc away from your dog unless you are there to play with him. It's important that he learn that this special toy is there only for the two of you. If he has one of his own, he'll soon grow tired of it.

Aim the Disc Correctly

When you start throwing the disc, be extremely careful not to aim it right at your dog and risk hitting him with it. The first throws should be low, flat, and easy to catch. It may take several months for your dog to learn to catch a disc in flight. Next, start throwing the disc at increasing distances, and throw it higher and higher over his head until he learns to leap and spin after it. Jump training is a very special element. Dogs need to learn to land with all four feet on the ground to prevent a spine-crushing vertical landing. Some trainers do this by teaching their dog to jump through hula hoops, which encourages a four-square landing.

Additional Organizations

Australian Canine Disc Association (ACDA)
www.frisbeedogs.asn.au
Canadian Disc Dog Association (CDDA)
www.geocities.com/cddadiscdog

Chapter 19

Herding

Definition

A herding trial is a competitive sport in which dogs move sheep or other flocking animals around a field, fences, gates, or enclosures under commands from their handlers. Herding tests are similar but are not competitive. Both trials and tests require dogs to be obedient to their handlers yet use their own initiative and judgment. It is not surprising that herding breeds consistently rank at the top of dog intelligence tests!

History of Herding

Dogs have been herding sheep and other animals for thousands of years. Their natural instinct is actually to kill these animals as prey, but they have been selectively bred not to do so. In other words, herding is really a modified prey instinct. The modern herding dog works behind the shepherd and at both sides of the flock to make sure that even the last sheep is included in the group and that no one goes his own way.

The American Herding Breed Association's (AHBA) program began in 1986, while the American Kennel Club's (AKC) herding program began in 1989.

Overview

Herding adds a different dimension to dog sports. Unlike obedience, agility, or skijoring—and somewhat akin to field trials—a third party is added to the human-canine mix. In this case, it is sheep, cows, or ducks, all of which have a mind of their own and desires that don't match yours or your dog's. The basic principles of herding events are the same for all organizations, and herding tests and trials do roughly the same things—although the latter are at a higher level and competitive.

A dog must be able to leave his handler and fetch stock from a distance. He must remain in control of the stock and bring it back to the handler. In more advanced events, a dog should also be able to drive the stock away from the handler. Dog and handler must be able to combine forces to put the stock into a confined space, such as a pen or even a trailer. Some tests ask the dog to separate the flock or herd into two groups, following the instructions of the judge. This is called "shedding." A similar test is "singling," in which one animal is separated from the herd. In the penning, shedding, and singling parts of the trial, the handler may leave the "stake" (a pole or stick in the ground to mark where he is supposed to stay most of the time) and work with the dog to achieve the task. Some events feature brace dogs—two dogs working simultaneously with one handler.

The layout of each herding course is variable. The AKC sets a minimum size, depending on the test and the stock.

Requirements

DOGS

- agility
- independence
- intelligence
- obedience to basic commands
- responsiveness
- self-confidence
- stock sense

HANDLERS

- ability to "read sheep" or targeted stock
- excellent training skills

Equipment and Supplies

- crook
- herding stock
- open space

Crook: This is a hooked staff used by shepherds (the handler, in this case) to control sheep.

Herding Stock: Herding is not an easy sport to start in because you need access to potential herding stock. The easiest to find are ducks, and they are much simpler to work with than sheep or cattle. They are also cheap, easy to care for, and take up much less room than large herding animals. They are also very transportable. If you plan to be a serious herder, it's comforting

---

FUN FACT

Herding style depends to some extent on the breed. The Border Collie, for instance, uses his famous intimidating stare to encourage sheep to behave in the way desired. Even the stance of various breeds is different. Border Collies creep, while Australian Shepherds work in a more "upright" stance and with a "looser" eye.

Ducks are easier to find and simpler to work with than sheep or cattle.

to know that most of what a dog learns about ducks can translate to sheep or even cattle know-how.

Open Space: The layout of the space can vary a great deal. Some groups offer several different kinds of areas: arena trials, an open field "post-advanced" course, and a ranch or farm course, depending on the class, stock, and what skill is being tested.

Sponsoring Organizations

AMERICAN HERDING BREED ASSOCIATION (AHBA)

HERDING TESTS
The AHBA's test levels include the Herding Capability Test (HCT) and the Junior Herding Dog Test (JHD), both of which are run on a pass/fail basis and require two passing runs (legs) under different judges. Tests may be held with sheep, ducks, goats, or geese, and are open to

all herding breeds. Dogs are judged on style (gathering, driving), approach, eye, bark, temperament, interest, power, responsiveness, grouping of stock, balancing of stock with handler, and controlled movement, among other things.

HERDING TRIALS

The AHBA program offers three types of trial classes, each with three levels: Started (HTD I), Intermediate (HTD II), and Advanced (HTD III). The Herding Trial Dog Program, with levels HTD I, II, and III, takes place on a standard course with outrun, lift, fetch, wear (the side to side movement of the dog to keep the stock grouped, as well as fetching them back to the handler), and/or drive and pen. These trials may be held in arenas, although larger fields are preferred. The Herding Ranch Dog Program, with levels HRD I, II, and III, takes place on farm courses. The Herding Trial Arena Dog Program, with levels HTAD I, II, and III, takes place in arenas with set minimum and maximum sizes. Here, four courses are run, each of which includes an alternative of either a gather (compact group) or a take-pen (a pen), three obstacles of various types, a drive section at levels II and III, and a "sort" of varying kinds (in which the dogs are required to sort out the stock animals in different ways according to instructions from the handler). The titles require two qualifying scores under two different judges. Titles may be earned on sheep, goats, ducks, geese, turkeys, or cattle, with a small initial
after the title indicating the type of stock on which the title was earned.

Eligibility Requirements: AHBA trials are open to all herding breeds and herding breed mixes nine months of age or older. They may be spayed or neutered. Dogs at least six months of age may enter herding tests.

Titles: A dog may enter at any level for which he is trained. No title is a prerequisite for another. For each title, two qualifying scores are required, earned under different judges. Upon completion of the second leg, a certificate is issued awarding the title. Titles include Herding Trial Dog, first level (HTD1); Herding Trial Dog, second level (HTD2); and Herding Trial Dog, third level (HTD3). The official

AHBA HTD title can have up to four suffixes: -d for ducks, -s for sheep, -g for goats, or -c for cattle. The title will always have at least one of these suffixes. After a dog has earned at least one advanced title on one type of stock, he becomes eligible to earn points for the title Herding Trial Champion (HTCh).

Premier Events: Various events are held all around the United States. Specific breeds have championships available for their breed.

AMERICAN KENNEL CLUB (AKC)

HERDING TESTS

The initial test is called the Instinct Test, and it is a test held for the traditional herding breeds, as well as Rottweilers, Samoyeds, Standard and Giant Schnauzers, Pyrenean Shepherds, Swedish Vallhunds, Norwegian Buhunds, and Greater Swiss Mountain Dogs. Dogs need no special training for this class and may be handled by the judge, owner, or a designated handler. The judge is looking for the dog's ability to move properly and control livestock by fetching or driving. It should be noted, however, that these tests are not always a reliable gauge of herding ability because in many cases they are nothing more than a test of prey drive rather than herding talent.

Other AKC pre-trial events include the Herding Test and Pretrial Test. Both are Pass/Fail. In the Herding Test, the dog must move the stock across a ring between two cones in a deliberate fashion three times with a stop and recall at the end. Two qualifying runs are required to earn the title. In the Pretrial, the dog must move stock in a U- or J-shape

---

FROM THE EXPERT

Expert herder Richard Whorton notes that instinct certification indicates that you might have something to work with if you're interested in herding; it might also simply mean that the dog is having fun chasing sheep. He may never understand about herding balance, how to do an outrun, how to gather sheep, how to handle a single, and so on.

---

around the edge of the arena, turn around, and go back, passing through two panels each way. At some point the handler must pause the dog. Two passing runs are required for the title.

HERDING TRIALS

Three types of trial courses are offered at three different levels: Started, Intermediate, and Advanced. The "A" Course takes place in an arena and requires working livestock through obstacles and into a pen. The "B" Course is a modified Border Collie course requiring an outrun, lift, fetch, wear/drive, pen, and in the advanced class, a shed. The "C" Course is meant to reflect herding as done in Europe (especially Germany), with large flocks in unfenced areas. Sheep, goats, ducks, geese, or cattle may be used on certain courses.

Eligibility Requirements: The AKC program is open to recognized herding breeds, Rottweilers, and Samoyeds. All dogs must be at least nine months of age. Spayed and neutered breeds are eligible to participate.

Titles: The AKC currently offers five herding titles, including two "test" trials. The test trial titles include *Herding Tested (HT):* Requires two qualifying runs under two separate judges; and *Pre-Trial (PT):* Requires two qualifying runs under two separate judges. The three "trial" titles, all of which require three qualifying scores under three judges, include Herding Started (HS), Herding Intermediate (HI), and Herding Advanced (HX). Past the HX level, the Herding Champion (HCh) title is earned on a point system, based on defeating a certain number of dogs. AKC herding titles are neither stock- nor course-specific. Thus, a dog may earn a title on three different courses and types of stock.

Premier Events: Herding events are held all around the United States.

How to Get Started

Dogs must have exposure to livestock before embarking on either herding tests or herding trials. You don't want to find out at an event that your pet is a duck killer, for instance, or

A good herding dog knows how to keep stock on the move without panicking the animals.

terrified of sheep. The basic goal of all herding is to move stock efficiently from one place to another with the least possible stress. The stock must be kept as calm and "settled" as possible. Herding is not a rodeo; the dog must be able to intimidate the stock, not frighten it to death, which is a delicate balance.

EVALUATE YOUR DOG'S SUITABILITY

Livestock are a "prey species." They are used to being hunted and don't necessarily panic if they see a potential predator, like a dog—unless that dog is perceived to be actively hunting them. In that case, stock tend to become fearful and will take off at a blind run (or else decide to stand and put up a fight)—a situation that isn't good for anyone. A good herding dog knows how to keep stock on the move without panicking the animals. It is usually the first few seconds of stock dog interaction that sets the mood; the wrong attitude or wrong move on the part of the dog can destroy the entire run.

Successful herding dogs must also be able to work well

with people and have enough independence and drive to problem-solve a difficult situation on their own. They must not be overly aggressive to their charges but must have enough firmness to control a potentially recalcitrant animal.

GET YOUR DOG A CHECKUP

Herding is extremely demanding work that requires a dog to be in top physical condition. Have your dog checked by a veterinarian before embarking on this enterprise. Dogs can usually begin training when they are about a year old.

FIND A MENTOR

Undoubtedly, the best way to get involved in herding is to find an experienced mentor or trainer who will be able to give your dog the attention and instruction needed. Many clinics are offered around the country every year. However, try to find one that is familiar with your particular breed and the way it works. Trainers often work with several dogs at once, and you can get the benefit of watching other dogs at work. Herding clinics are also held from time to time, and they can be very helpful.

TRAIN YOUR DOG

For herding breeds, herding is an instinctive activity but one that requires refinement in training. Many clubs hold training series to help you shape your dog's natural abilities into something you can use in tests and trials. They often start with getting your dog acquainted with stock. Dogs are placed in a long line in the presence of stock and are rewarded for quiet behavior. Slowly, the dog is allowed to go closer toward the stock, and the line is loosened.

Give your puppy ample opportunity to chase things. Basic obedience skills, especially stopping on command and learning to stay, are also a must. Have your dog stay while you throw a favorite toy, like a Nylabone. Take your dog to a herding facility, so that he can get accustomed to the sight, sound, and smell of livestock.

As mentioned earlier, begin training with ducks—they are easy to find and care for and are simple to work with. Use as many ducks as you can because they like being together en masse; your dog will quickly learn to split

A good handler must know how to "read" stock, or understand their body language.

them into groups. Duck-break your dog in a large area away from the ducks' natural home so as not as not to terrify any babies.

DEVELOP VERBAL CUES

You'll also need to teach your dog some herding commands. These typically include:

- Away to me: Flank counterclockwise around the stock.
- Come by: Flank clockwise around the stock.
- Lie down: Lie down or stop.
- Steady: Slow down.
- Walk up: Approach the stock.
- Look back: Turn around and go back for more stock.

Strategies for Success

Knowing your breed and learning how to "read" stock will help you and your dog achieve herding success.

KNOW YOUR BREED

The most important thing is to know your breed. Every herding breed works a little differently, and most were bred to work on a particular kind of stock. Australian Shepherds, for example, were bred to herd sheep, while Corgis were bred to herd cattle. Learn the history of your breed and what its "strong points" in herding are. If you work with your breed's predilections instead of against them, you'll be much more likely to achieve success in this fun sport.

LEARN TO "READ" STOCK

To succeed at a herding event, the handler must have a great deal of knowledge. A good handler needs to know how to "read" stock. This means understanding their body language, which gives a good indication of which way the animals are about to move. It will then be easier to direct the dog (who is doing quite a bit of watching on his own). Many beginners make the mistake of being in too much of a hurry, which puts inordinate pressure on the dog and the stock. It's often a good idea to give the sheep a "breather" and let them resettle. In herding language, this means positioning the dog so that the line of escape is blocked, then halting for a few moments to let the stock relax and think about their situation. At this point, the idea is not to push them but not to let them get away either. This gives the dog a chance to relax and settle also. Remember that the stock tend to see the handler as equally as threatening as the dog—don't panic them.

ADDITIONAL ORGANIZATIONS

Canadian Kennel Club (CKC)
www.ckc.ca
International Sheep Dog Society (ISDS)
www.isds.org.uk

Chapter 20

Hunting Tests, Pointing Breeds

Definition

The pointer hunting test is designed to test a dog's ability to hunt upland game birds under natural conditions. Dogs do not compete against each other but rather attempt to show that they have the qualifications necessary to pass. Birds are killed at the higher levels of competition but not at the junior level.

Pointer hunting tests evaluate a dog's ability to hunt game birds under natural conditions.

History of Pointer Hunting Tests

The American Kennel Club (AKC) pointing dog hunting test was developed after the overwhelmingly favorable response to the AKC Retriever Hunting Test Program. Regulations for the hunting test were approved on March 11, 1986, and AKC pointing breed clubs were encouraged to begin holding tests. The Nebraska Brittany Club held the first pointing test in April of that year, with an entry of 43 dogs. The very first dog to receive a title was a German Shorthaired Pointer named Russo's Timberdoodle Jake.

The United Kennel Club (UKC) works with its subsidiary, the Hunting Retriever Club (HRC), to run tests for "hunting retriever dogs," the idea for which was born in 1983. The concept is not to judge dogs against each other, as happens in a field trial, but to judge each dog's individual ability to hunt. Its first event was held in September of that year, with 140 dogs participating.

Overview

Hunting tests for pointing breeds were developed so that people would have an opportunity to demonstrate their dogs' ability to perform under actual hunting conditions. Judges should evaluate a dog's natural abilities as well as those skills obtained through training. Unlike a field trial, all the participants must walk (except the judges—they can ride horses), just as people do in a regular bird hunt.

Dogs are run in braces (two at a time) as determined by a drawing. The purpose of bracing is to let the judge see whether a dog can hunt independently or is a trailer who simply follows his bracemate. Dogs are released into a very large (hundreds of acres, usually) bird field where birds have been "planted." The dogs are expected to find them and point at them.

As opposed to a field trial, dogs are not judged in competition with one another but are instead judged against a "standard" in order to "qualify." All of the dogs in a hunting test may qualify, as opposed to a field trial, in which only one "winner" is named. This is a real test in which everyone can pass!

AMERICAN KENNEL CLUB (AKC)

An AKC hunting test challenges dogs at three different levels: Junior, Senior, and Master. Dogs are tested on hunting, bird-finding ability, pointing ability, and trainability, and at higher levels, they are tested on retrieving and honoring as well. They must receive a certain number of passing scores to be awarded a title for each level. However, a dog is not required to title at a given level before being allowed to work toward a higher title. Scoring is based solely on how the dog's abilities compare to the written standards. There are no placements in hunting tests, only qualifying and nonqualifying scores. Dogs are judged in braces, to be determined by lot. Each dog in a brace must have a separate handler.

Dogs are tested on a single course, with or without a bird field, or they can be tested in a bird field only; regardless of the option chosen, a bird field must have sufficient cover to hold birds and must be of adequate size to permit a dog to hunt naturally without excessive hacking (constant yelling and commanding the dog). The bird field must be of at least five acres, and larger than five acres is strongly desired. In testing for Junior, Senior, and Master Hunting Tests, all handling

---

FUN FACT

Every pointing breed has a different quality, a different hunting style, and a different bird of expertise. There is no one best dog. The English Setter is a specialist on ruffed grouse, while the biddable Irish Setter is a generalist and the Gordon Setter is renowned for his superlative nose. The classic Pointer can outpoint anything but isn't crazy about retrieving. And the list goes on!

---

must be on foot. Horses may be used only by the judges and a judge's marshal.

UNITED KENNEL CLUB (UKC)

NATURAL ABILITY TEST (TAN)

In this test, dogs up to the age of three are issued TAN certificates for showing a natural desire to point, even though a lack of age or training may prevent them from competing in more rigorous field trials.

The dog is evaluated on his enthusiasm and his desire to find birds by scent as well as sight. Not too much importance is given to his manner or style. He must establish a point on at least one designated game bird during the TAN hunt, and the judge must determine that he is not gun-shy. (This program includes field trials; see Chapter 14.)

HUNTING RETRIEVER TEST

This test is held by the Hunting Retriever Club (HRC), which works with the UKC on this event. For pointers, the test is called an Upland Game Test, which requires dogs to be steady to wing and shot (not react adversely when a bird flushes and a shot is fired). The dog is required to locate and retrieve game as directed by the judge. They are also required to honor another dog.

A live bird is thrown or released in full view of the dog and within scenting distance. The distance from the bird to the dog should be within scenting distance when the bird is released. The dog should be eager to hunt all available cover diligently and be under control. The dog should immediately return to the previous hunting range upon being commanded by his handler. The handler will shoot the gun, and the gunners may kill the bird. If the dog does not immediately return to the hunting area, he fails the test.

It is recommended that all participants at an HRC/UKC-licensed event have participated in an approved hunting safety course.

Requirements

Dogs

- bird-finding ability
- honoring ability (depending on division)
- hunting ability
- obedience to basic commands
- pointing ability
- retrieving ability (depending on division)
- steadiness to wing and shot (depending on division)
- trainability

Handlers

- good physical condition
- gun-knowledgeable
- hunting experience (for higher levels)

Equipment and Supplies

- blank pistol
- bumper/dummy
- collar
- field
- lead
- whistle

Blanks/Starter Pistol: Most field trials and hunting tests require the handler to carry a blanks pistol while her dog is on the course. A blank pistol is one that has been manufactured specifically for firing only blank cartridges and has a solid barrel. Blanks pistols come in two calibers: .22 and .32. These pistols can be hard to get and are fairly pricey. The purpose

A bumper is an oblong-shaped item used to train a dog to retrieve.

of the pistol is to make a sound that simulates the sound of a shotgun. The judges observe to see if the dog is gun-shy.

Bumper/Dummy: A bumper is an oblong-shaped, stuffed canvas item used to train a dog to retrieve. Dummies may be shaped and colored just like game birds, or they may be of a simpler design.

Collars: Tracking collars (radio or GPS) are allowed unless the host club specifies on the premium list that they are not allowed. *Note:* A battle is raging within the AKC about the use of GPS tracking collars at pointing field trials. As of this writing, rules limit the use of tracking collars to devices weighing under 5 ounces (141.5 g), excluding the strap itself. The AKC ruled in December of 2008 that GPS collars are not allowed in pointing breed field trials or pointing breed hunt tests at present.

Field: The field is a large, open, or partially wooded area. There are no set dimensions, although many fields are of a couple hundred acres in size.

Leash: Hunting test rules require that you unleash your dog, but most handlers use a short (3- or 4-foot [1-m]) lead to bring their dog into the field and to allow him to walk comfortably by their sides.

Walking Shoes/Hiking Boots: It's best to get something sturdy with traction soles—you'll be doing a great deal of walking.

Whistle: Don't count on being loud enough for your dog to hear you—you need a whistle. The whistle can be made of any material except metal. Metal tends to freeze to your mouth when it's really cold, and it can get hot enough to burn in the direct sunlight of summer. The important thing is that it has a good loud sound that will travel over distance. It's a plus if the whistle can make different sounds; with luck, you and your dog can recall what each of them means. It's even better if the whistle is distinct enough so that your dog can distinguish its sound from the whistles other handlers will be blowing.

Sponsoring Organizations

AMERICAN KENNEL CLUB (AKC)

AKC dogs work at three different levels: Junior, Senior, and Master. Junior dogs are expected to be bold and hunt independently of their bracemate. They are expected to find game and point at it until the handler gets within shooting range. A blank shot is fired by the handler to show that the dog is not gun-shy. Seniors must have all of these qualities and be steady to wing; they are allowed to break at gunshot. Seniors are expected to honor their bracemate and retrieve to their handler. A senior who "steals a point" from his bracemate cannot qualify. At the Master level, the dog must produce a finished performance, being under control of his handler at all times. He must do everything a Senior dog does, plus be steady to wing and shot and retrieve perfectly, all without too much advice from his handler.

Eligibility Requirements: Hunting tests are limited to pointing breeds, including the Brittany, German Shorthaired Pointer, English Setter, Gordon Setter, Irish Setter, Irish Red and White Setter, Pointer, Spinone Italiano, Vizsla, Weimaraner, and Wirehaired Pointing Griffon. Dogs must be at least six months of age and AKC registered or have an Indefinite Listing Privilege (ILP) number to participate. Spayed and neutered dogs are eligible.

When training your pointer to hunt, you must help him develop his natural birding instinct and learn to obey your commands.

Titles: Junior hunting tests are scored from 0 to 10 in four categories: hunting, pointing, bird-finding ability, and trainability. In Master and Senior tests, a dog is scored on two additional categories: honoring and retrieving. To receive a qualifying score, a dog must achieve a minimum score of no less than 5 points on each category and average overall a score of no less than 7. Titles include Junior Hunter (JH), Senior Hunter (MH), and Master Hunter (MH).

Premier Events: Tests are held all around the United States.

UNITED KENNEL CLUB (UKC)

In the Hunting Test Program, three tests are designed to evaluate the different levels of a dog's ability, and the dogs are judged against a standard for that level of test, not against each other. The four test levels are Started (dog must perform two single marks on land and two on water), Seasoned (dog must perform one double mark on land, one double mark on water, and a blind retrieve on land and water), Finished (among other requirements, a dog must perform one multiple mark on land, one multiple mark on water, and a blind retrieve on land and water), and Grand (same as the Finished but over tougher conditions and usually in multiple steps over several days); these levels are similar to the AKC levels of Junior, Senior, and Master. Unlike AKC tests, however, titles are awarded based on the total number of points a dog has accumulated.

In the TAN test, dogs up to the age of three are issued TAN certificates for showing a natural desire to point, even though a lack of age or training may prevent them from competing in more rigorous field trials. With regard to steadiness, dogs must establish a point on their own for a period of at least three seconds.

Eligibility Requirements: A hunting retriever or purebred gundog of any age or sex may participate. Dogs do not have to be registered.

Titles: Three titles are possible: Hunting Retriever (HR), Hunting Retriever Champion (HRCH), and Grand Hunting Retriever Champion (GRHRCH). Two Grand passes and 300 points are required for the GRHRCH title.

How to Get Started

Most sporting breed clubs have a strong contingent of field trial and hunt test enthusiasts. Your easy entry into this invigorating sport is to join the club and get to know them.

FIND A MENTOR

If you are new to hunting but dog-wise, seek out someone who is an experienced hunter. If the opposite is true, look for someone with lots of dog savvy. Whatever you do, don't try to go it alone. This is a complex activity in which you can benefit from the advice of an old hand.

GET YOUR DOG A CHECKUP

As with all strenuous sports, your dog needs a vet checkup before embarking on a hunting test. Pointing dogs run hard all day and must be in tip-top condition. Because they are out and about and exposed to other dogs (and ticks), they should be up to date on all vaccines as well.

TRAIN YOUR DOG

Your pointing dog must master two sets of skills that are in many ways opposite to each other. First, he must develop his

FROM THE EXPERT

My neighbor, Lloyd Maple, an experienced bird hunter, told me: "Most of the time dogs go crashing around in the bush making a bunch of noise. When all of a sudden everything goes ghostly still, you can bet your dog is on point. Trust him on that—he's found a bird."

natural birding instinct. That's the easy part. If he is not a natural birder and shows no interest in fluttering feathery things, it would be better to explore a different sport. Second, your dog must learn to obey your commands, even when his instinct may be "pointing" him in a different direction. Most of your training time will be spent on this aspect.

To get these skills just right, you must be prepared to do some drill work. However, you have to be dog savvy enough to stop drilling and do something else when you see his interest start to flag. Basic puppy obedience can be worked on in 15-minute segments twice a day. Field work, where skills are honed, takes longer. Because it's best to practice in different fields, join a hunt club that has extensive grounds in which to practice. You should work about an hour per session once in the field. Unless you really have plenty of time to devote to this activity, choose a different one.

If, while you are out in the field, your dog startles a rabbit rather than a bird, don't punish or scold him, but don't praise him either. Save your praise for when he pays attention to birds. The sensitive pointing dog will soon pick up the message. If he actually points at anything (even a cat), praise him. You want to work on hunting instinct before pointing expertise—that comes later.

You will also need to introduce your dog to gunfire, an absolute necessity. Start with a blanks pistol and fire when he is at a distance. As he becomes more accustomed to the sound, you can move in closer. Your dog should also get used to water. Even though many hunting trials don't include water, some do. You dog should not be afraid to plunge in!

Next, work on retrieving, which is just another fetch game. Use your dog's favorite toy or a training dummy. It's important when teaching the retrieve not to grab the dummy as soon as he brings it back to you. That will only encourage him to hold onto it longer next time or even try to run off with it.

Strategies for Success

Always trust and believe in your dog. If he is on a solid point, you can bet that there is a bird in the brush, even if you can't see it. Do what you can to flush it out.

STAY AWAY FROM ELECTRONIC COLLARS

Many people believe that pointing dogs must be trained with electronic collars, in which case it's hard to see how our ancestors, who developed these breeds in the first place, ever managed to shoot anything. The truth is that you can teach your dog hunting skills without pain and force—it may take longer, but your dog will remember what he learns better and will forge a relationship with you based on love rather than fear.

WEAR A HAT

Wear a hat to all pointing events. Why? Because when your dog goes into that nice brilliant point, you can wave it enthusiastically at the judges and yell: "POINT!" They might miss it otherwise.

BE A GRACIOUS COMPETITOR

When you leave the field, be sure to thank everyone involved—even if you lost. They have been hard at work from the earliest hours and will remember a kind word and good sportsmanship. It may not help you today, but people tend to remember gracious behavior.

ADDITIONAL ORGANIZATIONS

Canadian Kennel Club (CKC)
www.ckc.ca

Chapter 21

Hunting Tests, Retrievers

Definition

The retriever hunting test is a noncompetitive sporting event designed to test a dog's ability to hunt birds under natural conditions. Each entrant is judged against a standard, not each other, so all entrants at a particular hunting test may pass or fail. This is a blood sport in which birds may be killed for the purpose of the test.

The retrieving hunting test evaluates a dog's ability to hunt birds under natural conditions.

History of Retriever Hunting Tests

Retriever hunting tests were developed not only because many owners thought that field trials were too expensive and too competitive but also because field trials presented conditions that were not much like what a hunter would naturally encounter in a day's hunting. Retriever hunting tests are designed to remedy all that. The American Kennel Club (AKC) hunting test program for retrievers was established in 1985. The first year saw 13 events; now there are hundreds.

The United Kennel Club (UKC) works with its subsidiary, the Hunting Retriever Club (HRC), to run tests for "hunting retriever dogs," an idea born in 1983. The concept is not to judge dogs against each other, as happens in a field trial, but to judge each dog's individual ability to hunt. Its first event was held in September of that year, with 140 dogs participating.

Overview

Land and water, seek and fetch—retrievers do it all. And they work well with their handlers! Retriever hunting tests make it possible for ordinary dog owners to assist their dogs in doing what they like most: retrieving.

AMERICAN KENNEL CLUB (AKC)

AKC hunting tests are usually put on by local clubs, which set the courses and "plant" the birds. Dogs are run in braces (pairs), with their handler on foot. The judge rides on a horse, and the gallery (spectators) may also be on horseback. Dogs are expected to perform equally well on land and water and are thoroughly tested in both.

Dogs are brought up to a line (the starting point); the birds are downed (shot—downed birds are also called "marks"), and the dog is expected to retrieve them gently to the hunter's hand. When ordered to retrieve, the dog is expected to move quickly to retrieve both marked falls or unmarked falls after the handler indicates the line for falls that the dog hasn't observed himself. If the dog pays no attention to the directions or whistles of his handler, he is marked weak in response and trainability. Dogs who find the bird unaided receive higher scores than those who have to be "handled" to the retrieve. After retrieving the bird, the dog must then sit and await further orders.

The skills of the candidates are graded on a point system of 1 to 10. There are two judges. Dogs can participate in three levels—Junior, Senior, and Master—and are graded on the following abilities: marking (memory), style, perseverance (courage, hunting), and trainability (steadiness, control, and response and delivery). The Junior

BLIND VERSUS MARKED RETRIEVES

If the dog did not happen to actually see the bird fall, he should be able to be guided to it by the hunter's voice and hand signals. This kind of retrieve is called a "blind retrieve" and is an important skill for every working retriever. A retrieve that a dog actually sees is called a "marked retrieve."

dog is judged only on marked retrieves, not blind retrieves. The dog need not be steady, he may be held. At the Senior level, the dog must be able to handle easy blind retrieves, honor another dog's retrieve, and be steady. At the Master's level, the dog must retrieve difficult marking situations such as three or more downed birds prior to being sent to retrieve, and he must be able to honor another dog's retrieve. All test levels should be designed to simulate, as closely as possible, real-life hunting situations, including natural hazards, obstacles, and decoys.

UNITED KENNEL CLUB (UKC)

HUNTING RETRIEVER TEST

The Hunting Retriever Test is held by the HRC, which works with the UKC on this event. For pointers, the test is called an Upland Game Test, which requires dogs to be steady to wing and shot (not react adversely when a bird flushes and a shot is fired). The dog is required to locate and retrieve game as directed by the judge. They are also required to honor another dog.

A live bird is thrown or released in full view of the dog and within scenting distance. The distance from the bird to the dog should be within scenting distance when the bird is released. The dog should be eager to hunt all available cover diligently and be under control. The dog should immediately return to the previous hunting range upon being commanded by his handler. The handler will shoot the gun, and the gunners may kill the bird. If the dog does not immediately return to the hunting area, he fails the test.

It is recommended that all participants at an HRC/UKC-licensed event have participated in an approved hunting safety course.

Requirements

DOGS
- bird-finding ability
- honoring ability (depending on division)
- hunting ability
- obedience to basic commands

FUN FACT

It's bound to happen. Sooner or later, your retriever may be skunked! If this happens, be prepared with a commercial deskunker or a simple homemade mixture. To make your own, combine 1 quart (1 l) of hydrogen peroxide, 1/4 cup of baking soda, and 1 squirt of liquid dishwashing soap. Mix it up, rub it in, let it stand a few minutes, and then rinse your dog. Most of the smell will be gone.

- retrieving ability
- steadiness to wing and shot (depending on division)
- trainability

HANDLERS
- good physical condition
- gun-knowledgeable
- hunting experience (for higher levels)

Equipment and Supplies
- blanks pistol
- bumper/dummy
- collar
- field
- leash
- walking shoes/hiking boots
- whistle
- winger

Blanks/Starter Pistol: Most field trials and hunting tests require the handler to carry a blanks pistol while her dog is on the course. A blanks pistol is one that has been manufactured specifically for firing only blank cartridges and has a solid barrel. Blanks pistols come in two calibers: .22 and .32. These pistols can be hard to get and are fairly pricey. The purpose of the pistol is to make a sound that simulates the sound of a shotgun. The judges observe to see if the dog is gun-shy.

Bumper/Dummy: A bumper is an oblong-shaped, stuffed canvas item used to train a dog to retrieve. Dummies may be shaped and colored just like game birds or may be of a simpler design.

You can use a dummy to help your dog learn to retrieve on land and in water.

Collar: Although some trainers use shock collars to train their dogs, rules do not permit them in tests. GPS tracking collars are not allowed either. Because new technology is available all the time, check with the governing body before investing in a tracking collar to see if it is permitted.

Field: The hunting test field is simply a large area that contains a body of water.

Leash: Hunting test rules require that you unleash your dog, but most handlers use a short (3- or 4-foot [1-m]) lead to bring their dog into the field and to allow him to walk comfortably by their sides.

Walking Shoes/Hiking Boots: It's best to get something sturdy with traction soles—you'll be doing a great deal of walking.

Whistle: Don't count on being loud enough for your dog to hear you—you need a whistle. The whistle can be made of any material except metal. Metal tends to freeze to your mouth when it's really cold, and it can get hot enough to burn in the direct sunlight of summer. The important thing is that it has a good loud sound that will travel over distance. It's a plus if the whistle can make different sounds; with luck, you and your dog can recall what each of them means. It's even better if the whistle is distinct enough so that your dog can distinguish its sound from the whistles other handlers will be blowing.

Winger: A winger is a device that throws one (dead) bird at a time so that the retriever can mark the bird's arc and then retrieve it.

Sponsoring Organizations

AMERICAN KENNEL CLUB (AKC)

At the Junior level, the dog may be led to the line on leash or by his buckle collar. He may be restrained gently while honoring another dog's retrieve and until sent to retrieve. The Junior hunting test includes four single marked retrieves, two on land and two on water. The handler carries an unloaded shotgun on at least two of the marks but need not shoulder it.

At the Senior level, the test includes a minimum of four hunting situations: one land blind, one water blind, one double mark on land, and one double mark on water. ("Double" means two birds down to retrieve before the dog is sent for the first one and then the second.) At least one diversion shot (a shot in which no bird is thrown; it is used to test the dog's ability to pay attention to the task at hand) is fired at this level.

At the Master level, numerous decoys are used, and the dog is tested in a minimum of five hunting situations. A Master Hunting Dog is expected to honor other dogs' retrieves, and trainability is evaluated more stringently than in Senior hunting tests.

At the Senior and Master levels, the dog must come quietly and steadily up to the line and honor a working dog's retrieve off leash and without a collar. On these levels, the handler carries and shoulders an empty shotgun.

Eligibility Requirements: All registered dogs at least six months of age of the following retrieving breeds are eligible for testing: Chesapeake Bay Retrievers, Curly-Coated Retrievers, Flat-Coated Retrievers, Golden Retrievers, Irish Water Spaniels, Labrador Retrievers, Nova Scotia Duck Tolling Retrievers, and Standard Poodles. Spayed or neutered dogs are eligible to compete.

Titles: To receive a qualifying score at the Junior level, which is scored on a 1 to 10 scale, a dog must acquire a minimum average at least 5 points in each skill, with an overall average score for the entire test of at least 7 to earn the title of Junior Hunter (JH). Senior dog hunting requirements are divided into six categories, also scored on a 1 to 10 scale. The Senior Hunter (SH) title requires qualifying scores in five Senior hunting tests or a Junior Hunter title plus four qualifying scores in senior hunting tests. The dog with a Master Hunter (MH) title is a finished, experienced hunting companion. As with the Senior level, requirements are divided into six categories, scored on a 1 to 10 scale. To earn the Master Hunter title, a dog must earn qualifying scores in six master hunting tests or earn the Senior Hunter title plus qualifying scores in five Master hunting tests. In both the Senior and Master level, a dog must receive an overall average of at least 7 for the entire test and also receive separate scores of not less than 5 in each category related to marking, as well as separate scores of not less than 5 in each category related to blinds.

Premier Events: Hunting tests are held all around the United States.

UNITED KENNEL CLUB (UKC)

In the Hunting Test Program, three tests are designed to evaluate the different levels of a dog's ability, and the dogs are judged against a standard for that level of test, not against each other. The four test levels are Started (dog must perform two single marks on land and two on water), Seasoned (dog must perform one double mark on land, one double mark on water, and a blind retrieve on land and water), Finished (among other requirements, a dog must perform one multiple mark on land, one multiple mark on water, and a blind retrieve on land and water), and Grand (same as the Finished but over tougher conditions and usually done in multiple steps over several days); these levels are similar to the AKC levels of Junior, Senior, and Master. Unlike AKC tests, however, titles are awarded based on the total number of points a dog has accumulated.

Eligibility Requirements: A hunting retriever or purebred gundog of any age or sex may participate. Dogs do not have to be registered.

Titles: Three titles are possible: Hunting Retriever (HR), Hunting Retriever Champion (HRCH), and Grand Hunting Retriever Champion (GRHRCH). Two Grand passes and 300 points are required for the GRHRCH title.

Premier Events: Hunting tests are held all around the United States.

How to Get Started

Before you get started, download or buy a copy of the AKC or UKC rule book and read it carefully. Then observe a few hunting tests to see if this is something you'd like to try for yourself. This can be an expensive, time-consuming sport—retriever training is often done by professionals, so if you want to do it yourself, you must be willing to commit the time.

GET YOUR DOG A CHECKUP

Running and swimming in cold water in arduous, so take your dog to the vet to make sure that he is up to it, as well as current on all of his vaccines.

FIND A MENTOR, JOIN A CLUB

It's best if you can enlist the help of an experienced person to help you; nothing replaces a guiding hand. Also, join a local retriever club and get active! The more you run your dog, the more likely it is that you will achieve your goal.

FROM THE EXPERT

Well-known retriever trainer Jerry Holden suggests a good way to teach your puppy to retrieve: Use your hallway. When you throw the ball or bumper down the hall, your puppy is almost bound to bring it back to you—he has nowhere else to run to.

Don't overtrain your dog for this sport, or he may become bored and stop paying attention.

TRAIN YOUR DOG

Start training your dog are early as possible. You will have the greatest success if you begin with a puppy or young dog. Introduce him to birds. If there are no waterfowl around, you may have to resort to barn pigeons, which can be purchased commercially at a game farm or hunting preserve for a low price.

Make sure that your dog is obedience trained; hunting ability is nothing unless your dog follows your commands, hand signals, voice, or whistle. (Retrievers are generally taught to sit and come by a whistled signal.) In addition, your dog will need to learn to heel in and out of the field.

Learning a reliable retrieve and to honor another dog's retrieve are very important skills. (Before you even start to teach this, make sure that your dog has a healthy mouth!) Most retrievers love to fetch, and you can simply work on refining your dog's natural skills. If your dog doesn't seem to get it, then you will require the help of a mentor.

Don't overtrain your dog. Dogs are highly intelligent animals who get bored quickly. Early training sessions should last no longer than 20 minutes. Although AKC trials are open to pups as young as six months, many experts recommend not starting with real game until dogs are ten months old or more.

Strategies for Success

Some of the best strategies for success include positively training your dog and keeping your dog to himself.

DON'T USE ELECTRONIC COLLARS

While using electric shock collars (euphemistically called training collars) may produce fast "results," reward training is a surer and purer road to sweet success. Using "pain to train" results in a fearful dog, not a reliable partner.

KEEP YOUR DOG TO HIMSELF

When at an event, never introduce dogs to each other without the other handler's permission, and never attempt to handle, talk to, or control another handler's dog. (This is considered lack of etiquette. The dogs are expected to be all business and keep their minds on the task at hand.)

ADDITIONAL ORGANIZATIONS

American Hunting Dog Club (AHDC)
www.ahdc.org
Canadian Kennel Club (CKC)
www.ckc.ca
North American Hunting Retriever Association (NAHRA)
www.nahranews.org

Chapter 22

Hunting Tests, Spaniels

Definition

Hunting tests are designed to evaluate the abilities of flushing spaniels by testing them against a standard, not against each other. Spaniels are judged on their natural and trained ability to hunt, flush, and retrieve their game on both land and in water. This is a blood sport in which birds may be killed for the purpose of the test.

In a hunting test, spaniels are evaluated on their ability to hunt, flush, and retrieve game.

History of Spaniel Hunting Tests

The idea for spaniel hunting tests began simply as a request for an American Kennel Club (AKC)-sanctioned event to be known as the "Spaniel Gun Dog Qualification." The purpose was to gauge a dog's natural abilities during an event that resembled real hunting conditions more accurately than the more competitive field trial. A Spaniel Hunting Test Advisory Committee was formed and met on March 9–10, 1985, in New York City. Today, about 80 hunting tests are held every year all around the United States.

The United Kennel Club (UKC) works with its subsidiary, the Hunting Retriever Club (HRC), to also run tests for "hunting retriever dogs," an idea born in 1983. The concept was not to judge dogs against each other, as happens in a field trial, but to judge each dog's individual ability to hunt. Their first event was held in September of that year, with 140 dogs participating.

Overview

During a spaniel hunting test, dogs are judged on their ability to demonstrate the performance of a properly trained spaniel in any real-life situation in the field. The test occurs on land with some amount of cover. The "planter" plants birds in the field, and the field marshal then calls the first handler and dog to the starting line. Spaniels are known for their "quartering pattern," in which they go back and forth over the search area rather like a windshield wiper. Judges watch this movement carefully.

AMERICAN KENNEL CLUB (AKC)

In an AKC hunting test, dogs are scored on their hunting ability, bird-finding ability, flushing ability, trained abilities, and retrieving ability. The test has three levels: Junior, Senior, and Master. Elements of the test include:

Field: The dog is expected to cover the ground in a relatively efficient manner to locate and retrieve any birds (shot or caught) back to the handler. Ideally, each dog will have the opportunity to find, flush, and retrieve two birds.

Hunt Dead: This task occurs on land and simulates a situation in which someone has shot a bird that has landed in a location not seen by you or your dog. You are expected to send your dog to the general location so that he can retrieve the bird back to you.

Water Retrieve: The dog must retrieve a dead bird in the water. Although the bird is already dead, someone fires a gun to test if the dog is gun-shy.

Water Blind: This skill is only required at the Master Hunter level. Unlike in the Hunt Dead category, the dog must cross a body of water to find this retrieve. Along the way, he is expected to respond to commands from the handler in an efficient manner that gets him to the bird as quickly as possible, rather than simply being sent on a single command to cross the water and be left to his own devices to find the bird. This skill demonstrates his obedience and control.

Successful hunting test spaniels have flushing and hunting ability.

UNITED KENNEL CLUB (UKC)

HUNTING RETRIEVER TEST

This test is held by the HRC, which works with the UKC on this event. For pointers, the test is called an Upland Game Test, which requires dogs to be steady to wing and shot (not react adversely when a bird flushes and shots are fired). The dog is required to locate and retrieve game as directed by the judge. They are also required to honor another dog's retrieve.

A live bird is thrown or released in full view of the dog and within scenting distance. The distance from the bird to the dog should be within scenting distance when the bird is released. The dog should be eager to hunt all available cover diligently and be under control. The dog should immediately return to the previous hunting range upon being commanded by his handler. The handler will fire a gun, and gunners may kill the bird. If the dog does not immediately return to the hunting area, he fails the test.

It is recommended that all participants at an HRC/UKC-

licensed event have participated in an approved hunting safety course.

Requirements

DOGS
- flushing ability
- hunting ability
- obedience to basic commands
- retrieving ability
- trainability

HANDLERS
- firearms proficiency
- hunting experience (for higher levels)
- good physical condition

Equipment and Supplies
- blanks pistol
- bumper/dummy
- collar

Obedience training your spaniel is instrumental to his future success in the field.

- field
- leash
- walking shoes/hiking boots
- whistle

Blanks/Starter Pistol: Most field trials and hunting tests require the handler to carry a blanks pistol while her dog is on the course. A blanks pistol is one that has been manufactured specifically for firing only blank cartridges and has a solid barrel. Blanks pistols come in two calibers: .22 and .32. These pistols can be hard to get and are fairly pricey. The purpose of the pistol is to make a sound that simulates that of a shotgun. The judges observe to see if the dog is gun-shy.

Bumper/Dummy: A bumper is an oblong-shaped, stuffed canvas item used to train a dog to retrieve. Dummies may be shaped and colored just like game birds or may be of a simpler design.

Collar: Although some trainers use shock collars to train their dogs, rules do not permit them in tests. GPS tracking collars are not allowed either. Because new technology is available all the time, check with the governing body before investing in a tracking collar to see if it is permitted.

Field: Tests take place in a large open field with plenty of brush.

Leash: Hunting test rules require that you unleash your dog, but most handlers use a short (3- or 4-foot [1-m]) lead to bring their dog into the field and to allow him to walk comfortably by their sides.

Walking Shoes/Hiking Boots: It's best to get something sturdy with traction soles—you'll be doing a great deal of walking.

Whistle: Don't count on being loud enough for your dog to hear you—you need a whistle. The whistle can be made of any material except metal, which tends to freeze to your mouth when it's really cold and can get hot enough to burn in the direct sunlight of summer. It must have a good loud sound that will travel over distance. It's a plus if the whistle can make different sounds; with luck, you and

FUN FACT

Each spaniel has his own particular hunting style. The American Water Spaniel, for instance, works at a steady pace, moving from side to side in a sweeping fashion. The Boykin Spaniel has a characteristic "hesitation flush." The Clumber moves slowly, in an almost casual (but no less effective) way. The Cocker Spaniel is animated and often looks to his handler for advice; once he finds the bird, he flushes boldly. The English Cocker Spaniel is described as a merry and enthusiastic dog who changes his pace with changing conditions. The English Springer Spaniel is flashy yet biddable, with a hard-driving flush. The Field Spaniel has an efficient ground-covering trot, and he will often abandon a strict quartering pattern. The Welsh Springer Spaniel is brisk and methodical, alternating between air and ground scenting. The Sussex Spaniel moves easily through thick cover, with his head to the ground.

FROM THE EXPERT

According to James B. Spencer's book *Hup: Training Spaniels the American Way,* retrieving to human beings is not a natural behavior. Dogs do want to retrieve, but they want to bring the object (including dead birds) back to their lairs, not to a person. The human's job is to waylay the errant pup and con him into giving up the object.

your dog can recall what each of them means. It's even better if the whistle is distinct enough so that your dog can distinguish its sound from the whistles other handlers will be blowing.

Sponsoring Organizations

AMERICAN KENNEL CLUB (AKC)

As mentioned earlier, the AKC hunting test has three levels: Junior, Senior, and Master. The Junior Hunter must pass the Field and Water Retrieve portions of the test; the Senior Hunter Must pass the Field, Hunt Dead, and Water Retrieve portions of the test; and the Master Hunter must pass the Field, Hunt Dead, Water Retrieve, and Water Blind portions. A dog does not have to complete a lower level before going on to a higher one. At each level, dogs are tested on both land and water. Unlike in field trials, dogs are not braced for quartering work. A typical spaniel test takes only one day, and judges evaluate each dog according to the appropriate hunting style standards for his breed.

Eligibility Requirements: All flushing spaniels are eligible to participate; these include the American Water Spaniel, Boykin Spaniel, Clumber Spaniel, Cocker Spaniel, English Springer Spaniel, Field Spaniel, Sussex Spaniel, and Welsh Springer Spaniel. Dogs must be at least six months of age. Rescue dogs (purebred) or purebred dogs without registration paperwork may apply for AKC Indefinite Listing Privilege (ILP) to be able to compete in events. Spayed or neutered dogs are eligible.

Titles: Available titles are Junior Hunter (JH), Senior Hunter (SH), and Master Hunter (MH). Each level has a written standard of expectations that must be met before a qualifying score can be given. Dogs are scored 0 to 10 in the categories of hunting ability, bird-finding ability, flushing ability, trained abilities, and retrieving ability. To receive a qualifying score, a dog must acquire a minimum average of not less than 5 points on each of these categories of abilities. The overall average score may not be less than 7.

Premier Events: Hunting tests are held all over the United States.

UNITED KENNEL CLUB (UKC)

In the Hunting Test Program, three tests are designed to evaluate the different levels of a dog's ability, and dogs are judged against a standard for that level of test, not against each other. The four test levels are Started (dog must perform two single marks on land and two on water), Seasoned (dog must perform one double mark on land, one double mark on water, and a blind retrieve on land and water), Finished (among other requirements, a dog must perform one multiple mark on land, one multiple mark on water, and a blind retrieve on land and water), and Grand (same as the Finished but over tougher conditions and usually done in multiple steps over several days); these are similar to the AKC levels of Junior, Senior, and Master. Unlike AKC tests, however, titles are awarded based on the total number of points a dog has accumulated.

Eligibility Requirements: A hunting retriever or purebred gundog of any age or sex may participate. Dogs do not have to be registered.

Titles: Three titles are possible: Hunting Retriever (HR), Hunting Retriever Champion (HRCH), and Grand Hunting Retriever Champion (GRHRCH). Two Grand passes and 300 points are required for the GRHRCH title.

Premier Events: Hunting tests are held all around the United States.

How to Get Started

With the right dog, getting started in a spaniel hunting test is a fun way to strengthen your relationship.

GET YOUR DOG A CHECKUP

A hunt test involves vigorous physical activity. You'll need to get your dog checked out by his vet to make sure that he can handle it. He should also be up to date on his vaccinations because he will be around other dogs.

FIND A MENTOR

The easiest and most effective way to get started in this sport is to find a mentor. Your local kennel or field trial club can help you locate a knowledgeable mentor. These clubs are your one-stop place to find essential information, training tips, and moral support.

JOIN, ATTEND, OBSERVE

Getting a good start in hunting tests is a 1-2-3 process. The first step is to join a dog club that holds such trials. The second step is to attend a hunting test seminar offered by one of the sponsoring organizations. This will give you training tips and thoroughly acquaint you with the rules. The third essential step is to observe actual hunting tests as often as possible; watching a real event is a great way to learn.

TRAIN YOUR DOG

Training a spaniel proceeds in several stages. First is regular puppy training, which includes housetraining, walking calmly on a leash, and being socialized. Second is obedience training, which includes learning the basic commands and play retrieving.

Next, teach your puppy to retrieve. When he brings back the dummy to you, reward him with play so that he understands that the work is followed by reward. If he doesn't retrieve, don't chase him; he'll just turn the session into a game of keep-away. Try simply walking away from him, relying on his instinctive desire to chase you. If this behavior is a recurring problem, attach a 30-foot (9-m) leash (don't hang onto it when your dog is running after the dummy) and then draw him gently and slowly toward you, encouraging him at the same time.

Finally, after he has learned to retrieve, your spaniel should be introduced to birds and water. He will also need to be acclimated to the sound of gunfire.

Strategies for Success

For optimal hunt test success, obedience train your dog
without overwhelming him with too many commands.

OBEDIENCE TRAIN YOUR DOG

Obedience is critical. Spaniels work close to their handlers
and are expected to be under control at all times, especially
when they are working in the uplands. To be successful
in training, set up a schedule—even just five or ten
minutes once or twice a day is fine—but don't be
haphazard about it.

KEEP YOUR COMMANDS SIMPLE

Keep commands simple, and don't overwhelm your puppy
by "overhandling." The following are essential for spaniels
to learn:

- Come in: Come back from running around in the
  bushes (taught with voice and whistle).
- Down: Lie down, normally from a *sit* position.
- Heel: Walk beside the handler, usually on the left
  side.
- Hup: Spanielese for "sit."
- Kennel!: Go into the run or kennel.
- Release: Get up from previous position.
- Stay: Remain in that spot, freeze.

ADDITIONAL ORGANIZATIONS

American Hunting Dog Club (AHDC)
www.ahdc.org
Canadian Kennel Club (CKC)
www.ckc.ca
North American Hunting Retriever Association (NAHRA)
www.nahranews.org/

Chapter 23

Lure Coursing

Definition

Lure coursing is a sport specifically developed for sighthounds. This fun (and fast!) event tests a dog's ability to hunt by sight or coursing instinct.

OTHER SIGHTHOUND EVENTS

In addition to lure coursing, a number of speedy events are available to the sighthound aficionado. One such event is offered by the Large Gazehound Racing Association (LGRA). This group has no connection with the commercial racing industry. In this event, the hounds race 200 yards (183 m) on a straight, flat track. There are three programs, with heats made up of a maximum of four dogs. A variety of sighthound breeds are eligible.

History of Lure Coursing

Lure coursing dates back to ancient times and has been a much-loved sport throughout the ages. Murals of long-legged, regal hounds have been found adorning the walls of 4,000-year-old Egyptian tombs. In the Middle Ages, the sport was a favorite pastime reserved only for royalty, so much so that commoners were not permitted to own Greyhounds or other sighthounds. Today, however, the sport has become a major performance event for dog enthusiasts, both young and old, around the globe.

In the United States, the modern form of lure coursing dates back as far as the late 1800s. Known as "closed park coursing," competitions were held in which sighthounds were simply let loose in an enclosed space to chase live game, such as a rabbit. Around 1920, the mechanical lure (as seen in Greyhound racing) began to replace most live-game coursing, although it took away from the excitement of watching a sighthound's sharp twists and turns as he pursued his prey.

Enter Lyle Gillette, dog enthusiast and avid sighthound breeder. In the early 1970s, he developed a new kind of lure that not only did away with the need for live game but that was portable and would simulate the twists and turns of live game. By 1973, Gillette and other California sighthound enthusiasts had organized lure coursing under the American Sighthound Field Association (ASFA). It wasn't until almost 20 years later that the American Kennel Club's (AKC) Board of Directors finally voted to approve lure coursing regulations and to sanction the sport. A new era in lure coursing had begun.

Overview

Lure coursing is a performance event that gauges a sighthound's ability to hunt by sight rather than scent. These events can be either competitive or noncompetitive. The tests are conducted over an open-field course 500 to 1,000 yards (457 to 914.5 m) in length and sometimes longer. When released, each dog is judged (and awarded points) on his speed, agility, endurance, and overall ability in the field; dogs are also judged on how well they follow the lure (instead of taking shortcuts to try to head off the lure).

A mechanical white plastic lure is attached to a braided line connected to a pulley system. The lure is pulled along the course, simulating the motion of a rabbit darting around in a field. The object is for the hounds to chase the lure for the specified distance and keep their interest focused on the lure until they have run the course.

Most runs are conducted with three dogs of the same breed running against each other. The dogs wear different-colored blankets (yellow, pink, and blue) to distinguish them from one another. Yellow always starts on the left, pink in the middle, and blue on the right.

Requirements

Dogs

- agility
- endurance
- speed
- strong chase instinct

Handlers

- ability to sit back, relax, and watch your dog have fun

Equipment and Supplies

- blankets
- field
- lure
- portable lure coursing system
- quick-release collar

Dogs are allowed to tear up the lure at the end of a run as a reward for their efforts.

Blankets: These colorful cloths are worn by dogs participating in the event to distinguish them from one another. The colors used are bright pink, blue, and yellow.

Field: The field used is 600 to 800 yards (549 to 731 m) for the AKC and 500 to 1,000 or more yards for the ASFA (457 to 914.5 m).

Lure: The lure is usually made of white plastic; a white plastic bag works just fine. Even though these dogs hunt by sight, evolution never taught them to distinguish a bag from a rabbit.

Portable Lure Coursing System: These consist of a pulley and a machine (which can be battery powered) to run the "rabbit." They are expensive, but you don't have to own one yourself. The sponsoring organization will provide it. Very few people have a big enough yard for this activity anyway.

Quick-Release Collar: These are wide, decorative collars specifically designed for small-headed sighthounds; the collars can be quickly released during a lure coursing event. Many use large D-rings on the sides of the neck piece. Some come with a matching lead.

Sponsoring Organizations

AMERICAN KENNEL CLUB (AKC)

The AKC offers three regular stakes (classes): Open, Specials, and Open Veteran. The Open Stake is open to all sighthounds who have earned the title of Junior Courser or other qualifying performance title. Special Stakes are open to hounds who have earned the status of AKC Field Champion and are eligible to enter the Open Stakes. Open Veteran Stakes are open to those dogs eligible to enter the Open or Special Stakes and who meet the age requirement designated by the breed's parent club. Veteran Stakes are optional events held by the host club.

Eligibility Requirements: Afghan Hounds, Basenjis, Borzois, Greyhounds, Ibizan Hounds, Irish Wolfhounds, Italian Greyhounds, Pharaoh Hounds, Rhodesian Ridgebacks, Salukis, Scottish Deerhounds, and Whippets are eligible. The AKC also permits certain Foundation Stock Service (FSS) breeds that meet specific criteria to participate in lure coursing events, including the Azawakh, Portuguese Podengo, Sloughi, and Thai Ridgeback. Dogs must be one year of age or older and in good health. Spayed and neutered dogs are eligible to participate.

Titles: *Junior Courser (JC):* To be awarded this title, dogs must run alone in two events under two different judges or panels. The course is a distance of 600 feet (183 m) and incorporates at least four turns. To earn the title, the dog must run the entire course without stopping. A "pass" or "fail" is given rather than a numeric score. *Senior Courser (SC):* A dog competing for the SC title must run with at least one other hound. This title is awarded based on the dog's performance, earning qualifying scores in four AKC field trials under two different judges or judging panels. *Master Courser (MC):* The title of MC is awarded after a dog has acquired the Senior Courser title and has earned an additional 25 qualifying scores (with competition)

FROM THE EXPERT

Bob Mason, AKC senior executive field representative, writes in his article "Luring Coursing 101" that he begins encouraging his pups to chase when they are only ten weeks old. He attaches a 3-foot (1-m) nylon cord to a fishing pole and ties a toy to it. After a few days, he replaces the toy with a plastic garbage bag like those they will be soon chasing. Soon he lets them begin to actually run 50 or 75 yards (45.5 or 68.5 m), although he cautions that you not let your dog overexert himself.

in either Open, Open Veteran, or Special Stakes. *Field Championship (FC):* To be awarded the FC title, a dog must have earned 15 championship points, including two first placements (3 points or more) under two different judges. At least one of these points must have been earned in competition with a dog of the same breed. *Lure Courser Excellent (LCX):* This is a cumulative title awarded to a dog who has also been awarded the FC title and has earned 45 additional championship points. Each time the dog earns 45 championship points, the title increases in level.

Premier Events: The AKC holds a National Lure Coursing Championship.

AMERICAN SIGHTHOUND FIELD ASSOCIATION (ASFA)

The ASFA offers three regular stakes: Open, Field Champion, and Veteran. The Open Stake is open to dogs who have been certified by a licensed judge to compete or have previously participated in an Open Stake. Hounds who have received a lure coursing or racing title from another recognized organization are also permitted to compete. Field Champion Stakes are open to dogs who are recorded as Field Champions. Finally, dogs who are at least six years of age (for Irish Wolfhounds, five; Whippets, seven) and who have not previously been entered in either the Open or another regular stake in the same trial are eligible to participate in the Veteran Stakes.

In addition to the regular stakes, a number of optional stakes may be held at the discretion of the host organization. These can include Singles, Limited, Best in Field, Kennel, and Breeder Stakes.

Eligibility Requirements: Afghan Hounds, Basenjis, Borzois, Greyhounds, Ibizan Hounds, Irish Wolfhounds, Italian Greyhounds, Pharaoh Hounds, Rhodesian Ridgebacks, Salukis, Scottish Deerhounds, and Whippets are eligible. The ASFA requires that participating dogs be registered with the AKC or National Greyhound Association (NGA). It will also allow dogs to participate who have a Critique Case Number (CCN) from the Saluki Club of America (SCOA) or are registered with an AKC-recognized foreign registry. A hound must be at least 11 months old to run in a certification course. Spayed and neutered animals may participate.

Titles: *Field Champion (FCh):* A dog must have accumulated 100 points that include either two first placements or one first placement and two second placements. *Veteran Field Champion (V-FCh):* This title is awarded to hounds who have attained 75 championship points in Veteran Stake competition. These championship points must be earned in competition and include two first placements or one first placement and two second placements. *Lure Courser of Merit (LCM):* This is awarded to a hound who has received the title of FCh and has continued to compete. To receive merit, the dog must earn four first placements in competition and 300 additional points in an ASFA Field Champion Stake. This is a cumulative title; each time the hound earns an additional four first placements and 300 points, the level of merit increases. *Veteran Lure Courser of Merit (V-LCM):* The Veteran merit is awarded to a hound who has received the title of Veteran Field Champion and has continued to compete.

Lure coursing is a confidence-building sport that will also help channel excess energy.

The dog must earn four first placements in competition and 200 points. This is also a cumulative title; each time the hound earns an additional four first placements and 200 points, the level of merit increases.

Premier Events: Events are held throughout the year, all around the United States. There are regional invitationals, as well as an annual Grand National and a National Greyhound Specialty.

How to Get Started

Lure coursing builds confidence and gives your dog an acceptable channel for his excess energy. Most of all, it's fun and an excellent way to bond with your pet.

GET YOUR DOG A CHECKUP

This is a very strenuous event, requiring not only bursts of speed but also sharp twists and turns. (This can be hard on a young dog's joints; it's important that your dog is fully mature before he competes in earnest.) Make sure that your dog is checked thoroughly by his vet before embarking on this endeavor. Also, because he will be around other dogs, he must be kept current on his vaccinations.

FIND A MENTOR

Possibly the best (and most often given) advice for getting started in lure coursing is to seek out someone who already participates in these events. Lure coursing veterans, while a competitive bunch, are usually more than willing to give pointers to someone interested in becoming involved with the sport. Speaking with someone knowledgeable in the sport is a great way to gauge whether you (and your dog) will enjoy it.

GO TO EVENTS

To be successful in the sport of lure coursing, take the time to attend actual events. Don't just limit yourself to one event—go to many, and go often. By observing both handlers and dogs in action, you can better acquaint yourself with the sport and pick up a few tricks along the way.

While at the event, don't limit yourself to asking only one handler for her take on the best way to train your dog. Be brave! Ask as many people as are willing to talk to you. Get opinions from handlers of a variety of dog breeds and dispositions. By doing so, you will arm yourself with knowledge of the sport and be able to incorporate many different training techniques into your own regimen.

TRAIN YOUR DOG

Opinions on how to train your sighthound for lure coursing vary. Factors such as breed, size, age, and the dog's personality all contribute to how well he will respond to different training methods. And of course, natural predilection is important: Some dogs will literally bolt out of their handler's grasp at the sight of the lure; others are simply not interested.

Although dogs should be mature when they begin competing, many believe that training should begin during puppyhood. Start by playing simple chase and fetch games with your dog. These are a great way to exercise him and enhance his instincts and physical potential. Socialization is an

FUN FACT

The lure coursing equipment perfected for sighthounds is now used by several zoos to exercise and condition African wild dogs and cheetahs. Falconers also use lure coursing equipment to train and condition their short-wing hawks (raptors that hunt game on the ground) and to perform educational demonstrations of hawk hunting techniques and flight abilities without sacrificing live game.

absolute must as well. If your dog becomes so dependent on you that he won't leave your side, he won't run after the lure.

Simulating the lure course experience is rather easy. Simply attach a piece of plastic to the end of a fishing pole rigged with yarn. As you reel it in, encourage your dog to chase the lure across the lawn. Play this game with him often, but also remember to make the game short so as not to bore him.

It is also a good idea to introduce your dog to a real lure course, usually at around six months of age or older. Start out slowly, opting to have your dog run only a portion of the course—especially if he is still a puppy. About 40 yards (36.5 m) or so should be more than enough for training purposes.

Once your dog is continually chasing the lure as you play, incorporate a "friend" into your fun and games. Because competitive events have three dogs running after the lure at the same time, you will want to ensure that your dog is able to remain focused on the lure and not enticed to chase those running beside him. Seek out a skilled canine companion, preferably of the same breed as your dog, and don't get discouraged if at first your dog exhibits more interest in his playmate. Remember, praise and practice are important!

Sighthounds are bred for running and have an instinct for hunting by sight, so these are skills that you must concentrate on as you train. The key to success is your dog's ability to remain focused on the lure and ignore anything that may distract him.

Strategies for Success

As with any other sport, the smartest thing you can do is to watch how the experts handle their dogs. Don't be afraid to ask questions, follow the commands of the judge immediately, and be a good sport!

KEEP YOUR DOG SAFE

Probably the most important thing to consider in all sports is safety. Injuries can happen very easily if you do not observe most basic safety practices. Remember to keep your pooch hydrated, especially on hot days. Some handlers even add a small amount of infant electrolyte solution to their dogs' water, but it is wise to test this prior to competition to make sure that your dog does not experience any unwanted side effects.

Don't feed your dog for several hours before competition. Sighthounds are prone to bloating and other gastric problems, and food in the stomach can increase the potential for these problems.

WARM UP YOUR DOG

Warm up your hound before an event by going for a long walk so that he can stretch his legs. Doing so will help prevent serious injury and muscle strain. If your dog does injure himself, don't ignore it. Have a vet look him over and treat the injury if necessary.

ADDITIONAL ORGANIZATIONS

Canadian Kennel Club (CKC)
www.ckc.ca
Fédération Cynologique Internationale (FCI)
www.fci.be
Mixed Breed Dog Clubs of America (MBDCA)
http://mbdca.tripod.com

Chapter 24

Obedience

Definition

Obedience tests the training of a dog as he works through a series of exercises on command. Several levels of competition exist, from basic commands to scent discrimination and directed retrieves over jumps.

History of Obedience

It has always been important for dogs to learn to obey, of course, but formal obedience training was developed in the 20th century to school military and police dogs. Most early (and sometimes harsh) theories of training came from this same source, and contemporary companion dog training is just beginning to emerge from under this shadow. Newer theories of training rely on operant conditioning and positive reinforcement (which became popular when training sea mammals). Helen Whitehouse Walker devised the first obedience test in Mount Kisco, New York, in 1933, to show the intelligence of her Poodles. The first American Kennel Club (AKC)-licensed obedience trial was held in 1936, with approximately 200 entries in 18 trials. The United Kennel Club (UKC) offered its first sanctioned obedience trials in 1979.

Overview

Obedience competition tests pretty much what it says it does: the ability of the dog to heed and follow instructions from his handler. At lower levels, simple *come*, *sit*, and *heel* are tested, while at higher levels, dogs are tested for retrieval ability over jumps and scent discrimination.

Each level of obedience competition (Novice, Open, and Utility) requires mastering a specific set of skills that increase in difficulty before advancing to the next level. Dogs begin a competition with a possible score of 200; points are deducted for mistakes or omissions. Each level of competition is divided into A and B divisions. Handlers who have never earned an obedience title or have never owned

TOP BREEDS

Retrievers, especially Golden Retrievers, excel at obedience—they were developed to work closely with people and remain true to that heritage. Herding dogs like Border Collies and Shetland Sheepdogs are naturals. Poodles also do well. However, any dog of any breed can succeed; you just have to be patient and creative.

a dog with an obedience title compete in the A Division. Handlers who have earned an obedience title in the past or who do not own the dog with whom they are competing participate in the B Division.

AMERICAN KENNEL CLUB (AKC)

In the Novice Class, exercises include heel on leash and figure-eight, heel free, stand for examination, recall, long sit (one minute), and long down (three minutes). The Open Class includes heel free and figure-eight off leash, drop on recall, retrieve on flat, retrieve over high jump, broad jump, long sit (three minutes), and long down (five minutes). The Utility Class includes signal exercise (handler uses hand signals to direct the dog to perform obedience commands), scent discrimination (dog must find handler's scent among a pile of articles), directed retrieve (dog must follow signal to retrieve a glove), moving stand and examination (dog must perform obedience commands as handler moves away, then accept judge's examination), and directed jumping (dog must clear jump indicated by handler and then return).

UNITED KENNEL CLUB (UKC)

The UKC's obedience exercises are similar to the AKC's. In the Novice Class, exercises include honor exercise, heel on leash and figure-eight, stand for examination, heel off leash, recall over high jump, and long sit group exercise. The Open Class includes honoring, heel off leash and figure-eight, drop on recall, retrieve on flat, retrieve over high jump, broad jump, and the long sit group exercise. The Utility Class exercises include signal and heeling, scent discrimination, directed marked retrieve, directed signal retrieve, consecutive recall, and directed jumping.

Dumbbells can be plastic or wooden and must be properly sized.

Requirements

Dogs

- accuracy
- adherence to hand signals
- good natural movement
- precision
- responsiveness
- retrieving ability
- scent discrimination
- sit, heel, stay, fetch, jump on command

HANDLERS

- consistency
- discipline
- patience

Equipment and Supplies

- collar
- dumbbells
- jumps
- leash
- scent articles

Collar: The rules call for slip (choke) or buckle/snap collars. No prong collars or head collars are permitted. Martingale collars are allowed as long as you can detach the leash from the collar. However, because so many different types of collars are available, the rules actually say that any collar must be "approved by the judge." If you are uncertain, bring a couple of different options with you to the show.

Dumbbells: Dumbbells, which can be plastic or wooden, must be properly sized. A dumbbell should fit snugly in the mouth just behind the canine teeth. It should be high enough so that the dog's chin does not touch the ground during pickup but not so high that it interferes with his vision.

Jumps: Obedience jumps are portable and lightweight (usually made from PVC). They include the broad, bar, and high jumps.

Leash: The leash must be made of fabric or leather and need only be long enough to provide slack on the heel on lead exercise.

Scent Articles: The handler must provide three predominantly white gloves for the directed retrieve, which must be approved by the judge. (Dirty gloves may not be accepted, so wash them.) Gloves come in various sizes— even little ones for toy breeds.

Sponsoring Organizations

AMERICAN KENNEL CLUB (AKC)

As mentioned earlier, the AKC has three classes: Novice, Open, and Utility. Novice exercises are simpler and are geared

FROM THE EXPERT

According to the American Kennel Club (AKC), the best advice is to start training early. Training a puppy is easier than training an adult dog because a puppy is more open to new ideas and has not yet developed bad habits.

toward the beginner dog. A dog in this class must demonstrate good canine companion skills such as heeling both on and off leash, coming when called, standing for a simple physical examination, and staying in both a *sit* and a *down* position with a group of dogs. The Open Class presents more challenging exercises done off leash, including retrieving and jumping, and teach a dog to perform a variety of tasks and follow commands either by voice or signal. The Utility Class is the third and highest level of obedience and includes scent discrimination, directed retrieves, jumping, and silent signal exercises.

Eligibility Requirements: Dogs must be registered with the AKC or listed with the AKC Indefinite Listing Privilege (ILP) program. Dogs must be six months of age or older. Spayed and neutered dogs are eligible.

Titles: In the Novice Class, dogs earn an AKC Companion Dog (CD) title after receiving a qualifying score under three different judges. In the Open Class, dogs earn an AKC Companion Dog Excellent (CDX) title after receiving a qualifying score under three different judges. In the Utility Class, dogs earn an AKC Utility Dog (UD) title after receiving qualifying scores from three different judges. A dog completing the UD title may earn the Utility Dog Excellent (UDX) title by receiving ten passing scores in both Open B and Utility B at the same show. The highest honor of all is the Obedience Trial Championship (OTCH) title, the so-called PhD of obedience. To obtain it, a dog and handler team must receive 100 points by placing first, second, third, or fourth in the Open B or Utility B class and a first place in Utility B and/or Open B three times. The AKC National Obedience Championship (NOC) title is awarded to one dog each year. To compete, dogs must be the top OTCH and OTCH-pointed dogs in each breed.

Premier Events: The AKC holds various regional events plus the AKC National Obedience Invitational, a two-day event in which dogs compete for the title of National Obedience Champion (NOC).

UNITED KENNEL CLUB (UKC)

Many UKC obedience exercises are geared toward working (especially hunting) dogs, and these exercises also bear a resemblance to the AKC's Canine Good Citizen® (CGC) Test. Novice, Open, and Utility Classes are offered.

Eligibility Requirements: Dogs must be at least six months of age and permanently registered with UKC or have a valid Temporary Listing (TL) number as of the day of the event.

Titles: Three obedience titles are awarded, similar to the corresponding AKC titles: Companion Dog (U-CD), Companion Dog Excellent (U-CDX), and Utility Dog (U-UD). In 1996, a fourth competitive title was added: Obedience Trial Champion (U-OCH). To obtain this title, the dog must have a U-UD and qualify in both Utility B and Open B classes at the same trial, as well as have earned a certain number of championship points.

Premier Events: The UKC offers an Obedience All-Star Invitational.

How to Get Started

To get started with obedience, begin with the AKC's CGC test; passing this will assure that your dog has the basic skills needed to advance to higher levels.

GET YOUR DOG A CHECKUP

Although dog obedience is not as rigorous a sport as agility or flying disc, your dog still needs to be in good condition and up to date on his vaccines. Make sure that he gets a complete checkup by your veterinarian.

ATTEND AN OBEDIENCE CLASS

Obedience is really a mental sport! If you are starting with a puppy, get him into classes that are geared toward competitive obedience, not just a "good manners class." The main trick is to keep your dog happy and anxious

To be successful in obedience competition, your dog will need to know basic commands, including the *down*.

to learn. A depressed or wary dog will never earn an obedience title.

TRAIN YOUR DOG

Many methods of training exist, and the popularity of one sort or another shifts according to fashion. Nowadays, the emphasis is on positive reinforcement, in which a dog is rewarded for behaving in the desired manner. Research has shown that dogs learn best at between two and four months of age, so this is the ideal time to start training. As with all training, keep sessions fun and short.

At the Novice level, dogs are expected to display simple obedience skills, including *heel, sit, down, stand, stay, down-stay*, and *recall*. Some general guidelines for training at the Novice level are as follows:

Heel: *Heel* training is a good place to start. Begin with the leash held tightly in your right hand and loosely in your left. With your dog on your left side, say "Fido, heel!" and give the leash a very gentle tug as you start moving. Walk in different directions and at different speeds; keep telling your dog to heel, and use the leash to keep him with you in the proper position. Be lavish with your praise whenever he performs correctly. Keep the lessons short, and reward him with extra petting, praise, treats, or play with a favorite toy, such as a Nylabone, when you are done.

Sit: Start with your dog at your left side. Hold a treat in front of his nose, then slowly raise it. As his nose comes up, his rear goes down. Voilà. Be lavish with your praise when he performs correctly. A few repetitions are usually enough for a dog to get the idea.

Down: *Down* (meaning lie down) starts from the sitting position. While your dog is sitting, hold the treat lower and lower in front of his nose between his forelegs. This should lure him into a *down*. Praise him when he is in proper position on the ground. Chances are it will take longer to learn the *down* than the *sit*, but be patient. (The *down* is a more vulnerable position than *sit*, so make sure that no other dogs are around when you start teaching it.)

Stand: To teach *stand*, pretend that you are going to walk in the *heel* position, but don't move after he gets up. Say "Stand" instead of "Heel." As always, be lavish with praise and treats when your dog does what you want him to do.

Stay: Teaching *stay* will probably require a little time. Start from the *heel* position. When he is standing quietly, put your hand in front of his muzzle, say "Stay," and walk a step or two away. Keep your distance from him for only a few seconds at first. Praise him lavishly while he is staying. Be patient. He naturally wants to be with you, so staying in one place while you move away is difficult for him. Work on increasing the time you stay away before working on longer distances. As he gets used to the idea of staying, you can move farther away; eventually, you will be able to walk some distance away and even move around behind him.

Down-Stay: A variation of the *stay* is the *down-stay*. Start with a *down* command and then say "Stay," just as you did when teaching the regular *stay*. Gradually increase the time he stays down and the distance you can be away from him.

Recall: The desired response is for your dog to come to you quickly. Use a small treat in your open palm as bait. As

325

When teaching an obedience skill, like the *heel*, break it down into the smallest possible components.

soon as he arrives, praise him quickly with a single word. Later, the word will replace the treat. In the obedience ring, the dog is expected to return directly to you without pausing, sniffing, or deviating from the path, so reward him appropriately. Gradually add a *sit* command after he returns because upon return, he must sit directly in front of his handler.

Strategies for Success

The most important thing you can do to improve your chances of qualifying at an obedience trial is to listen very carefully to the judge's instructions and follow them to the letter. Also, attend a few trials as an observer so that you can get firsthand knowledge of how they work before you actually enter.

TEACH COMPLEX SKILLS GRADUALLY

When teaching a complex obedience skill, break it down into the smallest possible components. Your dog will understand small steps more readily than more complex directions. You may have to guide him with your hands the first few times through an exercise. Then use food or some other reward to get him to do the exercise on his own. Numerous repetitions will probably be needed before he masters the steps. As his training advances, include distractions such as calls from a "bystander" or unusual sights and sounds. Also, train in different areas and under different conditions so that he won't become confused when he gets into a strange show ring. As the handler, you must be consistent in your directions. If your body language changes when you get into the ring, your dog will sense it and may become confused.

INDULGE YOUR DOG

Because dogs can get "ring-sour," make sure that your obedience dog gets a good open run a day or so before an obedience class. Find something he really enjoys doing—your Labrador Retriever may want to swim, your Gordon Setter may enjoy hunting birds, or your terrier may want to dig around in a hole. Indulge your dog's hobby, and he will repay you when it's showtime.

ADDITIONAL ORGANIZATIONS

American Mixed Breed Obedience Registration (AMBOR)
www.ambor.us
Australian Shepherd Club of America, Inc. (ASCA)
www.asca.org
Canadian Kennel Club (CKC)
www.ckc.ca
The Kennel Club
www.thekennelclub.org.uk
Mixed Breed Dog Clubs of America (MBDCA)
http://mbdca.tripod.com

Chapter 25

Rally

Definition

In rally competition (also known as rally obedience and rally-o), a dog-handler team demonstrates basic obedience skills while negotiating a course. Signs are posted around the course, each indicating what maneuver the dog is to perform at that station. Communication between dog and handler, either verbal or by hand signal, is encouraged, although the handler is not allowed to actually touch the dog.

History of Rally

Rally obedience was developed from formal obedience
trials in 1998 by Charles L. "Bud" Kramer, a professor
of biology/mycology at Kansas State University and an
experienced obedience trainer. (He was also active in
developing agility.) The Association of Pet Dog Trainers
(APDT) was the first to sponsor rally competition in
2000. The beginning of rally by the American Kennel Club
(AKC) was a public demonstration as a special attraction
during the lunch break of the 2000 National Obedience
Invitational Competition. From this demonstration, rally was
given Non-Regular Class status, which meant that no titles
could be earned from competition in the activity. Despite
the handicap of no titles being available and the almost
total lack of support, participation in the sport continued to
grow. Finally, in 2005, the AKC designated rally as a regular
class competition, complete with titles. In less than a year,
it became the AKC's second most successful activity. More
recently (in November 2008), the United Kennel Club
(UKC) began to offer rally competition.

Overview

Rally is deceptively simple and endlessly complicated. It
is made up of a series of known activities constituting a
positive approach to training responsive, attentive dogs.
When these known activities are arranged in an unknown
sequence, it creates an entirely new and exciting challenge to
be met by both dog and handler each time they compete in

Top Breeds

Any dog can succeed in rally. The classic "obedience"
breeds, like retrievers and herding dogs, stand out of course, but
because you are allowed to offer more encouragement, breeds
that prefer more stimulus and owner participation also do very
well. This is truly a sport where even stubborn, independent
breeds like Bulldogs and Basset Hounds can achieve greatness.
What is more, many rally dogs go on to successfully compete in
obedience.

Rally signs tell the handler what skill must be showcased at each station.

rally. Also, because unlimited communication by the handler during competition is not only allowed but encouraged, rally is a natural way of relating to a dog, when compared to the stark commands of obedience competition.

Unlike regular obedience competition, dog-handler teams proceed around a course (designed by the judge) of designated stations with the dog in the *heel* position (which has a much more relaxed definition here than in regular obedience). Unlike in traditional obedience, handlers may give instructions or praise to the dog, either verbally or by hand signal, as they proceed along the course. Actual contact between dog and handler, however, is prohibited.

Rally courses consist of numerous numbered stations laid out in a pattern similar to agility courses. The team proceeds around the course performing the exercise indicated on a sign at each station. Courses are performed on or off lead and vary according to the level of competition and the sponsoring organization. The handlers may familiarize themselves by walking the course without their dogs before the competition begins. Teams are scored according to how accurately and smoothly the dog performs each exercise; attitude and enthusiasm are also considered by the judge.

Dozens of different exercises might be used in a rally course. Most of these are variations on basic *heel* exercises and other novice obedience skills, including slow/normal/fast pace heel, halt, left/right/about turn, and finish right/left. Others are simple extensions of these exercises, such as 270- and 360-degree right/left turns, straight figure-eight, and send over jumps. Higher levels have more stations and more difficult exercises.

APDT rally uses slightly different exercises from the AKC and UKC and includes some additional ones, such as a retrieve. The APDT also allows dogs to be rewarded with food during the competition, unlike the AKC or UKC.

FROM THE EXPERT

Roger Ayres, AKC Senior Executive Field Staff Representative, recommends that "both handler and dog must become proficient in the steps and maneuvers required by rally, but the overall focus should be on teamwork. As in any partnership, there must be a leader and a follower. The handler must learn the part that satisfies the requirements of an exercise, and the dog must learn to follow the handler's lead. In some ways, it's like dancing. It's the handler's job to lead the dance and the dog's job to follow the handler's lead. Once the handler has learned the details of the exercises required of the handler, then effort and concentration may be focused on getting the dog's attention and establishing a sense of teamwork through practice of the exercises. A useful skill to teach the dog in practice is "body awareness." The dog should know how to move not only his front but also his rear as well. This skill helps in several rally exercises, such as the halt, side step right exercise, the left pivots, and the back up three steps."

Requirements

Dogs
- basic obedience on and off lead
- jumping ability
- pace-changing ability

Handlers
- reasonably good shape

Equipment and Supplies
- collar
- jumps
- leash
- pylons or posts
- rally signs

Collar: The preferred collar is a simple snap or buckle type. The exhibitor must bring a collar (and leash) to the event.

Jumps: Jumps are a maximum height of 16 inches (40.5 cm), with smaller heights (8 and 12 inches (20.5 and 30.5 cm) for smaller dogs in the UKC and AKC. The APDT even has 4-inch (10-cm) jumps for tiny dogs. These are pretty much the same jumps used in obedience, although the UKC does not use a broad jump in rally.

Leash: The leash must be made of fabric or leather and long enough to provide some slack. Six feet (2 m) is the suggested length, and this length is required in the AKC's honor exercise. The exhibitor must bring a leash (and collar) to the event.

Pylons/Posts: Pylons or posts are present at a rally event to guide the dog through the required spiral turns. These posts are 12 to 18 inches (30.5 to 45.5 cm) in height and colored red or yellow.

Rally Signs: Rally signs are signposts and directional signals that tell a handler what skill is expected to be showcased at each station. They can be bought singly or as a set—or you can make your own for practice runs or fun matches.

To be a successful rally competitor, both you and your dog must know all of the exercises and be able to perform them.

Sponsoring Organizations

AMERICAN KENNEL CLUB (AKC)

AKC rally has three levels: Novice, Advanced, and Excellent. Novice is the easiest class; the dog is on leash and there are 10 to 15 stations. Advanced is for dogs who have completed their Novice titles; dogs are judged off leash, over a course of 12 to 17 stations, including one jump. Excellent is for dogs who have earned an Advanced title; dogs are judged off leash (except for the honor exercise) and must complete 15 to 20 stations, including two jumps.

Eligibility Requirements: Any AKC-registered dog of at least six months of age may enter AKC-sponsored trials. Spayed and neutered dogs are eligible.

Titles: In AKC rally, a team starts with 100 points and the judge deducts points for mistakes. A dog earns a title by earning a qualifying score three times at each level.

In the Novice Class, a dog can earn the title Rally Novice (RN); in the Advanced Class, Rally Advanced (RA); and in the Excellent Class, Rally Excellent (RE). Additionally, there is the Rally Advanced Excellent (RAE) title, in which a team has to qualify in both the Advanced and Excellent Classes in ten trials.

Premier Events: The AKC does not currently hold national rally competitions.

ASSOCIATION OF PET DOG TRAINERS (APDT)

APDT rally has three levels: 1, 2, and 3. At Level 1, dogs are expected to halt, sit, stand, down, walk around at *heel* position, turn, spiral, serpentine, and about face. Level 2 is divided into two classes: A and B. The A class is for teams that are working toward earning their Level 2 title, while the B class is for teams that have earned their Level 2 title in the A class. The teams work on figure-eights, pivots, stepping backward, sending over jumps, and more. Level 3 is divided into two classes: A and B. The A class is for teams that are working toward earning their Level 3 title, while the B class is for teams that have earned their Level 3 title in the A class. This level includes recalls over jumps, moving backward, and more complex exercises. There are also Puppy, Veteran, and Junior courses.

Eligibility Requirements: All dogs of any breed, as well as mixed breeds and even dogs with disabilities, may compete in APDT-sponsored trials. They must be registered with APDT rally and may be spayed or neutered. Dogs must be at least six months of age.

Titles: In APDT rally, the team starts with 200 points, and the judge deducts points for mistakes and adds bonus points for optional exercises. Three levels of titles are given by the APDT, and there are additional titles for multiple qualifications at various levels. *Level 1 (RL1):* The dog must earn three qualifying scores of 170 or better, earned under two different judges in the A class. *Level 2 (RL2):* The dog must earn three qualifying scores of 170 or better, earned under two different judges in the A class. Teams must earn a Level 1 title before entering Level 2. *Level 3 (RL3):* The dog

---

FUN FACT

Rally is for everyone, not just the young and fit. A 96-year-old woman who was legally blind entered a rally trial with her Bichon Frise. She could see well enough to negotiate the rally course but could not read the rally signs, so a helper was allowed to follow along with her and call out the requirements of each sign on the course. Then there was an 84-year-old woman who had one knee fused, walked with a cane, and had never owned a dog in her life. She entered rally trials with a rescue Chihuahua she took in from the local animal shelter and earned the Rally Excellent (RE) title with her new friend!

---

must earn three qualifying scores of 170 or better, earned under two different judges in the A class. Teams must earn a Level 2 title before entering Level 3.

Premier Events: Various events are held all around the United States. However, all dogs competing in rally events are eligible to earn points toward annual APDT Rally National Ranking Awards. Awards are given to the top 20 dog–handler teams in each title level each year.

UNITED KENNEL CLUB (UKC)

UKC rally obedience consists of three levels, 1, 2, and 3, and two sections, A and B. At each level, the exercises become more complex and demanding and will vary to some extent. The standard ring size is 40 by 70 feet (12 by 21.5 m) and may be indoors or out. Rules and required exercises are similar to those of the AKC and APDT. Jump heights are determined by the height of the dog at the withers and may be 8, 12, or 16 inches (20.5, 30.5, or 40.5 cm).

Eligibility Requirements: Dogs must be at least six months old and registered with the UKC.

Titles: Titles include *United Rally Obedience (URO1, 2, and 3):* The dog must earn three qualifying scores at three different UKC trials under at least two different judges. *United Rally Obedience Champion (UROC):* The dog must accumulate 100 championship points.

Premier Events: This is a brand-new sport for the UKC, so there are no premier events as of this writing.

How to Get Started

The Canine Good Citizen test is the perfect starting point for rally. (See Chapter 5.) Your dog will learn basic skills and socialization and learn to look up to you as a fair and trustworthy leader. Get your dog enrolled in a basic puppy or beginner obedience class and go for it!

GET YOUR DOG A CHECKUP

Rally is a fairly low-stress event, but your dog still needs to be in reasonably good shape—take him to the vet for a checkup. Because he'll be around lots of other dogs, make sure that he is up to date on his vaccinations.

LEARN THE FUNDAMENTALS

Because rally looks so easy to do, many people skip the most important step of all: learning the fundamentals. You must know the exercises, and your dog must know how to perform them. Through practice, your dog will develop a sense of teamwork with you. As with any activity, the more time invested in rally fundamentals, the more fun and enjoyable it will be.

TAKE A CLASS AND GO TO TRIALS

If one is available, take a rally class with a local dog-training organization. If possible, attend a rally trial and visit with the competitors. Most rally handlers are more than happy to share their knowledge and experience. Check with a local dog-training club to find out when and where a rally trial is scheduled for your area. Take time to prepare your dog for the new environment of a rally trial. Dogs in some ways are just like people—they often become tentative and cautious when faced with new and different situations. Taking your dog (on a leash) to new and different situations will build his confidence so that when the trip is made to a rally trial, it will be just another visit to something new and interesting.

TRAIN YOUR DOG

Successful dogs will heel on a loose lead, jump, serpentine, turn, halt, back up, sit, stay, and down on command. These are simple obedience exercises that you and your dog can learn from any class or good book, but the secret of rally is

The judge is looking for a harmonious relationship between handler and dog.

to move smoothly through them, one into another, while following the various rally signposts. Unlike obedience class, the judge does not give commands. Verbal commands and signals from the handler are allowed, but overall the team should demonstrate smoothness.

Because it is a requirement that all dogs be on leash at a rally trial, consider teaching your dog to relieve himself on leash and on command.

Strategies for Success

Before attending a rally event, become familiar with the rule book. The more you know, the more successful you will be!

FOSTER YOUR RELATIONSHIP WITH YOUR DOG

This event capitalizes on a loving, trusting relationship between partners, so the best way to get ready is to do everything you can to foster that relationship. Lots of walks together, along with practice of the various skills, will help immeasurably—it doesn't have to be formal training every single time. Because teams are penalized for harsh corrections, just preparing for the event will help you think of kind, gentle ways to help your dog learn what you want.

MAKE A GOOD IMPRESSION

How you and your dog appear at an event can make the difference between a good and bad impression. Your dog should be clean and well brushed. The judge is looking not just at mechanical obedience but at a flowing relationship. Keeping your dog clean and well groomed shows that you are a caring dog owner and that you respect the event. It's also a good idea to dress up a little bit yourself. You don't need an evening gown or a suit and tie, but clean, pressed clothes will show the judge that you are serious and interested in making a good impression. That counts for more than you might think.

ADDITIONAL ORGANIZATIONS

Canadian Association of Rally Obedience (CARO)
www.canadianrallyo.ca
Canadian Kennel Club (CKC)
www.ckc.ca
United Kennel Club (UKC)
www.ukcdogs.com

Chapter 26

Schutzhund

Definition

The word "Schutzhund" is German for "protection dog," and this sport covers the areas of tracking, obedience, and protection. In other words, this is training suitable for police work. Schutzhund is not "attack dog" training or "guard dog" training—it is protection training. This same sport is called Working Dog Sport by the American Kennel Club (AKC).

History of Schutzhund

The history of Schutzhund is linked to the history and development of the German Shepherd Dog. This versatile dog was originally developed as a herder and all-working dog, and Schutzhund trials were developed to make sure that the breed kept these valuable characteristics. The first Schutzhund trial was held in Germany in 1901. Only those German Shepherds who had passed a Schutzhund or herding test were allowed to breed. This is still true in Germany. In 1970, the first US Schutzhund trial was held in California. Working Dog Sport was recognized by the AKC in 2006 for four designated breeds (Bouviers des Flandres, Rottweilers, German Shepherd Dogs, and Doberman Pinschers) to test their abilities in scent and protection work, coupled with obedience. The United Schutzhund Clubs of America (USA) is another sponsoring organization for the sport of Schutzhund.

Overview

Modern Schutzhund (and Working Dog Sport) consists of three tests (Schutzhund [Sch]1, Sch2, and Sch3) given in a single day: tracking, obedience, and protection. A dog must earn passing scores on all three parts in a single trial to be awarded a Schutzhund title. Each part is judged on a 100-point scale, with 70 points required to pass. Dogs exhibiting poor temperament may be dismissed at any time.

TOP BREEDS

Originally, Schutzhund trials were limited to German Shepherd Dogs, but now various breeds may compete for Schutzhund titles, depending on the organization. The most successful competitors traditionally include German Shepherd Dogs, Belgian Malinois, Rottweilers, Doberman Pinschers, Giant Schnauzers, Bouviers des Flandres, and Dutch Shepherd Dogs. There are minimum age requirements to enter your dog in these Schutzhund events, so check with the sponsoring organization.

TRACKING

A track is laid across a field, with several small articles dropped along the way. The dog's handler may lay the track for a Sch1 test; strangers lay the track for Sch2 and Sch3. At some later time in the day, the dog is told to follow the track, indicating each of the dropped articles as he finds them. Indication is achieved when the dog lies next to the article, usually with his paws around it. Scoring is based on how well the dog follows the track and locates the articles. For Sch2 and Sch3, the tracks are longer, older, and have more turns and objects to find than in Sch1. Dogs are expected to follow the scent exactly and not "air scent," which may lead to dogs to cut corners and drift off the track.

OBEDIENCE

Obedience testing is held in a large open area, with one handler working with two dogs. One dog is commanded to lie down away from his handler, while the handler works in the field with the other dog. After the first dog completes his exercises, the dogs switch places. The dogs are put through several heeling exercises, both in the open and through a group of people. During the heeling part of the test, the dog's reaction to loud noises is tested by one or more gunshots. The test also includes recalls, retrieves, and a "send out," in which the dog is directed to run in the opposite direction from the handler and lie down on command. Scoring is based on accuracy and attitude. Retrieves for Sch1 tests are over flat ground, while Sch2 and 3 may add a 6-foot (2-m) wall. Dogs are expected to participate enthusiastically.

PROTECTION

This part of the test gauges the dog's ability to protect himself and his handler and requires courage, agility, and strength. The trial includes a search of hiding places, finding a hidden person (an assistant wearing a padded sleeve), and guarding that person while the handler approaches. The assistant will try to escape, and the dog must pursue the assistant and securely hold him. The assistant will then attempt to "attack" the handler; the dog is expected to stop the attack by biting the assistant on the padded arm. The

343

In higher-level obedience phases, the dog must retrieve over a wall.

dog is also threatened with a padded stick. The dog must release the sleeve on command, and failure to do so results in disqualification. The handler's ability to control her dog is a critical part of the test.

Requirements

Dogs

- courage
- high level of obedience skill
- intelligence
- perseverance
- strength
- strong bond with handler
- strong desire to work
- tracking ability
- willingness to attack on command

Handlers

- ability to be a leader

- consistent
- strong character

Equipment and Supplies

- agitation collar or harness
- bite sleeve
- bite tug toys
- choke collar
- dumbbells
- leash
- stick/whip
- tracking articles
- tracking line
- trial jacket

Agitation Collar or Harness: An agitation collar or harness distributes tension from the leash over a wider area than does a regular collar and keeps a dog from being choked while training. (These collars/harnesses are really quite comfortable.) Although not a requirement, you should invest in two harnesses: one for tracking and one for protection training. They can be nylon or leather, and the lead must attach to the harness with a snap.

Bite Sleeve: Bite sleeves come in different degrees of toughness to help your puppy develop the proper bite. At an actual event, they are used to protect the handler's helper from the dog's bite. Several models are available. (You can also purchase scratch pants, which will protect your legs.)

Bite Tug Toys: Toys and tugs are used as training tools to help motivate a puppy. They can also be used to prepare the dog for the sleeve. They should be sturdy but not so hard that the puppy can't squeeze them.

Choke Collar: This is a requirement for some parts of the test and is permissible in all. These collars are not used as chokes. When

FROM THE EXPERT

Dennis Helm, an experienced Schutzhund trainer, reminds us that dogs recall the last important experience of the training session. This is why they need to leave a session in a positive frame of mind.

The bite sleeve is used to protect the handler's helper from the dog's bite.

the leash is attached in trials, it is to the dead ring, which bypasses the choking action. A flat or buckle collar is not allowed.

Dumbbells: The dog must retrieve the dumbbells on a flat surface, over a hurdle, and over a slanted wall. Schutzhund has specific dumbbell requirements for each level.

Leash: You will need a short (3-foot [1-m]) standard leash. The handler must carry a lead at all times, including when the dog is working off lead. It must hang loosely and should be small enough to conceal or to be carried over the shoulder. Leather is preferred.

Stick or Whip: Used by the helper to attempt to intimidate the dog. The dog is not hit with these items.

Tracking Articles: Articles for tracking include items of wood, leather, plastic, or carpet. Schutzhund regulations specify specific sizes for trials. When starting a young dog, use something that holds scent well.

Tracking Line: The tracking line is used for the tracking portion of the test and should be light, nonslip, and 33 feet (10 m) long. The lead may be placed over the dog's back, along his side, or between the forelegs and hind legs. Trackers may opt not to use the lead but must stay 33 feet (10 m) behind the dog.

Trial Jacket: Schutzhund rules state that the helper must wear a jacket while doing the helper work in a trial. The jacket must provide protection to the arm that does not wear a bite sleeve.

Sponsoring Organizations

AMERICAN KENNEL CLUB (AKC)

AKC Working Dog Sport is both a competitive event and one in which the dog is judged against a standard. The test is designed to show a dog's suitability in serving humans in police work, narcotics detection, and homeland defense. It is also a good test for a breeder who wishes to preserve these characteristics in his stock. Basically, the rules are the same as for Schutzhund, from which this event was derived.

Dogs are tested on three phases: tracking, obedience, and protection. A dog must score 70 points (out of 100) to qualify. In addition, dogs in the protection program are rated on drive, self-confidence, and resilience; they are graded as Insufficient (I), Satisfactory (S), or Pronounced (P). In the temperament test, which is required before a dog can participate in any of the other phases, he is required to heel on and off lead; encounter people, bicycles, and cars; and behave properly when left alone. It is similar to the AKC Canine Good Citizen test.

In tracking, dogs are evaluated on a calm start, finding and indicating articles, staying on track, and responding appropriately to any wild animals that dart across the path. Occasional praise is permitted. The difficulty is increased at each level (Working Dog 1, 2, 3). In obedience, dogs begin in the *heel* position to the left of the handler, retrieve a dumbbell, go over a hurdle, scale a wall or A-frame, do a send-away, go into a *down* under distraction, defend, and attack. The handler may praise the dog after every exercise. In the

347

protection phase, the dog must "search" for the helper (who is hidden behind a blind), hold the helper there, and bark.

Eligibility Requirements: The AKC admits registered Bouviers des Flandres, Doberman Pinschers, German Shepherd Dogs, and Rottweilers. All of these breeds have a distinguished history of working as guard and protection dogs. Spayed and neutered dogs are eligible. Dogs must be 18 months for Working Dog I (WD I), 19 months for Working Dog II (WD II), and 20 months for Working Dog III (WD III). For the temperament test, dogs must be 15 months of age or older.

Titles: The AKC offers Working Dog I (WD I), Working Dog II (WD II), and Working Dog III (WD III) titles. The qualifier "TT" indicates that a dog has been temperament tested.

Premier Events: Each of the four parent clubs (Bouvier des Flandres, Doberman Pinscher, German Shepherd Dog, and Rottweiler) is separately responsible for holding its own event. Each may hold up to five events in one year.

UNITED SCHUTZHUND CLUBS OF AMERICA (USA)

This is the largest Schutzhund organization in the United States. Despite its name, the USA is a German Shepherd Dog breed club but sponsors all-breed Schutzhund clubs and trials. Their events are similar to the AKC's, but the temperament test is included in the tracking portion. The Schutzhund trials consist of three parts: tracking, obedience, and protection.

The tracking phase includes a temperament test by the judge to assure the dog's mental soundness. A track is laid, and the dog is expected to scent the track and indicate

FUN FACT

Most police departments and other organizations that make use of working dogs require the dogs to be neutered. Schutzhund dogs provide the breeding stock for these working dogs. Without Schutzhund, the abilities of many working breeds would deteriorate, and it might be difficult to find suitable dogs for police work, bomb detection, or search and rescue. People participate in Schutzhund not only to have a great time but also to serve society by guaranteeing the future of its protection dogs.

During the protection phase, the decoy threatens the dog with a stick and charges at his handler.

the location of the objects, usually by lying down with the found object between his front paws. The tracking phase is intended to test the dog's trainability and ability to scent, as well as his mental and physical endurance.

The obedience phase includes a series of heeling exercises. During the heeling, a gunshot test is performed to assure that the dog is not gun-shy. There is also a series of field exercises in which the dog is commanded to sit, lie down, and stand while the handler continues to move. With dumbbells of various weights, the dog is asked to retrieve on a flat surface, over a hurdle, and over a slanted wall. The dog is also asked to run in a straight direction from his handler on command and lie down on a second command. Finally, each dog is expected to stay in a *down* position away from his handler, despite distractions, at the other end of the obedience field, while another dog completes these exercises. All of the obedience exercises are tests of the dog's temperament, physical condition, efficiencies, and

RINGSPORT

A similar sport to Schutzhund is ringsport, which developed in France about 100 years ago. Unlike Schutuzhund, there is no tracking element in ringsport, but extra elements of agility are added. Ringsport dogs are primarily trained for guarding and protection.

willingness to serve his owner.

The protection phase tests the dog's courage, physical strength, and agility. The handler's control of the dog is absolutely essential. The exercises include a search of hiding places, finding a hidden person (decoy), and guarding that decoy while the handler approaches. The dog is expected to pursue the decoy when an escape is attempted and to hold the grip firmly. The decoy is searched and transported to the judge with the handler and dog walking behind and later at the decoy's right side. When the decoy tries to attack the handler, the dog is expected to stop the attack with a firm grip and no hesitation. The final test of courage occurs when the decoy is asked to come out of a hiding place by the handler from the opposite end of the field. The dog is sent after the decoy, who is threatening the dog with a stick and charging at the handler. All grips during the protection phase are to be firmly placed on the padded sleeve and stopped on command or when the decoy discontinues the fight.

Eligibility Requirements: Schutzhund tests are for German Shepherd Dogs, but other breeds, such as Belgian Malinois, Rottweilers, Doberman Pinschers, Giant Schnauzers, Bouviers des Flandres, Dutch Shepherd Dogs, American Bulldogs, and Boxers may also participate. Spayed and neutered dogs are eligible to compete. For Schutzhund 1 (SchH1), the dog must be at least 18 months old; for Schutzhund 2 (SchH2), the dog must be at least 19 months old; and for Schutzhund 3 (SchH3), the dog must be at least 20 months old.

Titles: There are three Schutzhund titles: Schutzhund 1 (SchH1; novice), Schutzhund 2 (SchH2; intermediate), and Schutzhund 3 (SchH3; advanced). The USA also offers tracking degrees, Advanced Tracking (FH1) and Superior

Tracking qualification (FH2), and a basic protection degree (WH), which includes basic obedience. It also offers the Ausdauerprüfung (AD), which is a 12.5-mile (20-km) endurance test and includes obedience. The USA also offers six separate obedience and tracking titles that reflect the routines for SchH1, 2, and 3 levels.

Premier Events: This organization holds the USA Working Dog Championships.

How to Get Started

People in Schutzhund must be prepared for the long haul—to get a dog ready for competition realistically takes about two years.

GET YOUR DOG A CHECKUP

Only dogs who are structurally sound can participate in this rigorous event. Have your veterinarian give your dog a checkup to ensure that he is able to compete successfully.

In higher-level obedience phases, the dog must retrieve over a wall.

Schutzhund is a complex sport that should only be undertaken by experienced trainers.

FIND A CLUB

The best source of training information is a good Schutzhund club; however, these are few and far between in the United States. In addition, Schutzhund clubs tend to be small, as only a few dogs can be trained in one session. Proper training methods for guard and attack dogs are controversial, and experts disagree among themselves. However, because improper training in the protection area can utterly ruin a dog or severely injure a person, this is not something to undertake on your own. Hence, most Schutzhund clubs concentrate most on protection training.

TRAIN YOUR DOG

This is a very complex sport that should be undertaken only by experienced trainers. If you have never trained a dog before, it's best to start with basic tracking and obedience before you attempt Schutzhund. Protection training, unless done properly, can result in an aggressive dog who is not safe around other people (or maybe not even safe around you). All Schutzhund dogs need to be good citizens first and completely responsive to their owners' commands.

Strategies for Success

For the best chance of success, remember that training must be more difficult than the trial; in this way, your dog won't become overwhelmed at the actual event. It will all be old hat to him.

FIND THE RIGHT PUPPY

The most essential requirement is the right puppy—and indeed, you must start with a puppy. In this respect, you'll need a mentor to help you select an experienced breeder who specializes in working stock. Your chosen puppy should demonstrate self-assurance, prey drive, dominance, and fight drive. (Because these are not the same qualities you want in the average family pet, know that you are in for a handful.) A properly trained Schutzhund is a perfect dog, but one mistake can ruin both of you.

LEARN BODY LANGUAGE

To be successful, you'll have to know your dog's body language and your own as well. Dogs are masters at reading humans, and they can tell what you are saying with your body as well as with your words. Make sure that you are giving your dog the same message consistently.

ADDITIONAL ORGANIZATIONS

Fédération Cynologique Internationale (FCI)
www.fci.be
Deutscher Verband der Gebrauchshundsportvereine (DVG)
www.dvg-hundesport.de
Schutzhund Australia
www.schutzhundaustralia.com
Verein für Deutsche Schäferhunde (SV) e.V.
www.schaeferhund.de

Chapter 27

Scootering

Definition

Dog scootering (also known as footbiking) is a sport in which one or more harnessed dogs pull a wheeled vehicle (scooter) with a passenger on board. It is similar to bikejoring but uses a scooter instead of a bicycle. Although scootering is often an urban sport using sidewalks and paved trails or roads, many dog scooters use mountain bike trails and backcountry roads.

History of Scootering

The history of scootering dates back to 1900, with the first scooters being made of wood and iron. However the question of when our canine friends began pulling the load, so to speak, remains a mystery. It is quite possible that the dog-powered scooter came about in an innocuous way—most likely as a warm-weather training method for mushers who wanted to keep their dogs in top physical condition during the off season. Whatever its origin, scootering is a wonderful pastime enjoyed by many dogs and dog lovers around the world.

Overview

With the right training, most dogs consider this sport a fun activity to enjoy with their owners. This eco-friendly activity can be done on city streets or backwoods trails.

Scootering is an ideal way to exercise your dog (and yourself), as well as to spend time with him. Dogs get plenty of exercise pulling the scooter, but sometimes the rider has to help push, particularly up hills. Your dog's ability to pull depends mostly on his individual strength and athleticism, although scooters offer very little resistance. Some dogs have been known to pull a scooter at up to 20 miles per hour (32 kph)! This sport can also serve as a wonderful outlet for highly energetic dogs.

Although most people dog scooter for fun, some musher types participate in scootering as a "dryland sport"—a chance to work out their sled or skijoring dogs when no snow is available. Scootering fun runs, for instance, are held by scootering clubs. In addition, the International Sled Dog Racing Association (ISDRA) offers some scootering competitions in which participants race against each other.

TOP BREEDS

Any strong, well-conditioned dog who loves to pull and run can participate in this sport. Successful breeds include Alaskan Malamutes, German Shorthaired Pointers, Siberian Huskies, Giant Schnauzers, Rottweilers, and others.

Scooters in which the dog pulls from the side rather than from the front are easy to ride and give you exceptional control.

Requirements

Dogs
- ability to follow directional commands
- endurance
- pulling ability (strength)
- speed

Handlers
- good physical condition

Equipment and Supplies
- harness
- safety gear
- scooter
- tugline/neckline

You may also want to bring a scooter repair kit, just in case.

Harness: You'll need a pulling harness—remember, scootering is a dog-powered sport. It should be either an X-back, H-back, or Y-back harness made of synthetic webbing. The collars are fitted to lie at the base of the neck, and the "pull" comes on the breastbone via the chest strap that goes between the front legs. These harnesses are easily kept in place, and most importantly, don't restrict the dog's gait when he is running.

Safety Gear: A fast dog can achieve speeds of 25 miles per hour (40 kph). To stay safe, wear a helmet, wrist guards, knee and elbow pads, and safety goggles to protect your eyes from debris. Bring booties to protect your dog's feet from getting scraped or cut; reflective vests for you and your dog may be a good idea as well.

Scooter: The scooter (sometimes called a kick bike) should preferably have at least 16-inch (40.5-cm) diameter air-filled tires for off-road and rough trail use. The scooter should also have a footpad large enough to accommodate your feet, good brakes, and front shocks. Fenders are optional and may be purchased and installed by any qualified bicycle shop. Razor-tired scooters should not be used because of their instability. Some scooters are designed so that the dog pulls from the side rather than from the front; these are easy to ride and give you exceptional control of the dog, but the attachments are wide, making this arrangement unsuitable for very narrow trails.

Tugline/Neckline: You'll need a 4- to 6-foot (1-to 2-m) leash or bungee tugline that can be safely wrapped around or attached to the stem of the scooter. The tugline connects the harness to the scooter, usually by wrapping around the down tube and snapping into a D-ring. A slide snap then attaches to the loop or D-ring in the harness.

Sponsoring Organizations

ISDRA scooting competition may be divided into one- and two-dog classes, Pro or Novice, and Adult and Junior. Competitors may be started individually in multiples or groups. Distances may range from 2 to 5 miles (3 to 8 km),

Pulling can often be much more fun for your dog if he has a friend to run alongside him.

and the courses are run over fairly level terrain on grass or dirt. The line between the dog and scooter is usually mandated at between 4 and 7 feet (1 and 2 m). Events usually last two or three days, and a competitor's final time is based on the accumulated time from each heat. Competitors must use the same dog in all heats of the event.

Eligibility Requirements: Events are usually open to any breed of dog (even mixed breeds) that is safely able to pull. The size of the dog is not as important as one might think, although medium or larger breeds are ideally suited for pulling. It is important to note that small terriers and toy breeds, regardless of how much energy they may have, are not built to pull heavy loads (such as their owner).

Titles: No titles are available.

Premier Events: Most events are noncompetitive fun outings. Sanctioned by the ISDRA, the East Meets West Dryland Challenge event takes place late in the year at Brainerd International Raceway in Brainerd, Minnesota. This is one of the more prestigious events in dryland racing.

How to Get Started

In scootering, the proper safety precautions, as well as the right amount of training, can ensure a safe and fun experience for you and your dog.

PUT SAFETY FIRST

Make sure that your dog is in good health and free of any debilitating ailments before beginning. A vet checkup is always a good idea.

You can begin training the rudiments of scootering to a puppy as young as four to six months. At nine months, puppies can begin very short runs, but no puppy should pull any weight until he is a year old.

It is also important to realize that this sport can be dangerous, and therefore you should take precautions to ensure that you and your dog do not run the risk of injury. Keep your dog hydrated—according to most musher manuals, a 3 percent dehydration level in a dog can cause a 20 percent drop in his performance. To prevent dehydration, give your dog 2 cups of water every 1.5 to 2 hours. Also, keep an eye on him for signs of fatigue or overexertion, and never run him when temperatures are too hot. Doing so can quickly overheat your dog, putting him at risk of serious health problems or even death.

TRAIN YOUR DOG—AND YOURSELF

To experience success from the beginning, first get your dog used to the feel of wearing a harness. This can be done simply by putting the harness on him and taking him for walks. This will help him become accustomed to wearing it, as well as to associate the harness (the same one that sled dogs wear) with an enjoyable and fun activity.

Next, get your dog used to dragging something behind him as he walks (or runs). Choose something lightweight, such as a small tree branch or bike tire. Use a variety of different items each time you walk, preferably things that produce different sounds and levels of noise. It is also a good idea to vary your terrain as you train (dirt, gravel, pavement).

Once your dog has become accustomed to pulling something small, you are ready to begin training with the actual scooter. A good way to start is to choose a trail that your dog is familiar with, such as at a local park or your normal walking route. He should be able to associate the route with a fun activity or getting a reward afterward. A great way to keep your dog focused on the trail is to have someone running or riding a bicycle ahead of you, a technique often referred to as using a "rabbit."

Start slowly, training for only a few minutes at a time. It will take a while for your dog to build up the muscle and stamina to pull for an extended period. Make sure that he always pulls the tugline taut and remains in front of you at all times. If not, the tugline could wrap around the front wheel or your dog's leg and potentially cause serious injury to both of you. *Never* allow the scooter to coast beside your dog. Of

FROM THE EXPERT

Expert dog scooterer Daphne Lewis says, "Take the time to ground train your dog to pull. The dog pulls when the snap is snapped to the harness. The dog does not pull when the snap is attached to the collar. When the snap is snapped to the harness, the dog is in work mode. Do not allow him to sniff, go say hi, or pee. He must ignore distractions when commanded to pull. Teach and enforce the *on by* command. The dog must not stop to visit other dogs. Do keep your eyes on the dog and your hands ready to use the brakes so that the tugline is always tight. Should the dog slow down, you must use the brakes to keep the line tight."
As for the best breed? "It depends, of course. If you want to win at scooter races, choose Pointers or Alaskan Huskies. If your child is riding the scooter, choose a gentle breed like a springer spaniel. For most people, though, the best breed to introduce to the sport is the breed they already have and love."

FUN FACT

Recently, a revolutionary scooter/harness combination has been invented that works by having the dog push rather than pull (using an outrigger device) and leaves the steering and braking control in the hands of the rider. (See photos on pages 357 and 359.) This makes scootering less hazardous and keeps the dog securely at your side. The scooter is customizable for one to three dogs. For more information, go to www.dogpoweredscooter.com.

course, nature must always take its course, and eventually a novice dog will feel the need to sniff or to relieve himself. It is a good idea to steer a bit to the side of your dog (with the line taut) just in case you cannot stop in time.

Conditioning is not limited to your dog. If you have little experience riding a scooter, you may want to start practicing before you hitch him to the end of the line. Practice on hills, curvy and bumpy terrain, and straightaways. Have someone (your "rabbit," perhaps) pull you with the tugline. Learn to use your brakes for coasting and stopping. You should be comfortable riding the scooter before ever hitching your dog to it.

DEVELOP VERBAL CUES

The following very basic commands can not only be lifesavers while on the trail but can also be carried over into other pulling sports, such as bikejoring and canicross. The beauty of teaching your dog commands is that the more often you use them, the more quickly he will learn them. Make sure to use them whenever you take him for a walk, and your dog will be responding correctly in no time at all!

- Hike! or Pull!: Go forward.
- Whoa: Come to a smooth stop.
- Gee: Turn right.
- Haw: Turn left.
- This way: Run in the direction the scooter is pointing.
- On by: Ignore distractions.
- Line out: Stand still with the tugline tight, facing

forward.
- Easy: Go slower.
- Hup hup: Go faster.

Strategies for Success

Teach your dog that a harness means business—don't let him play around when it is put on. This will reduce your chance of a nasty spill.

MAKE IT FUN

It is very important that your dog have fun taking part in this activity. Don't let him get overtired, and be sure to take out some time before and after for a little off-lead relaxation. (When your dog is relaxed, he is less apt to go chasing after squirrels and strange people.) It is best to measure success in time spent together rather than distance traveled.

USE MORE THAN ONE DOG

Another idea for success is to not limit yourself to having one dog pull. Pulling can often be much more fun for your dog if he has a friend to run alongside him. Make sure that the dogs are trained individually before hitching them together—otherwise, you may crash into a tree before you even make it a short distance. Of course, don't go overboard; more than four dogs is really overdoing it, so sticking to just two playful pooches is probably a good idea.

ADDITIONAL ORGANIZATIONS

Dogs Across America
www.dogsacrossamerica.org
International Sled Dog Racing Association (ISDRA)
www.isdra.org

Chapter 28

Search and Rescue

Definition

Search-and-rescue (SAR) dogs use their noses to find children and adults lost in the woods, people buried in avalanches or collapsed buildings, and many others in distress. It's a very rewarding activity, but it's a lot more than following your dog while he does all of the work. Creating a serious search-and-rescue team (that's you and your dog) requires a major commitment on your part to learn everything your dog can't, including map reading, compass and radio skills, and advanced first aid.

History of Search and Rescue

Saint Bernard of Menthon built an inn and monastery at the summit of what is now known as the Great St. Bernard Pass in the year 980 CE. The monks of this institution often aided travelers in distress and gradually came to recognize that the dogs guarding the monastery (starting in the 17th century) were better at finding lost or buried victims than they were themselves.

The beginning of modern SAR may be traced to the winter of 1937/1938 in Switzerland, when a dog showed repeated interest in a spot already searched after an avalanche, leading rescuers to find a buried victim still alive. After this incident, the Swiss Army trained four German Shepherd Dogs to help search for avalanche victims.

After World War II, the Swiss Alpine Club began using trained dogs to supplement their traditional method of probing avalanches with long poles to find buried victims. This effort led to the establishment of avalanche dog training centers throughout the Alps.

Rescue dogs have been used in many disaster situations, including by the Red Cross during World War I to find injured

TOP BREEDS

Theoretically, any breed can do search and rescue (SAR), but as a practical matter, only the larger breeds and mixes, those over 40 or 50 pounds (18 or 22.5 kg), are truly successful. The larger working, herding, and sporting breeds are most commonly used in SAR work, especially the smaller members of those breeds, who are less prone to hip and shoulder problems. This isn't to say that a smaller dog can't do the job, just that small dogs usually have more trouble negotiating the often difficult terrain a SAR dog finds himself traversing. A small dog may have a great nose, endurance, and a good work ethic, but most would probably be limited to working in relatively open country. (Some small SAR dogs are carried to a likely spot where they can begin their search among rubble.) Very large dogs have the opposite problem: They can't fit into small spaces or go through dense brush as well as a smaller dog. They are also more difficult to transport.

Search-and-rescue dogs are trained to find victims in all kinds of weather.

soldiers on the battlefield and during the London Blitz in World War II to find victims buried in bombed buildings. The heroic work of SAR dogs during the aftermath of the terror attacks of September 11th, 2001, is equally memorable.

Overview

Wolves used their noses and outstanding hearing to find game and mates for millions of years before they became dogs. Today, SAR training develops a dog's natural tracking skills to help find missing persons. Your dog leads the way, but you follow behind with a map, compass, GPS device, radio, cell phone, and first-aid kit to get the wanderer back home safely. With their acute hearing and sense of smell, dogs can often dramatically reduce the time it takes to find a missing person. A good dog may be as effective as 30 people in a search.

The missing person may be a confused Alzheimer's patient, a lost and possibly injured hiker, or a child who has wandered away from her family's campsite. SAR teams help search for drowning victims and look for victims of various disasters, including earthquakes, avalanches, or floods. You and your dog may even be called on to assist the police in a missing person or possible homicide investigation. The prompt response by a well-equipped, well-trained professional SAR team can make the difference between finding the lost person alive or dead or even finding her at all.

SAR takes more than a skilled dog. It also requires a dedicated handler who can devote the time (generally about two years) and money (maybe several thousand dollars) needed to develop a good SAR dog. If you think that this is something you'd like to try, know that it will demand a serious commitment on your part. The training is extensive, often taking 2 years to achieve certification, working 15 hours or more a week. Expect to spend hours in uncomfortable environments and in all kinds of weather pretending to be lost while your dog (or someone else's dog) looks for you. This is in addition to learning the human

Canine search and rescue handlers must have land navigation skills—a GPS device will help you lead your dog back home.

portion of the skills that make a good SAR team and paying for the considerable amount of equipment, including camping and other outdoor gear, you will need. To proceed with training, you must find a sponsor, which in itself may be a daunting task. Hundreds of SAR groups exist around the country, so check with one in your area.

Search dogs generally get to work when their team is called upon by a police department. They may have to travel many hours or days to arrive at the search site, often a camp set up in the middle of nowhere. The search dog must be able to find the targeted scent to the exclusion of everything else, no matter what the weather or terrain. Unlike tracking dogs, a SAR dog scents by both air and ground. He is seeking the infinitesimal particles of dead skin constantly flaking off a human body. These float in the air, sink to the ground, and even float in water.

Requirements

Dogs
- ability to concentrate on tasks
- ability to problem solve
- endurance
- friendly with other dogs and people
- obedience to commands
- tracking ability
- trainability

Handlers
- ability to attract sponsors
- enjoyment of the outdoors
- time to participate in what may be long searches at an inconvenient hour
- land navigation, map and compass reading, radio communication, and first-aid skills
- physically fit

Equipment and Supplies
The amount of equipment and supplies that might be useful on a SAR mission is nearly endless. What you actually carry will

FUN FACT

Dogs can search for more than human beings. We all know about drug- and bomb-sniffing dogs, but their expertise goes even further. Some dogs can detect an oncoming epileptic seizure in their owners, while others can sniff out cancer. A Portuguese Water Dog named Rocco sniffs out peanuts and saves his young owner from contact with an allergen that is lethal to her. More peanut-sniffing dogs are in the works. Beagles have been used to sniff out termites from buildings and pesky pythons in the Everglades. Most interesting, perhaps, are poop-sniffing dogs. An Australian Shepherd named Gator locates cougars, bears, jaguars, and wolverines by searching for their droppings, and a police school flunk-out Labrador Retriever has found his calling by sniffing out whale poop. He sits on the bow of the search ship and gets excited when he smells whale dung, allowing researchers to locate and tag orcas.

depend on where you are going and what kinds of conditions you expect to encounter. A list of some of important items includes extra clothing (especially dry socks) suitable for the terrain and weather conditions expected to be encountered, two-way radio, flashlight and extra batteries, knife, pliers, water purification kit, water bottles, drinking cup, extra food, matches, sunglasses, compass, mirror, and whistle. Climbing gear may also be necessary, and a notebook and pen may come in handy. In addition to his collar and leash, your dog will need a protective vest, a drinking cup, and enough food for at least one day.

If you are traveling by helicopter, carry earplugs, a helmet, and goggles. Pack a folding shovel for avalanche work, as well as your skis or snowshoes. Dog boots and vet wrap may also be needed, as well as your dog's vaccination and health records. A backpack tent will be useful if you expect to be out overnight, in which case you will also need a sleeping bag, sleeping pad, camp stove and fuel, mess kit, and enough food for however long you will be out.

Carry a first-aid kit with triangular bandages, Band-Aids, rolls of gauze and tape, gauze pads, elastic bandages, safety pins, scissors, tweezers, and aspirin or other nonsteroidal pain reliever. If you have room, pack some antiseptic, topical antibiotic, material for a splint, and a sting kit.

Sponsoring Organizations

NATIONAL ASSOCIATION FOR SEARCH AND RESCUE (NASAR)

The National Association for Search and Rescue (NASAR) is the main sponsoring organization, but many regional SAR organizations also exist.

Eligibility Requirements: There is no specific requirement for SAR work, although certain breeds have recognized "specialties." For example, Saint Bernards were bred for snow rescue work, while Bloodhounds are famous for their ability to follow a trail as long as four days old. Pedigree is not important—ability is. SAR dogs need to be trainable, agile, hardy, healthy, and amicable with people and other dogs. They must also have good endurance. Most are family pets.

Titles: There are no titles to be earned in SAR—just the satisfaction of doing a difficult, demanding, and extremely important job.

Premier Events: Few formal events are scheduled for SAR in the United States. There are, however, lots of training and certification exercises in which dogs and their handlers can participate.

How to Get Started

You must determine if your young dog has what it takes to be a SAR dog. After he has basic manners and obedience training, join an existing group. Be prepared to commit some time; it takes at least a year and a half before a dog completes his training.

CONDITION YOURSELF AS THE HANDLER

Any handler seeking to do SAR must enjoy working with dogs and be comfortable being outdoors in all kinds of weather. Sometimes this means camping in the wilderness while continuing to search. Handlers must also be physically

Search and rescue is tough and dangerous work, so your dog must be healthy and up for the challenge.

fit and have the time to participate in sometimes lengthy searches. It is also necessary to acquire several skills needed in SAR, including land navigation, map and compass reading, radio communication, and first aid.

Expect to spend at least one year (very likely two) training at least twice a week before being certified. Most SAR groups will require you to apprentice with them for a period while you and your dog complete your training. It would be very difficult, if not impossible, for a person to become fully qualified in SAR without this interaction with experienced rescue workers.

CHOOSE THE RIGHT DOG

The choice of a dog is critical for SAR work. While certain breeds, notably members of the American Kennel Club (AKC) sporting, working, and herding groups, are more successful than others, plenty of dogs of those breeds do not make good SAR dogs. There are no guarantees, although the offspring of good SAR dogs may have a better chance of themselves being good candidates. Provided that they have been well trained not to bite except on command, police dogs or dogs with Schutzhund or ringsport training may be used if they are nonthreatening and don't frighten the people they rescue.

Many handlers prefer to begin training with a young puppy, although an older dog who works well with his owner may also be suitable.

GET YOUR DOG A CHECKUP

SAR is tough, arduous, and dangerous work. It is a job, not a sport. Your vet must evaluate your dog's current health and structural ability to take on this lifesaving calling.

TRAIN YOUR DOG

SAR dogs are expected and encouraged to be outgoing and social, and SAR people have found that friendly dogs are excellent ambassadors for SAR. Begin socializing your dog just as you would any puppy—have him meet as many people in as many circumstances as possible.

Requirements vary somewhat among SAR groups, but dogs are initially trained in trailing, in which a leashed dog leads his handler along the trail with a particular scent, or in area searches, in which a dog ranges free and looks for any human scent he can detect.

Training for SAR skills is similar to that used for tracking dogs. When first beginning his training, start when your dog is a little hungry. This will give him an incentive to track—later on he will do it for fun. Drag a scented object along the ground and reward your dog when he finds it. Start with an easy search through short grass with no wind. Gradually make the trail more difficult. The idea is for your dog to follow the track, not the air scent. For area searches, encourage the opposite behavior; you want your dog to follow an air scent. Start with someone your dog knows, and reward him when he finds the person. For both kinds of searches, gradually make the distance longer, through underbrush, and over more broken ground.

After qualifying in trailing or area searching, the dogs may move on to more specialized missions, such as searching for

FROM THE EXPERT

Top Ten Ways to Tell If You Really Like K-9 SAR:
(Reprinted with permission of Denise Blackman, California Rescue Dog Association [CARDA])

10) You begin to think of ticks as fellow searchers.

9) You sleep with your pager.

8) You shower with your pager.

7) You just spent your entire vacation slipping down hillsides, getting slapped in the face by poison oak, and scratched by brush; and this was your idea of fun.

6) You have your vehicle, dog, and gear ready at all times, but you can't locate your work clothes.

5) You spend working hours fantasizing how you can become independently wealthy so you can search all the time.

4) When someone talks about "searching the Internet," you ask "Did they call a dog team?"

3) More of your coworkers know the name of your dog than know the name of your spouse.

2) Your Christmas list includes: an ammo box (for cadaver), 14-gauge wire (for your SAR-Tech II 24-hour pack), and a "super-screamer" whistle.

1) Your dog dances all around at the sight of your backpack, and you join him.

victims buried in avalanches, finding cadavers, locating dead bodies underwater, or working in collapsed buildings.

To become qualified in SAR not only requires that the dog be an expert tracker but that his handler also pass a series of tests. The requirements differ between SAR organizations, so check with the group you are planning to join. In general, the handler must demonstrate knowledge of advanced first aid and cardiopulmonary resuscitation, radio communications, helicopter safety, wilderness survival, and map and compass navigation. Annual certification may be required. The dog must be able to concentrate on tasks, track well, and be able to problem solve.

Strategies for Success

One of the best strategies for success is to get your dog trained in all of the basics. Most SAR organizations expect skills in obedience, tracking, air scenting, agility, and searching.

HAVE A GOAL IN MIND

You must have a goal in mind before you start. Many search organizations offer certificates in different areas: area search, trailing, land cadaver, water cadaver, avalanche, first-responder disaster, first-responder (human remains detection). An evaluator will help you decide what is needed in your area of interest, and what promise your dog shows. Bloodhounds, for example, are the best trailers. German Shepherds are tremendous at area searches. The ideal dog is cross-trained and can do several tasks well.

BE HONEST WITH YOURSELF

Be honest with yourself, above all. Although it's heartwarming to think of finding a missing child, many searches end up being cadaver searches—do you have the heart (and stomach) for this? SAR is one of the most rewarding of all dog-related activities, but it can be the most heartbreaking. Know what you and your dog are getting into. Some dogs became so dispirited during the 9/11 searches after finding nothing but dead bodies (or nothing at all) that volunteers pretended to be live victims simply to give the dogs a much-needed lift.

ADDITIONAL ORGANIZATIONS

National Search and Rescue Dog Association (NSARDA)
www.nsarda.org.uk
Search and Rescue Dogs Australia (SARDA)
www.sarda.net.au
Search and Rescue Society of British Columbia (SAR BC)
www.sarbc.org

Chapter 29

Skijoring

Definition

Skijoring is a sport in which a person on skis is pulled overland by a dog or dogs. In the United States, the word is usually pronounced SKI-joring, although the correct Norwegian pronunciation is closer to she-SHUR-ing, a word literally meaning "ski diving." It is the fastest-growing canine winter sport.

Variations of skijoring include snowboarding while hitched to a dog, grassjoring (skijoring over grassy fields), bikejoring, scootering, and so on. You can even skijor behind cars, horses, and snowmobiles, but skijoring with dogs is the most familiar (and safest) way to practice this sport.

Skijoring with your dog is a great way to get some exercise and strengthen your bond.

History of Skijoring

Although humans have been using sleds, skis, and dogs in various combinations for thousands of years, the modern sport of skijoring is only about 100 years old. Its original home is Scandinavia but it has spread very far. In this hemisphere, it is most popular in Alaska and the northern tier of the continental United States.

Overview

Skijoring is both recreational and competitive, depending on your interests. Skijor competitions are usually 3 to 10 miles (5 to 16 km) in length, although a few 20- and 50-mile (32- and 80.5-km) endurance events are hosted by the Alaska Skijoring and Pulk Association (ASPA). In the United States and Canada, skijoring races are frequently held along with sled dog races.

This sport can be divided into four categories: backwoods skijoring, endurance skijoring, recreational skijoring, and skijor sprint racing.

BACKWOODS SKIJORING

This is a solitary sport enjoyed by those who thrill to the stark beauty of the winter landscape over ungroomed trails and rough terrain. Like endurance skijoring, a knowledge of winter survival is essential, especially if a storm is brewing up. Using anywhere from one to three dogs is common in backwoods skijoring.

TOP BREEDS

Nordic breeds are popular skijoring partners, but other strong breeds, such as German Shorthaired Pointers, are also adept. Mixed breeds can also excel at this sport. Dogs used in skijor sprint racing are usually especially bred for the sport.

ENDURANCE SKIJORING

This is long-distance work, usually 20 miles (32 km), although the Alaskan Iditasport is a 320-mile (515-km) whopper. Skiers need all of their winter survival gear, and this sport should not be undertaken except by those who have excellent winter survival skills. Using anywhere from one to three dogs is common in endurance skijoring.

RECREATIONAL SKIJORING

Recreational skijoring is just that. It's for fun, not for training for another sport or for competition. There are no rules and no pressure to "win." It's all about fun, exercise, and companionship. Using anywhere from one to three dogs is common in recreational skijoring.

SPRINT RACING

Sprinters use ultra-light "skate skis," wear skin suits, and have up to three race-bred dogs harnessed up. Skijor sprint racers can move up to 30 miles per hour (48.5 km) and average more than 20 miles per hour (32 km) in a typical 5-mile (8-km) race.

Requirements

DOGS

- desire to pull
- obedience to directional commands
- speed (for racing)
- strength

HANDLERS

- competency as cross-country skier
- winter survival skills (for endurance and backwoods skijorers)

Equipment and Supplies

- booties
- cross-country ski gear
- harness
- helmet
- skijoring belt
- towline

Booties: Fleece-lined booties with Velcro closures will protect your dog's feet (from snow buildup between the pads) and help keep him warm.

Cross-Country Ski Gear: Unlike regular cross-country skiing, skijoring skis are hot waxed from tip to tail to keep from slowing the dog or dog team down. Backwoods skiing, undertaken in wilder areas, needs special wide "backcountry" skis and poles. Participants in skijor sprint racing use

---

FUN FACT

Skijoring was a demonstration sport in the 1928 Winter Olympics, and there are periodic attempts to bring it back.

---

special ultra-light "skate skis" and wear skin suits. Don't use metal-edged skis because they can be dangerous to your dog.

Harness: The skiing harness is just like those sled dogs use. The X-back design allows the pulling forces to be evenly distributed without constricting movement or breathing, and it supports the back and sides for increased stability. (This design is also hard for a dog to back out of.) Harnesses come in many different sizes; a good manufacturer will include proper measurements so that you can get exactly the right one for your dog.

Helmet: Helmets are always advisable to protect your head, and they are a true necessity when going downhill—especially if trees are involved.

Skijoring Belt: A skijoring belt for your waist attaches the towline and is designed for your comfort. Proper placement is low on the hips to reduce back injury and to keep your center of balance low.

Towline: The towline is made of poly rope and is usually at least 5 feet (1.5 m) long and hooked to the back of the harness. A longer line is used for a three-dog team. A bungee-type attachment is usually incorporated to reduce jerks. The best ones are reflectorized for easy visibility. Special quick-release hitches or hooks are available, used so that the skijorer may unhook the dog's lead rapidly. If you are using more than one dog (not recommended for beginners), you can choose a variety of ways to hook them up. Dogs in a single line rather than fanned out are better on narrow, single-track trails and on fresh snow for breaking trail. If you are skijoring with two dogs, you will need to add a neckline to hook them together.

Sponsoring Organizations

In the United States, the International Sled Dog Racing Association (ISDRA) sanctions many races. The International Federation of Sleddog Sports, Inc., (IFSS) World Cup sponsors races all over the world, as well as a world championship race every other year. At the IFSS World Championship event, skijoring races are separated into men's and women's and one-dog and two-dog categories.

You should be a competent skier before attempting to skijor with your dog.

Eligibility Requirements: Any strong dog who enjoys running and pulling is eligible. All dogs should be at least 1 year old before beginning serious training, and 18 months is ideal. Dogs should weigh at least 35 pounds (16 kg).

Titles: Some organizations offer one-, two-, and three-dog skijoring titles.

Premier Events: The 320-mile (515-km) Alaskan Iditasport Supreme is a premier event for long-distance skijorers. Sprint races are held in various localities all around the United States, and the Alaska Skijoring and Pulk Association (ASPA) holds 20- (32-km) and 50-mile (80.5-km) endurance races.

How to Get Started

If your dog loves to pull or has a strong chase instinct, he is a good candidate for skijoring. Most dogs have the basic instincts (chasing and running) that can be "harnessed," so to speak, to make a good skijoring prospect.

LEARN TO SKI

Learn to ski before you start skijoring. You should be able to "snowplow" proficiently and feel comfortable climbing and descending hills. Learning to step-turn corners, carve turns, and "hockey stop" is a plus.

PUT SAFETY FIRST

Of course, a thorough vet checkup is a requirement for this strenuous sport, which requires peak physical condition and the ability to withstand cold temperatures, often for a protracted period.

To keep both you and your dog safe, understand how skijoring equipment works, especially the towline quick release, which connects to your belt. Never ski with more dogs than you can control. Also, avoid icy or heavily trafficked areas, and tell someone where you are going and when you expect to return. Stay away from motorized traffic if at all possible. Wear bright clothing and protective gear. Never wrap a towline or tugline around your fingers—many a person has broken a bone this way. Ski the trail without your dog first, to ascertain what the conditions are. Dogs are complicating factors.

TRAIN YOUR DOG

Many people start training their dogs on foot in the summer. Using a skijor belt and bungee tug, the idea is to take off at a light jog. You can use this time not only to condition yourself and your dog but to teach the *gee* (turn right) and *haw* (turn left) commands. Travel well-defined trails that go only in the direction you want. When the weather gets cooler, some people hook their dogs up to wheeled carts. Once the snow begins, you have to exercise renewed caution. During this era of global warming, much snow cover is so thin that dangerous roots and sharp rocks can be a real problem.

As soon as you get up on your skis and are ready to go, call out "Hike!" or a similar phrase. If your dog doesn't "get it," you may want to resort to throwing something ahead of you to get him to chase it. It also helps to practice in a place where a ready-made trail stretches in front of you. A narrow flat ski trail with a berm at least 1 foot (2 m) high is perfect for starters. When your dog begins pulling, praise him. Keep the towline taut so as to get him accustomed to pulling. All of this is easier if you enlist the help of a friend to ski or skijor (or even walk) ahead of you so that your dog is encouraged to follow or chase. If you have a friend with an experienced pulling dog, hooking the dogs up together will give your dog a clear idea of what is expected of him.

Some skiers use a classic diagonal stride (cross-country) technique, while others prefer the faster skate-skiing technique, especially when racing.

DEVELOP VERBAL CUES

Dogs must be taught the traditional mushing commands. This is critical because you won't have much control over your dogs while on the trail—your voice is your only real tool. However, it's important to use these commands sparingly. If you talk too much, the dogs may stop paying attention.

- Come around: Turn 180 degrees.
- Gee: Turn right!
- Haw: Turn left!
- Hike: Start running.
- Line out: Stand out with a taut line to wait for the hike command.
- On by!: Keep going and don't pay attention to the distraction.
- Whoa!: Stop.

Strategies for Success

To be successful at skijoring, keep training sessions short and interesting, feed your dog well, and start training slowly.

KEEP TRAINING SESSIONS SHORT AND INTERESTING

Keep training sessions short and sweet, and teach one segment at a time. Don't overwhelm your dog, and if you see his enthusiasm flagging, let him rest and recover his zeal. You can also try altering speeds, distances, and routes.

FEED YOUR DOG WELL

Keep your dog well fed; most winter sports dogs require a much higher-calorie and higher-fat diet than do sedentary dogs. The cold, the pulling strain, and the speed and times worked all demand fuel. If your dog will be working hard, consider home-cooking some meals—a dry kibble will not be sufficient, especially for distance work

START TRAINING SLOWLY

When training, start at a slow and controlled pace; don't let your dog simply start running. It's not safe, and it doesn't teach him any control. Because some dogs get nervous at the idea of something attached to them, use an object like a tire instead of yourself. This is called "pull training" and must be mastered if your dog is to be successful at skijoring.

ADDITIONAL ORGANIZATIONS

European Sleddog Racing Association (ESDRA)
www.esdra.net
International Federation of Sleddog Sports, Inc. (IFSS)
www.sleddogsport.com
International Sled Dog Racing Association (ISDRA)
www.idsdra.org

Chapter 30

Sledding

Definition

Also called mushing, sledding involves the use of one or more dogs to pull a sled over snow. Sledding can be utilitarian, recreational, or competitive.

History of Sledding

The two breeds most closely associated with sledding are the Alaskan Malamute and the Siberian Husky, but their histories are quite different. Alaskan Malamutes originated with the Mahlemuit Eskimos (hence the name Malamute) near the Anvik River in Alaska. These very large, sturdy dogs were used for hauling food and other cargo around the widespread Mahlemuit communities. Siberian Huskies originated with the Chukchi people of northeastern Siberia and were used not just for hauling but also for transporting people on hunting trips. Siberians were smaller and faster than their Malamute cousins.

When Russian and American pioneers came to Alaska, they found a dog-mushing culture well established. Alfred H. Brooks, the head of the US Geological Survey, commented at the beginning of the 20th century, "Countless generations of Alaskan natives have used the dog for transport, and he is

Mushing is most popular in North America and northern Europe.

TOP BREEDS

"Sled dogs" live to do two things: run and pull. Unsurprisingly, the most successful sled dogs are members of Nordic breeds, such as the Siberian Husky, Samoyed, and Alaskan Malamute. Other breeds, less familiar in the United States, include the Euro Hound, Greenland Dog, Canadian Eskimo Dog, Chinook, Seppala Siberian Sleddog, and Akita. Best known for long-distance racing, however, is the Alaskan Husky, which is a crossbreed. The cross can vary, but usually the dog is partly Siberian Husky and partly something else, such as a pointer or Greyhound. However, any cross that works is okay—the only criteria are speed and endurance.

to Alaska what the yak is to India or the llama to Peru." The Russians developed the idea of a lead dog who would follow voice commands and keep the team in order.

Sled-dog racing began as a formal sport with the first All-Alaska Sweepstakes Race in 1908, and in the 1920s, returning gold miners brought the sport to New England, where it became popular. Sponsors were sought, and in the next two decades, professional mushers and teams traveled across North America to compete in races. Media attention increased the popularity of the sport, and in the 1932 Lake Placid Winter Olympic games, sled-dog racing was featured as a demonstration sport. In 1992, the International Federation of Sleddog Sports, Inc., (IFSS) was officially incorporated to coordinate local, national, and international organizations and to obtain the stated goal of Olympic recognition and organization on par with other sports.

Overview

Mushing, the state sport of Alaska, is practiced worldwide but is most popular in North America and northern Europe. Although dogsled racing gets the most publicity, informal recreational mushing is widespread and provides a healthy outdoor winter activity for many individuals and families.

Mushing for utilitarian purposes includes anything from hauling wood and delivering milk or the mail to rural travel and equipment hauling. Dogs have been replaced by snowmobiles in many places, but some trappers and other isolated users have gone back to sled dogs, finding them safer and more dependable in extreme weather conditions.

Events like the Iditarod grab the headlines, but many shorter and more informal races are offered over much of the United States and Europe. (In some places, wheeled carts replace sleds in the event of a lack of snow.) Generally, the length of the race depends on the number of dogs in the team, with 1 mile (1.5 km) per dog being the general rule. Therefore, a three-dog team can run 3 miles (5 km). Sometimes a club will allow an "unlimited" race, which can involve as many as 22 dogs. Many races are known as "sprints" and can range from 3 to 15 or more miles (5 to 24 km). Mid-distance races are from about 35 to 200 miles (56.5 to 322 km), while long-distance races cover 200 to more than 1,000 miles (322 to 1,609.5 km). The sprint and mid-distance races are frequently run in heats over two or three days.

Usually, to avoid a traffic jam of excited dogs at the starting line on the first day, teams are released at one-minute intervals. (Mass starts, however, are used in some events.) The trail is wide enough so that faster teams can pass slower ones. On the second day, teams are seeded according to the

The musher's main job is to steer and direct the dogs.

previous day's time, so the faster teams go first. The final score is based on the combined times of both days' racing.

Each dog on a team has a position name and a function. Lead dogs guide the team and set the pace. Modern teams usually have two lead dogs, although single leaders used to be more common. A few teams use a free leader, who runs loose and finds the trail for the rest of the team, but this is not allowed in races. Good lead dogs must be intelligent and have initiative, common sense, and the ability to find a trail under often adverse conditions. Directly behind the leaders are the swing dogs, whose primary job is to help guide the rest of the team around turns or curves. Big, strong team dogs are next and add power to the team. Nearest the sled are the wheel dogs. Wheel dogs also need to be strong, and a good wheeler must have a relatively calm temperament so as not to be startled by the sled bouncing around right behind him. The wheel dogs help guide the sled around tight curves.

The musher is along for the ride, and her main goal is to steer and direct the dogs. She is the ultimate leader and responsible for their combined safety. She is also required to "peddle" (stand with one foot on the runner of the sled and push it along), and on occasion, may have to get out to walk (or run) along with the dogs to lighten the load, especially when the going gets really tough.

FUN FACT

The term "mush" is said to derive from the French word *marche*, meaning "Go!", the command to the team to commence pulling. Nowadays, most sled dog drivers just say "Hike!" (obviously a football analogy). But they still call themselves "mushers."

Requirements

Dogs

- cold resistance
- endurance
- love of running
- strong

Sled-dog breeds love to run, and sledding gives them the perfect opportunity to do so.

HANDLERS

- ability to put the dogs first
- love of the outdoors
- understanding of snow and winter conditions

Equipment and Supplies

- booties
- pulling harness
- sled
- tugline

Basic equipment required for long-distance races includes an ax, warm clothing and sleeping bag, and adequate food for the musher and dogs. You may be out of contact with the "civilized" world for days, so it is best to be prepared.

Booties: Sled dogs almost always wear booties for paw protection. These are small sock-like coverings that are used over rough ice or when the team is traveling a long distance.

Pulling Harness: The harness should be padded around the front and fit perfectly. Two kinds of harness are available. Racers mostly use an X-back or H-back harness with the dogs connected in pairs to a central gangline or pulling line. Although the H-back harness might be optimal, beginners usually have more success with the easier-to-fit X-back harness. A fan hitch, with each dog connected directly to the sled with a tugline, is used in treeless areas or where the dogs need to spread out their weight over ice. This hitch is used on narrow trails and is mandatory in some races. The gangline consists of three components: the towline that connects to the sled and runs between the dogs; the tuglines, attached to (and braided into) the towline and attached to each dog's harness; and the neckline, which attaches to the collar to keep the dogs close to the towline. (The dogs don't pull on the neckline.) The collar should be a simple buckle collar, with a large welded O-ring. Never use a choke collar.

Sled: There are two basic kinds of sleds: basket sleds and toboggan sleds. Basket sleds are lightweight and are the most popular with recreational mushers and racers. They are also cheaper and easier to learn to handle, so they are best for the beginner. Toboggan sleds are heavier and less maneuverable and are more often employed for serious hauling. Both sled types have an emergency brake, or heavy metal snow hook, which is obviously of major importance in case the dogs get tangled up or out of control.

Sponsoring Organizations

Many local clubs sponsor events, sometimes under the auspices of the IFSS or International Sled Dog Racing Association (ISDRA). These events may include one-, two-, four-, six-, or eight-dog sleds for juniors and adults. Races can also be divided into sprints and long-distance runs.

Eligibility Requirements: Any large- or medium-sized dog who is cold-hardy and likes to pull can participate. Age restrictions can vary, depending on the sponsoring organization.

Titles: Titles are not given out in sledding events.

Premier Events: The most famous dog racing event is the 1,049-mile (1,688-km) Alaskan Iditarod (literally, a "far-off place"), although the actual length varies somewhat, as the route changes from year to year. The trail is part of an old mail route that was the site of the great serum run when, in January 1925, dog teams across Alaska formed a relay to carry life-giving diphtheria serum to a plague-stricken community. The race starts near Anchorage and ends in Nome, and the winners average between 9 and 12 days, depending on weather and trail conditions.

A more recent premier event is the Yukon Quest, which began in 1984. It follows the old gold-rush and mail-delivery routes. Every February, outstanding dog teams from around the world set out on an epic 1,000-mile (1,609.5-km) journey starting in Whitehorse, Yukon Territory, to Fairbanks, Alaska. Dog teams consist of 1 musher and 14 dogs. Not as widely known as the Iditarod, the Yukon Quest is regarded as the toughest dogsled race in the world.

How to Get Started

Sled-dog breeds love to run, and sledding gives them that opportunity. They are strong enough to pull you along for the ride as well! Whether your interest is racing or just recreational sledding, sledding is a fun sport for the entire family.

GET YOUR DOG A CHECKUP

Sledding requires a superlative athlete, and your dog must be in perfect condition. Have your vet give him a thorough checkup before even trying. Only adult (12 to 14 months) dogs should participate in racing, although you can start training puppies (8 to 10 months) to pull for recreation, as long you don't put any pressure on them. No dog should run in distance competition until he is at least three years old.

Each sled dog on a team has a position name and a function.

FIND A MENTOR

Although mushing itself is pretty simple, you'll need a mentor to help you with the harnessing and training aspects. A local club (or one of the many mushing boot camps that have sprung up) should be able to give you any advice you need.

While you can get some preliminary practice by doing bikejoring or skijoring, obviously this is a sport meant for snow, and if you live in Hawaii, it may not be the best event for you. If your area does have snow in the winter, join up with a local sled racing club or visit a competition.

TRAIN YOUR DOG

Sledding is not a weekend sport. To be successful, you'll need to work through the week to help your dog stay in condition.

The most important advice is to start young by getting your puppy used to wearing a harness and to start pulling things. Obviously, you'll begin with something light—a 6-inch-long (15-cm-long) piece of board is ideal. Just let him drag it around the house. If you have a natural puller, you'll

You must always be the leader of your sled-dog pack.

soon know it. The only thing you'll have to work on is to encourage the dog to keep the line taut. It's also important to get your dog used to the idea of being "staked," as this is a feature of races—waiting to start, resting, and so on. If you start when he's young, your puppy will soon accept the idea of a stakeout and not struggle against it.

To train your dog to start moving, stand behind him and say "Hike." If he doesn't walk ahead at your command, step forward until you are beside his head and gently encourage him to go forward. Then move back again. Don't stay in front of him; he needs to get the idea that he is to forge ahead. Once he succeeds with this, you can hook him up to a more experienced dog he already knows. If your puppy shows no interest, don't despair. Some dogs just need to grow up a little and become more self-confident.

Many mushers like to start on some kind of wheeled rig before the snow comes. Increase your mileage only in small increments. A good training schedule will include rest days, so your dog will have time to build muscle. Your dog should wear booties on rough trails; check them regularly.

Most places don't have snow year round, so in the summer you can practice on the various "dryland" sports, like bikejoring or canicross. This will keep you both in shape.

DEVELOP VERBAL CUES

Your sled dog is not only being controlled with a leash—your voice is his only guide, so he needs to listen to you. All commands should be spoken in a clear, firm voice. Do not shout or "overtalk" your dog, or he may stop listening to you. The basic commands are:

- Gee: Turn right.
- Haw: Turn left.
- Hike: Start moving.
- On by: Keep going straight ahead, don't stop.
- Out front: Go out to the end of the gangline and hold it taut.
- Whoa: Stop!

Strategies for Success

Although most professional mushers keep their dogs outside in kennels year round (many have 50 to 70 dogs), your house pet can also succeed in this sport. Just keep an eye on how he acclimates to cold weather. Your ideal dog is mellow at home but a "beast" on the mushing trail.

BE THE LEADER OF YOUR PACK

You must always be ready to be the true leader or alpha dog of your pack. If your dogs lose confidence in your ability to lead them, they will become unresponsive.

HONE YOUR SENSE OF DIRECTION

It may seem obvious, but a good musher needs a good sense of direction—or at least a GPS. Too many people have gotten lost, off track, and into trouble.

ADDITIONAL ORGANIZATIONS

European Sleddog Racing Association (ESDRA)
www.esdra.net

Chapter 31

Terrier Racing

Definition

A terrier race is just what it sounds like—a race among terriers. In a way, this is the terrier equivalent of lure coursing. The event is so much fun that it is often performed at various local fairs and other events.

Steeplechase races feature several short hurdles adjusted to the height of the competitors.

History of Terrier Racing

There isn't a lot known about the earliest history of terrier racing, but the sport probably developed as a recreational event held at foxhunting kennels during the off-season. Several "fun" events were staged, including conformation, a hound show, and a terrier show. Events such as these were used to keep the dogs occupied, limber, and in condition when they weren't hunting. The first races may have simply been pickup affairs between farmers or other terrier owners in recognition of their dogs' speed and competitiveness. More recently, the Jack Russell Terrier Club of America (JRTCA) began offering official terrier races in the early 1980s, and the United Kennel Club (UKC) began holding formal events beginning in May 2004.

Overview

Both the JRTCA and UKC sponsor two types of races: flat and steeplechase (hurdles).

Flat Races

Flat races take place on a straight course with a starting box at one end and a stack of straw or hay bales with a hole in the middle at the other. The finish line is at the exit point of the hole. The dogs are muzzled for safety (theirs and the catcher's, the person who catches the dog at the end).

A lure (usually a piece of scented fox or rabbit fur) is attached to a piece of string that is pulled along by a lure pulley. The gate is opened just as the lure starts away, and the dogs chase after it. The first dog through the hole in the hay bale is the winner. The muzzles come in handy here, as these feisty dogs don't always perfectly agree about which dog really has the right to enter the opening first.

Each race may be a series of heats, semis, and finals, and up to six terriers race at a time. Any race may be rerun at the judge's discretion.

Steeplechase Races

The steeplechase race usually features several short hurdles, adjusted to the height of the competitors. Otherwise, it is conducted just like a flat race. As in flat racing, the dogs chase after a lure pulled on a string.

Fun Fact

The world's most famous racing terriers are the Tricky Tykes, a British terrier racing display team. They have a tremendous following throughout the United Kingdom and have been invited many times to appears at Crufts Dog Show. These dogs are really the Harlem Globetrotters of the terrier racing world, and they put on a hilarious show as they negotiate hurdles and "outsmart" their trainers time and again.

Requirements

Dogs

- speed
- strong chase instinct

Handlers

- sense of humor

Equipment and Supplies

- hay/straw bales
- hurdles
- lure
- lure pull
- muzzle
- protective gloves (for catchers)
- race course
- racing collar
- starter box

Hay/Straw Bales: Straw bales or other suitable material must be placed around the lure pull motor to prevent access by the dogs. These bales also mark the end of the course and cushion the back of the catching area. The UKC allows the end barrier to be made of straw with foam padding or cushioned foam.

Hurdles: Hurdles—a minimum of four placed at least 20 feet (6 m) apart—are required for the steeplechase. The last hurdle should not be closer than 30 feet (9 m) from the finish line. Each hurdle should be lightweight and slant back from the direction of approach for safety reasons; it must be flush with the side fencing of the race course. For the JRTCA, the hurdles should be no taller than 8 inches (20.5 cm) for puppies and 16 inches (40.5 cm) for adults. The UKC requires that hurdles have a 6-inch (15-cm) maximum height for the under 10 inches (25.5 cm) class; an 8-inch (20.5-cm) maximum height for the 10 (25.5 cm) to under 12.5 inches (31.5 cm) class; and a 12-inch (30.5-cm) maximum height for the remainder of classes.

Lure: In the JRTCA, the lure is a piece of scent-drenched fur tied to several hundred feet (m) of string. The lure pull

The starter box—the place from which the terriers are released—has a wire or clear plastic front that allows the dogs to see the lure.

drags it down the race track for the terriers to follow. The UKC uses unscented lures.

Lure Pull: The lure pull is attached to an electric motor connected to a reliable power source.

Muzzle: Dogs must wear a muzzle when racing, and the muzzle must properly fit the dog. Soft, plastic, and wire basket-type muzzles with top straps are acceptable.

Protective Gloves: All catchers must wear protective gloves, regardless of whether the dog's owner is catching. It is recommended that all dog catchers wear heavy gauntlet-style gloves, such as welder gloves.

Race Course: The JRTCA race course consists of a 150- to 225-foot (45.5- to 68.5-m) straight track with a 15- to 20-foot (4.5- to 6-m) catch area. UKC track lengths are 175 to 250 feet (53.5 to 76 m). The best courses are designed to go slightly uphill. The sides of the course are generally made of plastic fencing.

Racing Collar: Each terrier must wear a colored fabric collar to help determine the order of finish. The colors should be easily distinguishable from each other to prevent confusion.

Starter Box: The starter box is usually made of wood, with either springs or hinges on the front. The front is made of strong wire (or clear plastic) to allow the terriers to see the lure. The floor of the box may be grass, dirt, or carpeting to provide good footing for the dogs.

Sponsoring Organizations

Jack Russell Club of America (JRTCA)

The Racing Division at a sanctioned trial consists of two sections: Flat and Steeplechase (Hurdle). Both contain Pups, Puppy Championship, Dogs, Bitches, Adult Championship, Veterans, and Veteran Championship classes.

Eligibility Requirements: The JRTCA admits Jack Russell Terriers only. Spayed and neutered dogs are eligible. Age requirements vary, depending on the class.

Titles: No official titles are awarded.

Premier Events: The JRTCA has a National Trial.

United Kennel Club (UKC)

The UKC offers separate divisions for Dachshunds; for American Hairless Terriers, Parson Russell Terriers, and Rat Terrier breeds (APR Classes); and an Open Division, which is for all other eligible breeds. The classes are identical for flat and steeplechase divisions and include Regular (for a dog who has not earned a race championship title of that race type), Champion (for a dog who has earned the Champion race title for that race type), and Grand Champion (for a dog who has earned the Grand Champion

---

From the Expert

The Jack Russell Terrier Club of America (JRTCA) reminds contestants to cool down their terriers after each race. You can use a spray mist bottle for this purpose. Find more tips at www.therealjackrussell.com/trial/racing.php

---

race title for that race type. Each of these classes is divided into Dachshund, APR, and Open Divisions.

Eligibility Requirements: The UKC admits Dachshunds (although they are not eligible to race in steeplechase) and the following terrier breeds: American Hairless Terriers, Australian Terriers, Bedlington Terriers, Border Terriers, Cairn Terriers, Cesky Terriers, Dandie Dinmont Terriers, Glen of Imaal Terriers, Jack Russell Terriers, Jagdterriers, Lakeland Terriers, Manchester Terriers, Miniature Schnauzers, Norfolk Terriers, Norwich Terriers, Patterdale Terriers, Rat Terriers, Russell Terriers, Scottish Terriers, Sealyham Terriers, Silky Terriers, Skye Terriers, Smooth Fox Terriers, Sporting Lucas Terriers, Teddy Roosevelt Terriers, Toy Fox Terriers, Welsh Terriers, West Highland White Terriers, Wire Fox Terriers, and Yorkshire Terriers. In some cases, spayed/neutered dogs and mixed-breed dogs, as described in the UKC breed standard, can be entered under the Limited Privilege (LP) Program. Spayed and neutered dogs are eligible to participate. Except for special puppy classes, dogs must be at least 12 months of age.

Titles: UKC terrier race titles must be earned successively. Titles earned in flat racing include United Flat Racer (UFR) and United Flat Race Champion (URCH). Steeplechase titles include United Steeplechase Racer (USR) and United Steeplechase Race Champion (USRCH).

Premier Events: Events are held all around the United States at which dogs can receive All-Star rankings.

How to Get Started

Most terriers have a strong prey drive that enables them to enjoy this sport and participate with gusto. Sophisticated training is not needed.

GET YOUR DOG A CHECKUP

This is a fast-paced sport that requires your dog to be in top condition. Be sure to get your vet to certify that your dog is healthy and ready to run, and in some cases, jump.

You can start training with a puppy who's only four months of age, although he will not be able to compete until he is at least six months old. Don't let him go over

Go to a couple of terrier races to see if it's something your dog may enjoy.

high jumps at first, as his bones and joints are still growing.

Go to a Terrier Race

Go to a couple of terrier races to see if this is something your dog (and you) might enjoy. You'll definitely need to join a local kennel club that participates in this sport; most people don't have a terrier racing track in the backyard.

Train Your Dog

To begin training your dog for a terrier race, simply get a sock and spray some artificial scent on it if needed (available in many hunting supply stores). Attach the lure to a 20-foot (6-m) piece of string. "Tease" him by shaking the fur in front of him to get his attention, and then run off in the opposite direction, trailing the lure behind you. Let your dog catch the fur so that he will have a sense of accomplishment and praise him mightily. Repeat until you think that he gets the idea—but don't tire him out, and don't let him get dehydrated.

To teach hurdles, drag the lure over them—your terrier will get the idea in a flash. Make sure that you keep the hurdles very low if you have a young dog because jumping could damage his growing bones and joints.

You may also want to start using a basket muzzle right away to get your dog used to the idea. Just put it on him and leave it there—he'll get used to it fast. As long as he is having fun training, he'll associate the muzzle with good things!

Strategies for Success

Letting your dog watch other dogs run and always remembering to be a good sport will help both of you succeed in terrier racing.

LET YOUR DOG WATCH SOME RACES

It's a good idea to let your dog watch some of the races before he participates; this is sure to get him all wound up and ready to run himself! Participate in a fun race to get in some needed practice.

BE A GOOD SPORT

Remember to be a good sport, and thank everyone involved (including the "catchers"). They have a tough job. Being friendly and polite won't win you races, but it will win you friends.

Chapter 32

Therapy

Definition

Therapy dogs visit institutions such as nursing homes, schools, and hospitals to provide comfort to and relieve stress for people in these difficult environments. This role of providing companionship and comfort distinguishes therapy dogs from service dogs, who actively assist people with various disabilities.

Two types of pet therapy exist: animal-assisted therapy (AAT) and animal-assisted activities (AAA). AAT is a goal-directed, documented intervention in which a trained therapist or health professional uses a dog or other animal as an integral part of the treatment to improve human physical and emotional functioning. A written, individualized treatment plan is designed. An example of AAT would be having a person lacking fine motor control handle a dog by grooming him and buckling his collar. The United States Army has recently begun using AAT dogs in the field to help seriously distressed soldiers. The soldiers often find it easier to talk to the dog, with the therapist listening, than to the therapist alone.

Unlike in AAT, AAA dog visits do not provide direct, goal-oriented therapy but seek to use the animal to make a person relax, improve their well-being, and open communication channels with a withdrawn person. A trained professional does have to be present during sessions, but the visits are less structured overall, with no records kept of the encounter.

In both AAT and AAA, therapy animals are not considered "service animals" by federal law, and they are not permitted to enter a "No Pets" area.

History of Therapy

Elaine Smith, a registered nurse, observed the effects of visits by a chaplain's dog on hospital patients while working in England. Upon returning to the United States in 1976, she founded Therapy Dogs International (TDI), a program to train therapy dogs for work in hospitals and other institutions. Today, these dogs work in all 50 states and Canada, providing free visits to people in need.

The Delta Society was formed in 1977 in Portland, Oregon, by Michael J. McCullock, MD, as a response to growing research that showed the healing power of the human–animal bond. For more than 30 years, the Delta Society has remained focused on improving human health through positive interactions with animals of all species.

Numerous other organizations also provide similar services through therapy dogs. And of course, some people

TOP BREEDS

Dogs of any breed or size can be therapy dogs. Some dogs are purebred, others were adopted from rescue groups or animal shelters. The only requirements are that the dog be calm, gentle, friendly, healthy, and nonthreatening. He should also be comfortable in all sorts of unusual environments and situations.

In general, older, calmer, less excitable, and less distractible dogs make excellent therapy dogs. Big dogs can stand next to a bed to be petted; smaller dogs can be put on someone's lap. If your dog is a little too old to start an active sport like agility, being a therapy dog might be an ideal activity for both of you.

do therapy work with their dog without belonging to any particular organization.

Overview

The company of dogs (and other pets) has been shown to have many therapeutic benefits, such as lowering blood pressure, increasing flexibility in arthritic fingers and wrists, and giving patients a more positive outlook. And the benefits of therapy dogs are not limited to physical health. Dogs provide a point of contact between the visitor and resident. They provide spiritual comfort and awaken the memory. Recently, dogs have even been used to help children with speech and reading problems; the dog listens patiently to the child without being judgmental, thereby lowering stress and anxiety and improving the child's performance.

Dogs bring sparkle into the facilities they visit, providing a lively subject for conversation and bringing back memories of previously owned pets. The volunteers in the program and the dogs who visit with them make a real difference in the quality of life for the people with whom they interact. The dogs provide real therapy, not just an amusing interlude in an otherwise dull day.

ANIMAL-ASSISTED THERAPY (AAT)

In AAT, therapy is integrated into the total care program the patient needs, and the visit is geared to helping the patient

In animal-assisted therapy (AAT), a trained therapist or health professional uses a dog to help improve human physical and emotional functioning.

progress in specific areas. To find out if your dog can assist in this program, contact the institution you are interested in working with to find out its specific requirements. These will differ from place to place.

ANIMAL-ASSISTED ACTIVITIES (AAA)

In AAA, the volunteer works mostly alone with the patient, staying for as long as desired. The volunteer may visit different people on different days or just one. There are no rules, and the benefits for the patient are mostly social and psychological. Some facilities require your dog to have been pre-approved by a national or local organization; others are more flexible and have no such prerequisites, although they way want to meet the dog and view his veterinary record first. Always call ahead and see what is required by the institution in which you have an interest.

Requirements

Dogs

- ability to take treats quietly without grabbing
- clean and well groomed
- enjoy interacting with strangers
- enjoy being touched by strangers, especially children
- obedience to basic commands
- quiet

Handlers

- empathetic
- friendly and outgoing
- good listener
- nonjudgmental
- polite

Equipment and Supplies

- brush/other grooming items
- collar
- leash
- treats

Brush/Other Grooming Items: You will need a brush or other grooming items if required by the program.

Collar: You will likely need a collar to take your dog into the institution. Most therapy dogs should be easily controlled with a plain buckle or snap collar, although smaller dogs are often walked on harnesses. You might also wish to use a head halter, which allows you complete but humane control of your dog's head (in case he's too inquisitive about sniffing).

Leash: You will likely need a lead to take your dog into the institution. It's usually best to select a 4-foot (1-m) leash, which helps keep your dog close to you—you

Fun Fact
Animal therapists give something special to enhance the health and well-being of those with whom they interact. It has been clinically proven that petting, touching, and talking with animals lowers blood pressure, relieves stress, and eases depression.

Therapy dogs can really make a difference in a person's quality of life.

certainly don't want him scampering down the hallway ahead of you. Specific programs and institutions may have special requirements.

Treats: Bring along some small, dry treats for the clients to hand out to your dog.

Sponsoring Organizations

DELTA SOCIETY

The Delta Society is a human-services organization dedicated to improving people's health and well-being. It does this by providing positive interactions with animals and by seeking to reduce the barriers that prevent the involvement of animals in everyday life and expanding the therapeutic and service role of animals in health, service, and education. Its Pet Partners Program, established in 1990, is the only national registry that requires volunteer training and screening of animal–handler teams. Animals with disabilities are welcome.

Eligibility Requirements: You can attend a workshop (scheduled throughout the year all around the United States) or complete the Delta Society's home study course. Your dog must pass a general physical exam, be up to date on vaccinations, and be free of parasites. He will be tested on his obedience to basic commands and controllability. A Pet Partners Aptitude Test (PPAT) is designed to simulate conditions you may encounter on a visit.

Titles: The Delta Society does not award titles.

Premier Events: Every visit to a lonely or sick person is a premier event.

THERAPY DOGS INTERNATIONAL (TDI)

TDI is a volunteer organization dedicated to the regulation, testing, and registration of therapy dogs and their volunteer handlers for the purpose of visiting nursing homes, hospitals, other institutions, and wherever else therapy dogs are needed.

Eligibility Requirements: TDI requires that prospective therapy dogs be at least one year old and have passed the American Kennel Club's (AKC) Canine Good Citizen (CGC) test. In addition, all dogs must be assessed by a certified TDI evaluator for temperament and suitability to become a therapy dog. This test also evaluates the dog's behavior around people who use service equipment, such as wheelchairs and crutches. A health record form must be completed and signed by a licensed veterinarian, and a negative heartworm test is required within the past year in areas where heartworm is present. (Dogs on heartworm preventive are exempt from this requirement.) In addition, hospitals and other institutions may have separate requirements for admitting therapy dogs to their premises.

Titles: No titles are awarded.

Premier Events: Every visit to a sick or troubled person is a premier event in the world of therapy dogs.

How to Get Started

Register with a national organization like the Delta Society or TDI or another organization that specializes in such work, or contact a local group. Many communities have their own

FROM THE EXPERT

"Mr. Whitlock hasn't spoken today," said the nurse sadly. Lizzie and I had just arrived at the nursing home for our weekly Fuzzy Buddy visit, and I was sorry to hear that our old friend, who suffered from Alzheimer's, was doing so poorly. Lizzie, however, seemed unfazed. Looking up impatiently, my 14-year-old Beagle was still robust, enthusiastic, and ready to take on any challenge. A few seconds later, I pushed open the door to Mr. Whitlock's room. He was in his wheelchair, staring at the wall. "Mr. Whitlock?" No response. Then Lizzie barked—the low, gruff bark of a very old dog who would not take silence for an answer. Mr. Whitlock turned slightly in his chair, and the blank look melted. "Lizard," he said. He always called her that—whether from mishearing her name or whether it was simply a whim of his, I was never able to determine. It didn't much matter, as Lizzie responded equally to either name. A smile cracked the wrinkles. "Hi, Lizard." The visit began.

easily accessible programs. The best way to find out what is available in your area is to call local hospitals and nursing homes, ask what programs they provide, who runs them, and how to contact them.

GET YOUR DOG A CHECKUP

All groups require dogs to be checked by a vet, especially for problems that he might pass on to ill people or children (like ringworm).

SOCIALIZE YOUR DOG

Early socialization is important for all dogs and especially for a therapy dog. Take your puppy with you whenever you can. Let him meet people of both sexes and every age and race. Have unknown people pet and talk to him and give him treats. Also, let him meet people who are using walkers, canes, or wheelchairs, and who are wearing all sorts of uniforms. It's a good idea for any puppy to meet 100 people by the time he is four months old.

When participating in therapy work, your dog may have to walk on unfamiliar surfaces or tolerate loud noises or people acting in unusual ways. He also needs to react calmly to any unexpected situation he may encounter. This is why socialization is so important for a therapy dog.

Be sure that your dog will react quietly to rough treatment—a child or older person may pull on fur or even an ear before you can run interference. Your dog should be able to put up with this without snapping or whining.

Strategies for Success

Letting your dog do the talking and scheduling regular therapy visits will help you help others.

BE A GOOD LISTENER

The best way to succeed at pet therapy is to be a good listener—let your dog do the talking. A quiet, nonjudgmental dog has a miraculous way of letting people open their hearts. It is amazing how much you can learn too!

SCHEDULE REGULAR VISITS

It's also a good idea to make your visit regular. If you can only go once a month, that's fine, but people depend on that once-a-month visit. People confined to prisons, nursing homes, and hospitals have little control over their lives, and a regular visit does tremendous things for their spirits. Being reliable and regular in your attentions will help develop trust among all concerned.

ADDITIONAL ORGANIZATIONS

Delta Society Australia
www.deltasocietyaustralia.com.au
Pets as Therapy
www.petsastherapy.org
Therapeutic Paws of Canada (TPOC)
www.tpoc.ca

Chapter 33

Tracking

Definition

Tracking is a sport designed to encourage a dog to make use of his scenting ability to find human beings. The dog uses his nose to follow a trail, and the object is to find an article left by a person—usually a leather glove. Dogs do not compete against each other but work to pass the test.

History of Tracking

Dogs were tracking game while they were still wolves, and human hunters have used the tracking abilities of dogs for thousands of years. Today, dogs find missing children, help capture escaped criminals, find drugs and bombs, and earn titles in tracking trials.

The first American Kennel Club (AKC)-sponsored tracking test took place on June 13, 1936, at the North Westchester Kennel Club all-breed show in Mount Kisco, New York. The first tracking test at which a dog could earn a tracking title (Tracking Dog [TD]) was held October 7, 1947. Until that time, tracking was part of the Utility Dog (UD) title earned in obedience. The first Tracking Dog Excellent (TDX) test was in 1980, and the first Variable Surface Tracking (VST) test was held in 1995.

Overview

The dog's nose is his most amazing organ, and it's been estimated that a dog can smell things at concentrations nearly 100 million times lower than people can, sniffing out, for example, a drop of blood in 5 quarts (4.5 l) of water. Finding a leather glove in a field should be a cinch!

Tracks are generally laid out on the day previous to the trial. Events almost always take place outside in a large field, although the Variable Surface Tracking (VST) test may take you indoors through buildings as well. On the day of the trial, a track layer follows the marked track, removing any extraneous material and leaving an article on the track as specified. The track is not the confused jumble likely left by the truly lost or those trying to cover up their whereabouts; instead, it is a fairly straightforward trail so that each dog can be assessed on a level playing field.

After a specified time, the dog and handler are directed to the track to

TOP BREEDS

Any breed can compete in tracking, with people-oriented breeds like German Shepherd Dogs and Labrador Retrievers doing especially well. Hounds have great sniffers but can get sidetracked by game.

In TD and TDX tests, dogs have to track either a leather wallet or glove.

proceed. The dog is expected to work without assistance from his handler and is required to find the "lost" article to pass the test. He then indicates that he has found it in some way. There are no rules about this—some dogs sit, some dogs bark at it, some dogs pick it up, and some just wag their tails. The quality of the work may also be assessed by the judge. A tracking title is awarded to the dog who fulfills all of the requirements for that title.

Requirements

Dogs
- determination
- focus

Handlers
- ability to read dog's body language

Equipment and Supplies

- landscape flags/stakes
- leash
- practice area
- tracking articles
- tracking harness
- treats

Landscape Flags/Stakes: These flag or stake indicators mark the start of the course.

Leash: Your dog must be on a 30- to 40-foot (9- to 12-m) leash. You have to walk well behind your dog—you are not allowed to give guidance.

Practice Area: You'll need a large open area to practice in, one that is not loaded with the scent of other humans and dogs. One or two acres is enough for early training, but advanced training may require up 20 acres or more to provide an adequate challenge for the dog.

Tracking Articles: In TD and TDX tests, the article that the dog must track is a glove or wallet, usually made of leather. The VST uses four different articles of four different materials: leather, plastic, metal, and fabric.

Tracking Harness: A tracking harness is a special nonrestrictive design devised just for tracking. They come in a variety of materials (usually nylon in this sport) and styles, but in most cases the loop for the lead is usually farther to the rear than on a walking harness because the handler must stay behind the dog at all times. Many have quick-release snaps on the rear legs. For correct sizing, measure the dog's

Fun Fact

The first Variable Surface Tracking (VST) test was held in 1995 on a beautiful, clear morning in Ellicott City, Maryland. Darlene Ceretto competed on track one (of six). The following weekend, Ceretto's female German Shepherd Dog, Sealair's Raggedy Ann UD TDX, received the first VST title at an event held by the Northwest Obedience Club of Glenview, Illinois. Thus, she also became the first Champion Tracker (CT), a designation awarded to dogs holding all three tracking titles.

girth at the broadest part of the chest behind the front legs.

Treats: For training, you will need soft, high-value treats. These may include cookies, cheese, or hot dogs cut into cubes.

Sponsoring Organizations

AMERICAN KENNEL CLUB (AKC)

When beginning in AKC tracking events, a dog must first earn a certification to compete. Certification is granted if the dog completes the basic TD track test under the observation of an AKC judge. After successfully completing the certification, the dog is awarded four certificates for official entries in tracking competitions. These certificates are good for one year. Each time a handler enters a dog in an AKC tracking competition, a certificate must be relinquished. (This means that a handler must be recertified after that year is up.) Once in competition, a dog only needs to complete one tracking trial successfully to earn a title, unlike in other AKC sports. The dog can then move on to the next level of tracking tests.

You'll need a large open area in which to practice with your dog.

With the right training, any dog can learn to track.

The TD test includes following a track 440 to 500 yards (402.5 to 457 m) long with three to five changes in direction. The track is aged between 30 minutes and 2 hours before the dog begins scenting. The TDX test includes following a longer and older track. This track is 800 to 1,000 yards (731.5 to 914.5 m) long and has been aged between three and five hours. There are also five to seven direction changes, and human cross tracks are added as an extra challenge. The VST test is one of the most difficult tests for a tracking dog and replicates tracking in a real-world situation. The VST challenges the dog to track on a three- to five-hour-old track over three different surfaces, such as vegetation, concrete, and sand. The track is 600 to 800 yards (548.5 to 731.5 m) long, with at least three 90-degree turns and four articles: leather, plastic, metal, and fabric. Between one-third and one-half of the track must be devoid of vegetation (to make it harder). Rain, snow, and various weather conditions may also add to the challenge.

Eligibility Requirements: Purebred dogs registered with the AKC who are at least six months of age are eligible to participate in trials. Spayed and neutered dogs are eligible to participate.

Titles: A dog can earn four titles: Tracking Dog (TD), Tracking Dog Excellent (TDX), Variable Surface Tracking (VST), and Champion Tracker (CT). After successfully completing all three AKC tracking titles (TD, TDX, and VST), a dog earns the prestigious and highest title of Champion Tracker (CT).

Premier Events: The AKC National Tracking Invitational is held every other year. This event provides owners of CT dogs an opportunity to participate in an event designed especially for them.

How to Get Started

Tracking is a sport that can be learned by any dog when the training is right. Puppies are easiest to train, but dogs of any age can learn. The hardest part for the dog is learning what to track and to stay with that scent and not change over to a different one. (Beagles, for instance, may have a hard time concentrating on a boring human scent when a rabbit scent crosses the tracking line.)

GET YOUR DOG A CHECKUP

Although tracking is not terribly rigorous, especially at the lower levels, your dog needs to be reasonably fit and of course healthy and up to date on his shots.

GO TO A TRACKING CLASS

Most local kennel clubs hold seminars and weekend classes on this sociable activity. Sign up and join the fun!

TRAIN YOUR DOG

It's always smart to start practicing when your dog is hungry—a well-fed dog has less incentive to track. Start when the conditions are best: no wind, early morning, moderate temperatures, and fresh green grass about 4

FROM THE EXPERT

According to expert Belgian tracker Guy Verschatse, it's a good idea not to say your dog's name when you command him to "Find it." After all, when you say his name he is likely to look up at you, and you want him to concentrate on the ground.

In the sport of tracking, you and your dog are a team.

inches (10 cm) tall.

To begin, lay out some flagged stakes. Place your dog in his harness and use an ordinary 6-foot (2-m) lead. Work with a track layer (which can be a friend) who will show a treat to the dog on top of the glove and then walk off, placing the treat at the base of the first flag. (Make sure that your dog is observing all this.) It helps if the wind is blowing in the dog's direction at this point. The ultimate idea is to encourage him to follow the track, not the air scent. (Following an air scent is called trailing and is not allowed in tracking events.)

The track layer should continue to walk to about 10 yards (9 m) away, putting a treat every few feet (m) in her footprints. At the furthest point, she should place the treat on the glove (making a big to-do over the whole affair). After moving a few yards (m) forward, she should then make a wide circle. Now it's your dog's turn. Encourage him with words such as "Find it!" while he walks along, sniffing for the treats in the footprints until he reaches the glove, at which point you should praise him. Most dogs will catch on to the fun very quickly.

As soon as your dog gets the basic idea, allow some time (45 minutes to 1 hour) to let the air scent completely blow away; the tracking scent will remain. All beginning tracks should be one hour old before you set your dog on the track again. You should also soon stop leaving food on the track because the treat smells stronger than the scent of the object. As soon as your dog gets the basic idea, reward him when he succeeds in tracking the article.

Strategies for Success

Remember that you and your dog are a team. If he makes a mistake and gets off track, guide him gently back the right way. Never get angry or irritated with him. Your job is to help him succeed.

ACKNOWLEDGE YOUR DOG'S CONTROL

One of the most difficult mental blocks to get over for some handlers is the realization that in this sport, the dog has control. After all, you don't know (or are not supposed to know) where the article is. This is a true team sport.

TRAIN ON THE STRAIGHT FIRST

Train your dog on the straight first—let him be very accurate there for 75 feet (23 m) or so before you begin working on corners. Hide the bait in the track by burying it. You want your dog to smell the bait, not see it. Remember, this is a test of your dog's sniffing ability. Start off by working only on cool, wet days; these conditions hold the scent longer and make it easier for him to find the article.

ADDITIONAL ORGANIZATIONS

Canadian Kennel Club (CKC)
www.ckc.ca
United Schutzhund Clubs of America (USA)
www.germanshepherddog.com

Chapter 34

Water Sports

Definition

Canine water sports test a dog's desire and ability to perform useful water work, and these events promote water safety and achievement opportunities for all dogs. They include activities such as boat towing, locating and retrieving articles, and water rescue.

History of Water Sports

Although dogs have been saving lives for centuries, only the national breed clubs of various water dog breeds had certification programs. Today, an organization called Canine Water Sports (CWS) exists to provide opportunities for various water sports for all breeds and mixes. The CWS was founded in 2001 by Deborah Lee Miller-Riley, who gained experience working with Portuguese Water Dogs.

Overview

Some water tests have their foundation in historic canine water service work, such as rescue, retrieving, and courier duties. Other tasks, like the team swim, boat work, and underwater scent searches, derive from modern canine work and recreational activities. The guidelines for this sport are easy to master, and all of the water tasks are functional and fun to learn. Most of the events are held in lakes.

Requirements

Dogs

- calmness
- obedience
- strength
- swimming ability

Handlers

- swimming ability

Equipment and Supplies

- canine life jacket
- floating articles
- submersion articles

Top Breeds

Newfoundlands, with their immense size and powerful swimming skills, excel at this sport, but other large breeds, especially retrievers and Portuguese Water Dogs, can also perform well.

A doggy life vest helps prevent drowning, keeps your dog warm, and encourages confidence.

- harness
- whistle

Canine Life Jacket: This doggy life vest is required for all CWS training programs. It helps prevent drowning, keeps your dog warm, and encourages confidence. Even very buoyant dogs swim better and longer with a life jacket. Some are designed for calmer waters, others for more turbulent areas. For the best fit, choose one that just covers your dog's rib cage. To measure for size, measure around your dog's rib cage at its widest point.

Floating Articles: These can be various floating items used for retrieve work or tow-lines. CWS accepts, for example, the Portuguese Water Dog Club of America (PWDCA) floatline, made for the Portuguese Water Dog water trial, or the very similar tug and fetch line. Both are essentially floating marine lines with brightly colored floats attached. You may also choose any floating toy your dog likes to grab, but the CWS requires that your dog show his stuff on three different retrieve articles, so go for variety.

Harness: The harness can be the same kind used by

search-and-rescue or skijoring dogs, but any harness that allows your dog to swim easily and that you can grab is fine. For water sports, harnesses are used in submersion work. (You can lift your dog out of the water by the harness.) The CWS sells a bright red one that makes for easy visibility in the water. Other harnesses are specifically designed for water work, too. Floating leashes are available to go with the harnesses.

Submersion Articles: Some exercises require your dog to fetch underwater. The CWS sell a variety of interesting, colorful articles, but you can use anything that sinks.

Whistle: Many handlers use a whistle to provide audible sound cues for commands during water work.

Sponsoring Organizations

CANINE WATER SPORTS (CWS)

Canine Water Sports, based in Connecticut, is divided into three test divisions: Single Tasks, Water Games, and Community Service. In all divisions, the dog–handler team is evaluated for technical and presentational aspects of a performance, which means that happy, willing, and confident dogs are recognized and rewarded for producing an inspiring performance.

The Single Tasks Division consists of entry-level evaluations in seven categories, including team swimming (dog and handler) ability and how well the dog retrieves, delivers objects, works while submersed, tows a boat or other object, finds objects in a wet-scent search, and demonstrates boating skills. (Each of the seven categories

---

FUN FACT

Some breed clubs, notably the Newfoundland Club of America (NCA) and the Portuguese Water Dog Club of America (PWDCA), offer water tests for their breeds only. The NCA showcases the lifesaving abilities of its breed by offering Newfoundland Water Rescue in three divisions. The PWDCA offers a water trial that illuminates the working heritage of its breed: retrieving objects and towing boat lines.

To participate in canine water sports, your dog must love the water.

includes several different tasks.) The team swim test must be passed before the other tasks may be attempted. The handler may then undertake any of the other tasks in any order or can enter the Water Games Division without completing any other single division tasks. There are two sets of standards for these categories: Group 1: giant, large, and medium dogs; and Group 2: miniature, toy, small, and dwarf dogs. Tow weight, article size, and distances are adjusted accordingly.

The Water Games Division is based on skills demonstrated in the Single Task Division and is also divided into the same two groups. The winner of each game wins a game point toward a Water Games Division title.

The Community Service Division is intended for dogs with advanced skills in the water. The division is divided into three service work areas, each with multiple tasks. The dog is required to show proficiency in water utility, rescue, and underwater scent search. The tasks must be completed consecutively, and all must be passed to qualify for a title. These tasks simulate real-life situations, and unlike in the other divisions, the dogs must be big and strong enough to perform the tasks in each category.

Eligibility Requirements: The CWS offers programs for dogs of all sizes; testing events are open to any water-loving dog six months of age or older. Dogs must be registered with the CWS to participate.

Titles: Single Task and Community Service titles are scored on a pass/fail basis. Single Task certificates are Certificate of Canine Team Swim Work (TSW), Certificate of Canine Water Retrieve Work (WRW), Certificate of Canine Water Delivery Work (WDW), Certificate of Canine Water Tow Work (WTW), Certificate of Canine Underwater Work (UW), Certificate of Canine Wet Scent Work (WSW), and Certificate of Canine Boatwork (BW). In the Community Service Division, a dog who qualifies in a Water Utility Trial earns a Water Utility Dog Title (WUD), a dog who qualifies in a Water Rescue Trial earns a Water Rescue Dog Title (WRD), and a dog qualifying in a Wet Scent Search Trial earns a Wet Scent Search Dog title (WSSD).

Premier Events: Events are held throughout the United States.

How to Get Started

To participate in canine water sports, your dog must love the water and be healthy—get him a vet checkup before you begin.

INTRODUCE YOUR DOG TO THE WATER EARLY

To maximize the chances of having a good water dog, introduce your puppy to water as earlier as possible, always making it a fun, nonfrightening experience. Let him play and splash in the shallows. He'll gradually want to go in deeper on his own.

TEACH YOUR DOG TO RETRIEVE

Start playing retrieving games in the water as well as on land to introduce your dog to some of the skills he'll need later. Start by throwing the object to be retrieved just a few feet (m) away. Gradually throw it farther, then start throwing more than one object and tell him which one to go after. Later, you can drop them from a boat. Reward him lavishly when he does what you want him to. You will have the most success if you select retrieve articles that stand out clearly from the environment.

TEACH YOUR DOG TO TUG

Tugging on a rope is a game most dogs love, and it is critical in retrieving games. You want your dog to grab the rope, not drop it. Tug-of-war will teach your water dog to grab a rope and hang onto it, at least until you ask for it. Start with him pulling light objects on land, gradually increasing the weight. Get him used to the idea of taking a line to someone by having him carry one end of a leash while someone pulls gently on the other end. As he gets older, start swimming with him and get him to pull you back to shore.

Strategies for Success

To be successful at canine water sports, vary your retrieve articles and find a mentor to help you.

USE DIFFERENT RETRIEVE ARTICLES

Work on a variety of retrieve articles with your dog—don't get him too used to just one. He'll need to be able to retrieve several different kinds in an actual test.

FIND A MENTOR

A mentor is a good idea for serious water rescue training. Join a local club if one is available, and camps and training classes are also helpful. The CWS offers several different workshops and classes.

FROM THE EXPERT

The experts at Canine Water Sports (CWS) emphasize the importance of selecting the right retrieve articles to ensure success. Small articles are easier to grab but harder to see and find. It's up to you to find the right balance for your dog. Dogs who retrieve largely by scent will do better with fabric retrieve articles that hold scent (including yours). Also, patterned objects create an illusion of movement and rolling that may be easier for a dog to see. Yellow, red, orange, and white obviously show up better in the water than green or blue.

Chapter 35

Weight Pulling

Definition

This sport challenges a dog to pull a loaded sled or cart (often bearing concrete blocks) for a short distance across grass, carpeting, or snow. In this event, some dogs can pull ten times their weight on a sledge and even more with a wheeled vehicle. A specified amount of time is allowed for each pull. In many cases, a completed pull is 15 or 16 feet (4.5 or 5 m) long and must be completed in 60 seconds.

History of Weight Pulling

Dogs have been pulling weights (in the form of sleds and carts) for centuries. However, the formal sport of weight pulling is comparatively new. The International Weight Pull Association (IWPA) was organized in November 1984 to promote this specialized event; the United Kennel Club (UKC) currently recognizes the sport as well.

Overview

In a typical weight-pulling event, the dog stays behind the starting line until the handler moves in front to call the dog forward. In some events, the handler has the choice of standing at the end of the 16-foot (5-m) course and calling her dog from in front, or she may stand behind the sled/cart and drive the dog. The decision about which method to use is based on the handler's individual training techniques and the dog's preference. Most organizations, including the IWPA and UKC, do not allow "baiting" or urging the dog forward with food.

Each dog may have between 5 and 12 "pulls" for a typical day's competition. A starting weight is increased by agreed-upon increments. The weights largely depend on how big the dog is in the first place (and what surface he is pulling on), but dogs have been known to pull 3,000 pounds (1,361 kg). Even 15-pound (7-kg) dogs can pull 300 pounds (136 kg). A handler may skip one or two weight increments (but no more than two) as a strategy or to conserve a dog's energy.

Pulling continues until only one dog succeeds in pulling the weight. If a tie occurs, the dog with the fastest time wins. In many events, if the dog does not pull the load within 45 seconds, needs help to move the load, or cannot pull the load at all,

TOP BREEDS

Although any dog can participate in weight pulling, including mixed breeds, sled dogs and pit bull-type breeds are often the most successful. In fact, sled dogs, Mastiffs, Rottweilers, and American Pit Bull Terriers are some of the breeds most often seen in competition.

In weight-pulling events, dogs wear a special harness that distributes weight evenly, minimizing the chance of injury.

it is considered a no-pull and the dog is eliminated from the day's competition. In the event of a tie, time can be used as a tiebreaker because all pulls are timed.

INTERNATIONAL WEIGHT PULL ASSOCIATION (IWPA)

The objective of an IWPA competition is to see which dogs (within their weight class) can pull the most weight 16 feet (5 m) within one minute. The weight vehicles operate on wheels or snow.

Dogs compete within their own weight class, of which there are eight: 0-20 pounds (0-9 kg), 21-40 pounds 9.5-18 kg), 41-60 pounds (18.5-27 kg), 61-80 pounds (27.5-36.5 kg), 81-100 pounds (36.5-45.5 kg), 101-125 pounds (46-56.5 kg), 126-150 pounds (57-68 kg), and 151 pounds (68.5 kg) and over. Snow and wheeled competitions are kept separate.

United Kennel Club (UKC)

In a UKC event, dogs are placed in a harness and pull a weighted cart for a prescribed distance. The weight vehicles operate either on wheels, on snow, or on a rail system. The dogs are scored based on how much weight they can pull and by the proportion of their body weight to the amount of weight pulled.

There are eight weight classes, separated according to the dog's weight in pounds: 0–20 pounds (0–9 kg), 21–40 pounds (9.5–18 kg), 41–60 pounds (18.5–27 kg), 61–80 pounds (27.5–36.5 kg), 81–100 pounds (36.5–45.5 kg), 101–125 pounds (46–56.5 kg), 126–150 pounds (57–68 kg), and 151 pounds (68.5 kg) and over. Sometimes there are very few dogs within a particular weight class, and in that case classes are combined. Even so, the dogs still compete only with others in their weight class.

In UKC weight pulling, you may not go behind the front edge of the vehicle while your dog is pulling, you may not touch any part of the vehicle or tuglines, and you may not touch your dog.

Requirements

Dogs

- endurance
- obedience to commands
- perseverance
- strength
- willingness to pull

Handlers

- ability to remain calm (the dog needs to concentrate!)

Equipment and Supplies

- harness
- sled/cart

Harness: You will need a specially constructed weight-pulling harness designed to distribute the weight evenly and minimize the chance of injury. These harnesses disperse the tension of pulling large loads over a larger area of the dog. The crisscross styling and tension bar, which goes behind the dog under his tail, greatly reduce the possibility of injury to the dog. The padded V-neck of the collar area pulls the harness down and away from the dog's

throat, allowing him to breathe freely while competing

Sled/Cart: A variety of sleds or carts are used. Typically, a wooden weight-pull sled is capable of holding 4,000 pounds (1,814.5 kg); these sleds have mountable, pneumatic wheels for when there is no snow. The IWPA uses two basic kinds of vehicles: sleds for snow surfaces and wheeled vehicles for everything else. The sled must have two runners at least 4 inches (10 cm) wide and 7 feet (2 m) long. The sled must be between 30 and 48 inches (76 and 122 cm) wide and be able to carry 4,000 pounds (1,814.5 kg).

The cart (for all other surfaces) must have four pneumatic tires 8 to 18 inches (20.5 to 45.5 cm) in height and be able to carry at least 4,000 pounds (1,814.5 kg) safely. The UKC allows all of the above and also requires a rail cart and rails (made from angle iron) that must be able to carry 4,000 pounds (1,814.5 kg).

Sponsoring Organizations

INTERNATIONAL WEIGHT PULL ASSOCIATION (IWPA)

The IWPA's season for sanctioned pulls runs from September through March; currently, it sanctions about 100 pulls a season throughout the contiguous United States and Canada. Membership currently runs at around 250 to 300, with around 400 to 600 dogs in competition.

Members' dogs earn points based on their completion position and the number of dogs they beat. Their five best pulls are used in the total points for the season. They compete only within their weight class and only within their region.

Eligibility Requirements: Participants must be a member of the IWPA to earn points. Competition is open to all dogs, including mixed breeds, and spayed and neutered dogs are eligible. All dogs must be at least 1 year of age and no more than 12 years of age.

Titles: On snow, a dog can earn *IWPA Working Dog (WD):* Dog must pull 5 times his own body weight in four different pulls; *IWPA Working Dog Excellent (WDX):* Dog must pull 10 times his own body weight in four different pulls; and *IWPA Working Dog Superior (WDS):* Dog must pull 15 times his own body weight in three different pulls. On wheels, a dog can earn *IWPA Working Dog (WD):* Dog must pull 12 times his own body weight in four different pulls; *IWPA Working Dog Excellent (WDX):* Dog must pull 18 times his own body weight in four different pulls; *IWPA Working Dog Superior (WDS):* Dog must pull 23 times his own body weight in three different pulls.

A dog can earn three levels of Working Dog certificates for pulling certain percentages of his own weight.

Premier Events: At the end of the season each year, a "pull-off" takes place that all first, second-, and third-place dogs are invited to attend.

UNITED KENNEL CLUB (UKC)
The UKC offers classes for sled, rail carts, and wheeled carts.

Eligibility Requirements: Dogs must be registered with the UKC and be between 1 and 12 years old.

Titles: Titles include *United Weight Puller (UWP):*

FROM THE EXPERT

Todd Tripp, owner of Pulldoggies.com, emphasizes never setting your dog up to fail or giving him more weight than he can handle. Once your dog can handle pulling his own body weight for 20 to 30 yards (18.5 to 27.5 m) at a time for an hour, you can begin working toward the shorter, heavier pulls that the dog will be doing when competing.

A dog must earn a qualifying leg at three different UKC-licensed weight pulls. *United Weight Pull Champion (UWPCH):* A dog must earn the UWP title and 100 additional championship points; *United Weight Pull Champion Excellent (UWPCHX):* A dog must earn the UWPCH title and 250 additional championship points; *United Weight Pull Champion Versatile (UWPCHV):* A dog must earn the UWP title, 100 points on one weighted vehicle, and an additional 100 points, which may be earned on any combination of at least two types of weighted vehicles; *United Weight Pull Champion Outstanding (UWPCHO):* A dog must earn the UWP title and 100 additional championship points each on two different types of weighted vehicles; *United Weight Pull Champion Supreme (UWPCHS):* A dog must earn the UWP title and 100 additional championship points on all three types of weighted vehicle.

Premier Events: Various events are held all around the United States.

How to Get Started

Before getting started, your best bet is to join a weight-pulling club for help and advice. Most people don't have the proper sleds and carts lying around the house, although you probably will once you get into the sport.

GET YOUR DOG A CHECKUP

You need a strong, healthy dog to participate in this sport. Get him a vet checkup to make sure that his joints and ligaments can stand up to the work.

ACCUSTOM YOUR DOG TO THE HARNESS

Get your puppy accustomed to wearing the harness. This can be done as early as 12 to 16 weeks, although a puppy shouldn't do anything strenuous until he is nine or ten months old. However, young puppies can get the idea of pulling, even if it's just a cereal box or an empty milk jug. Obviously, you don't want to do anything to strain his muscles, and dogs should not be entered in competition until they are a year old.

You need a strong, healthy dog to participate in weight pulling, so get a vet checkup to make sure that his joints and ligaments can withstand the sport.

CONDITION YOUR DOG

You can condition your weight-pull dog in several ways: bikejoring, skijoring, or even pulling a tire. Weights should be added in small increments every other day or so. Start adding the cart when your dog is used to pulling the weight, however long it takes; at this point, ask another person to help. This person is the "brakeman," so to speak, who will keep hold of the cart to prevent it from running into the dog when he has finished his pull. Start by asking your dog to pull the empty cart about 20 feet (6 m) to get him used to the idea.

Interestingly, many handlers in the sport don't advocate obedience training beyond basic good manners for weight-pulling dogs. Some feel that such training hinders a dog's initiative.

Use Food Rewards

Although food rewards (as well as noisemakers and
enticement props) are banned during the actual pull period
in many events, these make excellent training aids.

Strategies for Success

Learning to be patient and use tools, as well as adhering
to a schedule, will help your dog achieve weight-pulling
success.

Be Patient

Weight-pull dogs are often stubborn by nature, and there is
no way to make one pull a load he does not wish to pull.
When they get tired, they may simply sit down and "wait it
out." In this case, there is really nothing to do but wait for a
better day.

Learn How to Use Tools

Get handy with tools; if you must practice at home, most
people have to build their own weight competition carts.
Only a few commercial outfitters sell them, and most won't
ship them. Read the rules, check with the sponsoring club,
and build your cart according to specifications.

Stick to a Schedule

Keep your dog to a good weight-pulling schedule—every
other day is about right for most dogs. Practice about a
week at one weight before moving up to the next.

Additional Organizations

American Pulling Alliance (APA)
www.weightpull.com
United National Weight Pull Association (UNWPA)
www.unitednationalweightpullassociation.com

Glossary

agility: A timed obstacle race

article: Term used in tracking and obedience to denote a target object

babbler: In hound field trials, a hound that gives tongue when not on the trail

bait: Using food or a toy to attract a dog's attention

beater: One who walks through the bushes flushing out rabbits at field trials

benched show: A dog show in which all of the entrants are constantly in view

Best in Show: The dog who wins in the final round at a conformation dog show

bikejoring: Sport in which a dog pulls a bike ridden by his handler

bird field: In hunting tests, a marked-off area where at least two birds are planted per **brace** (q.v.)

bitch: A female dog

blind retrieve: A retrieve in which the dog is sent to retrieve a bird that it did not see fall. The dog is expected to take hand, voice, and whistle signals to direct him to the bird.

booties: Soft foot covering for dogs who run on ice, snow, pavement, or rugged terrain

brace: A pair of randomly assigned dogs that work simultaneously in field trials. In conformation, two of the same breed presented together as a pair.

bracemate: A dog's brace "partner"

break: In field trials, the action of the dog leaving the assigned spot (usually at handler's heel) without command when bird is thrown, shot, falls, or is flushed

breed standard: A written description of the ideal specimen for a particular breed of dog

bumper: A cylindrical plastic or canvas object, usually 2 or

3 inches (5 or 7.5 cm) in diameter, used to train the dog.

canicross: Sport of running across country with a dog attached to you and pulling you forward.

canine freestyle: A competitive sport that combines obedience and dance to display teamwork and rapport between dog and handler

Canine Good Citizen test: A ten-step pass/fail test to prove a dog's good manners

clean run: In agility, flyball, or similar events, when a dog and/or team completes the course without errors

cold nosed: Refers to a hound who is capable of following a "cold" scent, i.e., one that is either old and/or one that is difficult to find and follow

cold trailer: Refers to a hound, usually slow working, who has the inherent ability of nose as well as the desire, endurance, and tenacity to follow a cold trail, one that is either old and/or difficult to find and follow

command: In obedience, a verbal order given by the handler to the dog. Only one command may be given in a trial. The dog's name may be used once immediately before any verbal command.

conformation: A competitive dog sport in which dog is evaluated as to how well he matches the breed standard. Also known as a dog show.

dock diving: A competitive sport in which dogs race down a dock, then jump off the end and into the water, with distance being the goal

dog: A male of the species. Also used to describe male and female canines collectively.

draft: The act of weight pulling

dryland mushing: Fanciful name for carting

Dual Champion: A dog who has won both field and conformation championships, a very highly regarded honor

dummy: See **bumper**

earthdog: A sporting event that tests a dog's instincts and ability to work underground in search of quarry in timed courses designed to simulate hunting conditions. Some courses consist of actual underground tunnels, while others consist of artificially constructed aboveground passages.

eye: In herding, the amount of concentration shown by a stock dog

fetch: In herding, bringing of the sheep to the handler

field marshal: At field trials, the person who supervisors the **beaters** (q.v.)

field trial: A competition for specified hound or sporting breeds where dogs are judged according to their ability and style on following a game trail or on finding and retrieving game. There are separate field trials for pointing breeds, hounds, spaniels, retrievers, and coonhounds.

flank: In herding, the movement of the dog around the stock in response to a command from the handler

flush: To drive birds from cover, to spring at them, to force them to take flight

flushing breeds: Term applied to those spaniel breeds that typically flush or force a bird from cover

flyball: A competitive sporting event that involves relay races in which several teams of dogs compete against each other and the clock, jumping over hurdles to retrieve a ball released into the air

flying disc: A sporting event in which the dog races into the ring to leap and snatch a disc thrown high into the air and return it to the handler at the starting position. A time is set, and scoring depends upon the number of catches, distance, accuracy, and artistry of the dog within that time limit.

freezing: Dog holds onto bird and will not release it

gait: The way a dog moves

gallery: The spectators at field trials and hunting tests

gangline: A line that connects the tuglines and attached dogs to the sled

gather: In herding, when the dog collects the sheep into a compact group

gee: Command to turn right in mushing and other sports where the dog pulls a person

give tongue: This phrase is used as a synonym for bay, howl, or open—all terms meaning that the dog is vocal when he is following a scent trail

go by: In mushing events, the command to go straight ahead

go to ground: In earthdog events, to follow quarry into their dens

gun shy: Describes a dog who cringes or shows other signs of fear at the sound or sight of a gun

gundog: A dog who has been specifically trained to work with a human in the field for retrieving game that has been shot and for locating live game

gunner: In field trials, people who are given the job of shooting the birds after they are flushed

handler: The human part of the dog–human team

hard mouthed: A dog who grasps the game too firmly in retrieving, causing bites and tooth marks

haw: A command to turn left in mushing and other sports where the dog pulls a person

heat: In flyball, nite hunts, and some other events, a single "run" during a competition

heel: The position in which the dog's right shoulder and nose are aligned with the handler's left leg

heeling: In herding, when the dog works the stock from behind, usually nipping the lower leg to move the stock. This occurs most often when working cattle.

herding trial: A competitive sport in which the dogs move sheep or other flocking animals around a field, fences, gates, or enclosures under commands from their handlers

hike: What mushers really say (instead of "mush") when they want the dogs to move forward

honor: In field trials and hunting tests, the act of a dog sitting quietly off leash on or near the line while another dog retrieves

hunting tests: Noncompetitive events in which retrievers, spaniels, and pointing breeds are evaluated for their hunting ability

hup: Term used for "Sit!" in spaniel field tests

hurdle: Term for a jump used in flyball

lead: Leash

leg: A term often used to refer to one qualifying score in obedience and other events

licensed field trial: A field trial at which championship points may be awarded

lure coursing: Originally, a sporting event where sighthounds coursed after live game, although most modern contests use a rag or mechanical lure for the dogs to chase. Scoring is based on speed, agility, endurance, enthusiasm, and follow.

marked retrieve: A retrieve the dog has seen fall

match show: An informal conformation dog show at which no championship points are awarded

musher: Dog handler in sledding

nite hunt: Competition in which coonhounds attempt to find raccoons in trees.

non-qualifying score (NQ): In obedience and hunting tests, any score that is not passing

nonslip retriever: A dog not expected to flush or to find game; one who merely walks at heel, marks the fall, and then retrieves upon command

obedience trial: A licensed obedience trial is one at which a dog must perform a number of obedience commands, ranging from basic to advanced depending upon the event, with the goal being to earn a title

open trailing: When a hound begins baying as soon as he has found the scent (opens) and continues as long as he is on the trail

pedaling: In dog sledding, a one-legged push by the musher

point: The exaggeration of a dog's stalking game to the point where he stops moving and freezes in place.

qualifying: A passing score at a trial

rally: A competitive sport drawing on obedience and agility, in which the dog and handler must execute a course consisting of stations at which they must demonstrate specific skills. Courses become more difficult at higher levels of competition. Also known as rally obedience, rally-o.

sanctioned field trial: An informal field trial where dogs are not competing for championship points

scentline: The scent path of the rabbit or other game

Schutzhund: A performance event that tests the obedience, tracking, and protection work skills of working dogs. Courses demand stamina, high intelligence, and versatility and become more difficult at higher levels.

search and rescue: Search and rescue dogs are trackers who follow a human scent to locate missing persons using their senses of smell and hearing under all conditions in various environments. One search and rescue dog is equivalent to 20 searchers in a given area.

shagger: In field trials, one who carries the shot birds after they have been retrieved

shedding: In herding trials, separating the marked sheep from others, in accordance with the judge's instructions

singling: In herding, a test in which one marked sheep is separated from the herd

skijoring : A dog sport that combines cross-country skiing and carting, with the handler as a driver. Attached to the handler on a long bungee cord, the dog wears a pulling harness and must respond instantly to voice commands given by the skier during a race.

sledding: Competitive sled-dog racing that tests the performance ability of working dogs, especially huskies. The most celebrated race is the Iditarod.

slip lead: A slender rope or leash that slides through the o-ring on the dog's collar

snow hook: A "brake" used in dog sledding

specialty show: In conformation, a show limited to a single breed

stake: (1) A regular class held at field trials; (2) The handler's fixed position in a herding trial.

station: One of the locations on a rally course that contains a sign indicating the desired obedience skill to be performed

steady to wing and shot: In hunting tests, a completely trained dog who remains still while the bird is flushed and the gun fired

stock: Animals intended to be herded

sulky: Cart

therapy dogs: Dogs who visit nursing homes, hospitals, rehabilitation centers, and schools.

tracking: A competitive sporting event designed primarily to test a dog's ability to discriminate scent

trail: To hunt by following a trail scent

travois: In carting, a dragged load without wheels

treeing: The act of chasing an animal up into a tree and holding it there for a hunter to shoot; most often performed by coonhounds.

Triple Champion: A dog who has won a conformation show, a field trial, and an obedience trial.

tugline: In mushing, a line that connects each dog to the gangline

veteran: Older dog

water race: Coonhound event in which a scented lure in a cage is floated or suspended on water

weight pulling: A competitive sport designed to test strength and stamina. To earn titles, a harnessed dog must pull a sled or cart holding a specified weight for a prescribed distance within a set time limit.

whoa: Stop!

wool-pulling: In herding, nipping or gripping at the sheep. Biting at the body of any type of stock is a fault.

working: In earthdog events, digging, barking, growling, lunging, and biting at the quarry cage

Resources

Agility Association of Canada (AAC)
www.aac.ca

American Coon Hunters Association, Inc. (ACHA)
www.acha-wcchr.com

American Kennel Club (AKC)
5580 Centerview Drive
Raleigh, NC 27606
Telephone: (919) 233-9767
Fax: (919) 233-3627
E-Mail: info@akc.org
www.akc.org

American Herding Breed Association (AHBA)
www.ahba-herding.org

American Hunting Dog Club (AHDC)
www.ahdc.org

American Mixed Breed Obedience Registration (AMBOR)
P.O. Box 223
Anoka, MN 55303
E-Mail: ambor@ambor.us
www.ambor.us

American Pulling Alliance (APA)
www.weightpull.com

American Rabbit Hound Association (ARHA)
134 Rutledge Pike
P.O. Box 331
Blaine, Tennessee 37709
Telephone: (865) 932-9680
Fax: (865) 932-2572
E-Mail: joyce@nationalkennelclub.com
www.arha.com

American Sighthound Field Association (ASFA)
www.asfa.org

American Working Terrier Association (AWTA)
www.dirt-dog.com

Association of Pet Dog Trainers (APDT)
150 Executive Center Drive Box 35
Greenville, SC 29615
Telephone: 1-800-738-3647
E-Mail: information@apdt.com
www.apdt.com

Australian Canine Disc Association (ACDA)
Suite 102
Morayfield Shopping Centre
Morayfield QLD 4506
Telephone and Fax: (07) 5495 6700
E-Mail: damian@frisbeedogs.asn.au
www.frisbeedogs.asn.au

Australian Flyball Association, Inc. (AFA)
PO Box 4179
Pitt Town NSW 2756
E-Mail: info@flyball.org.au
www.flyball.org.au

Australian Shepherd Club of America, Inc. (ASCA)
6091 E. State Hwy 21
Bryan Texas 77808-9652
Telephone: (979) 778-1082
Fax: (979) 778-1898
www.asca.org

British Agility Association (BAA)
E-Mail: june @baa.uk.net
www.baa.uk.net

British Flyball Association (BFA)
www.flyball.org.uk

Canadian Association of Rally Obedience (CARO)
E-Mail: canadianrallyo@gmail.com
www.canadianrallyo.ca

Canadian Kennel Club (CKC)
89 Skyway Avenue, Suite 100
Etobicoke, Ontario M9W 6R4
Telephone: (416) 675-5511
Fax: (416) 675-6506
E-Mail: information@ckc.ca
www.ckc.ca

Canadian Disc Dog Association (CDDA)
www.geocities.com/cddadiscdog

Canine Freestyle Federation, Inc. (CFF)
E-Mail: secretary@canine-freestyle.org
www.canine-freestyle.org

Canine Freestyle GB
P.O. Box 7680
Alfreton, Derbyshire, DE55 9BX
E-Mail: cfgb@caninefreestylegb.com
www.caninefreestylegb.com

Canine Good Companion Programme
www.diydoggrooming.com/caninecompanionsoverview.php

Canine Performance Events (CPE)
E-Mail: cpe@charter.net
www.k9cpe.com

Canine Water Sports (CWS)
P.O. Box 842
Monroe, CT 06468
E-Mail: K9waterfun@aol.com
www.caninewatersports.com

CaniX UK
www.cani-cross.co.uk

Delta Society
875 124th Ave NE
Suite 101
Bellevue, WA 98005
Telephone: (425) 679-5500
Fax: (425) 679-5539
E-Mail: info@deltasociety.org
www.deltasociety.org

Delta Society Australia
Shop 2, 50 Carlton Crescent
Summer Hill NSW 2130
Telephone: (02) 9797 7922
Fax: (02) 9799 5009
Emails: glenn@deltasocietyaustralia.com.au
hollee@deltasocietyaustralia.com.au
amy@deltasocietyaustralia.com.au
www.deltasocietyaustralia.com.au

Deutscher Verband der Gebrauchshundsportvereine (DVG)
www.dvg-hundesport.de

DockDogs®
Telephone: 330-241-4975
Fax: 330-241-4976
E-Mail: info@dockdogs.com
www.dockdogs.com

Dogs Across America
www.dogsacrossamerica.org

European Canicross and Bikejöring Federation (ECF)
www.ecf.cc

European Sleddog Racing Association (ESDRA)
E-Mail: board@esdra.net
www.esdra.net

Federation Cynologique Internationale (FCI)
Secretariat General de la FCI
Place Albert 1er, 13
B – 6530 Thuin
Belqique
www.fci.be

International Agility Link (IAL)
Global Administrator: Steve Drinkwater
E-Mail: yunde@powerup.au
www.agilityclick.com/~ial

International All Breed Canine Association, Inc. (IABCA)
4742 Liberty Rd S #159
Salem, Oregon 97302
Telephone: (503) 316-9860
Fax: (859) 406-4608
E-Mail: iabcaofamerica@yahoo.com
www.iabca.com

International Federation of Sleddog Sports, Inc. (IFSS)
www.sleddogsport.com

International Sheep Dog Society (ISDS)
Clifton House
4a Goldington Road
Bedford
MK40 3NF
Telephone: 01234 352672
Fax: 01234 348214
E-Mail: office@isds.org.uk
www.isds.org.uk

International Sled Dog Racing Association (ISDRA)
E-Mail: dsteele@brainerd.net
www.isdra.org

International Weight Pull Association (IWPA)
E-Mail: info@iwpa.net
www.iwpa.net

Jack Russell Terrier Club of America (JRTCA)
P.O. Box 4527
Lutherville, MD 21094-4527
Telephone: (410) 561-3655
Fax: (410) 560-2563
www.terrier.com

Kennel Club Plovdiv
37, Tzar Boris III - Obedinitel Blvd.
4003, Plovdiv, Bulgaria
Telephone: (+359) 32/903 600
Fax: (+359) 32/902 432
E-Mail: fairinfo@fair.bg
www.fair.bg/en/events/CACIB08.htm

Mixed Breed Dog Clubs of America (MBDCA)
E-Mail: Libi-Lew@juno.com
http://mbdca.tripod.com

Musical Dog Sports Association (MDSA)
515 S. Fry Road
PMB # 301
Katy, Texas 77450-9100
E-Mail: musicaldogsport@gmail.com
www.musicaldogsport.org

National Association for Search and Rescue (NASAR)
Telephone: (877) 893-0702
Fax: (703) 222-6277
E-Mail: info@nasar.org
www.nasar.org

National Bird Dog Challenge Association (NBDCA)
32 County Road 30 SW
Montrose, MN 55363
Telephone: (866) 909-THTV
E-Mail: tournamenthunter@frontiernet.net
www.nbdca.com

National Search and Rescue Dog Association (NSARDA)
www.nsarda.org.uk

National Shoot to Retrieve Association® (NSTRA)
226 N. Mill Street, #2
Plainfield, IN 46168
Phone: (317) 839-4059
Fax: (317) 839-4197
E-Mail: nstrfta@ameritech.net
www.nstra.org

New England Drafting and Driving Club (NEDDC)
E-Mail: info@neddc.org
www.neddc.org

North American Dog Agility Council (NADAC)
E-Mail: info@nadac.com
www.nadac.com

North American Flyball Association, Inc. (NAFA)
1400 West Devon Avenue, #512
Chicago, IL 60660
Telephone and Fax: (800) 318-6312
E-Mail: flyball@flyball.org
www.flyball.org

North American Hunting Retriever Association (NAHRA)
E-Mail: nahra@starband.net, nahra1@gmail.com
www.nahranews.org

North American Versatile Hunting Dog Association (NAVHDA)
P.O. Box 520
Arlington Heights, IL 60006
Telephone: 847.253.6488
Fax: 847.255.5987
E-Mail: navoffice@navhda.org
www.navhda.org

Pawfect K9 Freestyle Club
E-Mail: ask@pawfect.jp
www.pawfect.jp

Pets as Therapy
3a Grange Farm Cottages
Wycombe Road
Saunderton
Princes Risborough
Bucks
HP27 9NS
Telephone: 01844 345 445
Fax: 01845 550 236
E-Mail: reception@petsastherapy.org
www.petsastherapy.org

Schutzhund Australia
www.schutzhundaustralia.com

Search and Rescue Dogs Australia (SARDA)
E-Mail: info@sarda.net.au
www.sarda.net.au

Search and Rescue Society of British Columbia (SAR BC)
E-Mail: sarbc@sarbc.org
www.sarbc.org

Skyhoundz
660 Hembree Parkway
Ste 110
Roswell, GA 30076
Telephone: (770) 751-3882
Fax: (770) 740-1665
E-Mail: info@skyhoundz.com
www.skyhoundz.com

South African Flyball Dog Association (SAFDA)
www.safda.netfirms.com

The Kennel Club
1 Clarges Street
London
W1J 8AB
Telephone: 0870 606 6750
Fax: 0207 518 1058
www.the-kennel-club.org.uk

Therapeutic Paws of Canada (TPOC)
www.tpoc.ca

Therapy Dogs International (TDI)
88 Bartley Road
Flanders, NJ 07836
Telephone: (973) 252-9800
Fax: (973) 252-7171
E-Mail: tdi@gti.net
www.tdi-dog.corg

United Beagle Gundog Federation, Inc. (UBGF)
www.ubgf.org

United Flyball League International (U-FLI)
PMB 169
4132 South Rainbow Blvd
Las Vegas, NV 89103
(509) 696-9176
www.u-fli.com

United Kennel Club (UKC)
100 E. Kilgore Road
Kalamazoo, MI 49002-5584
Telephone: (269) 343-9020
Fax: (269) 343-7037
E-Mail: pbickell@ukcdogs.com
www.ukcdogs.com

United National Weight Pull Association (UNWPA)
E-Mail: UNWPA_webmaster@q.com
www.unitednationalweight pullassociation.com

United Schutzhund Clubs of America (USA)
www.germanshepherddog.com

United States Dog Agility Association (USDAA)
P.O. Box 850955
Richardson, TX 75085
Telephone: (972) 487-2200
Fax: (972) 272-4404
www.usdaa.com

US Disc Dog Nationals (USDDN)
E-Mail: webmaster@usddn.com
www.usddn.com

Verein für Deutsche Schäferhunde (SV) e.V.
www.schaeferhund.de

World Canine Freestyle Organization, Inc. (WCFO)
P.O. Box 350122
Brooklyn, NY 11235
Telephone: (718) 332-8336
Fax: (718) 646-2686
E-Mail: WCFODOGS@aol.com
www.worldcaninefreestyle.org

Websites

Nylabone
www.nylabone.com

T.F.H. Publications, Inc.
www.tfh.com

Index

NYLABONE

Index

NYLABONE

Index

Index

Acknowledgments

Special thanks to my research assistant Kimberly Maske-Mertz for her invaluable assistance in writing this book. I am incredibly grateful to the team at TFH for all of their help and support, especially to Stephanie Fornino, whose eagle eye, insight, patience, and sense of humor made everything worthwhile.

About the Author

Diane Morgan writes books on animals and comparative religion and tries not to get them confused. She is a professor of philosophy and religion at Wilson College in Chambersburg, Pennsylvania, and lives in Williamsport, Maryland, with her human and animal family. She is shown here with her Gordon Setter conformation champion, Gambler.

Photo Credits

Anyka (Shutterstock): 178; Stacy Barnett (Shutterstock): 456; Camilla Berns: 40, 43, 47; Paul Brennan (Shutterstock): 286; LaDonna Brezik (Shutterstock): 204; R. Briggle, courtesy skijornow.com: 378, 382; Dan Briški (Shutterstock): 180, 189; Alex Brown (Shutterstock): 294; Joy Brown (Shutterstock): 78, 160, 164; Tim Callen (Shutterstock): 292; John Carnemolla (Shutterstock): 256; Andraž Cerar (Shutterstock): 131, 244; clearviewstock (Shutterstock): 264; Linn Currie (Shutterstock): 192, 199, 202, 216, 282, 468; cynoclub (Shutterstock): 220, 316; Jeff Dalton (Shutterstock): 298; Lindsay Dean (Shutterstock): 326; Fernando Delvalle (Shutterstock): 30; Baevskiy Dmitry (Shutterstock): 376; Doghouse Arts: 10, 14, 18, 22; Jean M. Fogle@jeanmfogle.com: 58, 62, 64, 68, 70, 80, 86, 88, 108, 112, 114, 118, 122, 124, 132, 136, 139, 143, 146, 151, 154, 159,